An Event, Perhaps

An Event, Perhaps

*A Biography of
Jacques Derrida*

Peter Salmon

VERSO
London • New York

First published by Verso 2020
© Peter Salmon 2020

1 3 5 7 9 10 8 6 4 2

Verso
UK: 6 Meard Street, London W1F 0EG
US: 20 Jay Street, Suite 1010, Brooklyn, NY 11201
versobooks.com

Verso is the imprint of New Left Books

ISBN-13: 978-1-78873-280-2
ISBN-13: 978-1-78873-283-3 (US EBK)
ISBN-13: 978-1-78873-282-6 (UK EBK)

British Library Cataloguing in Publication Data
A catalogue record for this book is available from the British Library

Library of Congress Cataloging-in-Publication Data

Names: Salmon, Peter, 1955– author.
Title: An event, perhaps : a biography of Jacques Derrida / Peter Salmon.
Description: London ; New York : Verso, 2020. | Includes bibliographical
    references and index. | Summary: "An introduction to the life and work
    of the philosopher Jacques Derrida"— Provided by publisher.
Identifiers: LCCN 2020021106 (print) | LCCN 2020021107 (ebook) | ISBN
    9781788732802 | ISBN 9781788732833 (US ebk)
Subjects: LCSH: Derrida, Jacques.
Classification: LCC B2430.D484 S275 2020 (print) | LCC B2430.D484 (ebook)
    | DDC 194 [B]—dc23
LC record available at https://lccn.loc.gov/2020021106
LC ebook record available at https://lccn.loc.gov/2020021107

Typeset in Sabon by MJ & N Gavan, Truro, Cornwall
Printed in the UK by CPI Group (UK) Ltd, Croydon CR0 4YY

To Fiona

I have sometimes been troubled by a doubt whether what is true in one case may not be true in all. Then, when I have reached that point, I am driven to retreat, for fear of tumbling into a bottomless pit of nonsense.

– Socrates (Plato, *Parmenides*)

I'd never say this in public – I still love beautiful books and believe in them.

– Jacques Derrida

Contents

Introduction

Perhaps something has occurred in the history of the concept of structure that could be called an 'event', if this loaded word did not entail a meaning which it is precisely the function of structural – or structuralist – thought to reduce or to suspect. But let me use the term 'event' anyway, employing it with caution and as if in quotation marks.

On 21 October 1966, a little-known thirty-six-year-old French philosophy teacher took to the stage at a conference on structuralism at Johns Hopkins University in Baltimore, to deliver a paper titled 'Structure, Sign and Play in the Discourse of the Human Sciences'.

The symposium, portentously titled 'The Languages of Criticism and the Sciences of Man', had been running for three days, and was a huge intellectual event, bringing together over a hundred philosophers, literary critics, ethnographers, anthropologists, psychoanalysts and other cultural theorists from eight countries. Speakers included Roland Barthes, Jean Hyppolite, Hans-Georg Gadamer, Northrop Frye, Tzvetan Todorov and Jacques Lacan, while the attendees included future intellectual stars such as Paul de Man and Joseph Hillis Miller. Of the preeminent names in structuralism, only Michel Foucault was absent.

The symposium was organised to introduce structuralism to

America. Structuralism was rapidly replacing the existentialism of Sartre, Camus and de Beauvoir as the dominant philosophical trend in France. Taking its lead from the linguistics of Ferdinand de Saussure and the anthropology of Claude Lévi-Strauss, and underpinned by Freud and Marx, structuralism rejected human-centred philosophy. Instead, it proposed that all elements of human culture, and all phenomena of human life, could only be understood as being part of a 'structure', and any explanation of motives, actions and behaviour had to overcome the illusion of a free subject. Everything could only be explained by its inter-relationship to other parts of the scheme.

These insights were applied across a range of disciplines. In literature, structuralism moved away from the model of autho-rial intention – the work as a creation of a single mind which knew what it was doing during the creative process and which produced a work whose effect corresponded, more or less, with 'what the author was trying to do' – to a model which saw the meaning of a work as being produced by its place within a system of shared narrative techniques, shared tropes, shared conventions and assumed worldviews. Meaning is produced by the work's place in a genre (or outside of one), by the circumstances of its production and by the social (and intellectual and cultural) posi-tion of the reader.

Derrida had only been invited to the conference at the last moment, after the Belgian anthropologist Luc de Heusch was unable to attend. He came on the recommendation of the director of the École normale supérieure, Jean Hyppolite, who provided what was hardly a ringing endorsement. 'I think', said Hyppolite, 'he would be somebody who would come.'[1]

Derrida was the final speaker on the final day. He remained a silent observer for much of the symposium. He looked on as Lacan rose to his feet with obscure questions at the end of each lecture, and as Barthes gently asked for clarification on various moot points. Eventually, however, Derrida, unused to speaking to large audiences, took to the stage, quietly shuffled his notes, and began, 'Perhaps something has occurred in the history of the concept of structure that could be called an "event"...' He spoke for less than half an hour. But by the time he was finished the entire structuralist project was in doubt, if not dead. An event had occurred: the birth of deconstruction.

Any biography of Derrida must, as a sort of contractual obligation to his thinking, foreground its caveats. Some are the caveats that any biography must include: an attempt to present a version of an individual's life and thought, whether one's own or that of someone else's, must by definition be partial, selective. Such an undertaking forms a narrative that could be told otherwise and that, presented in the form of a book with a beginning, middle and end, uses the structures of literature to present an object – a life – which is not ipso facto propitious to literary form, nor has any essential reason to mirror its tropes. The writer and the reader make a compact with each other – sign a contract of sorts – to ignore this deceit as much as possible, as the readers of fiction suspend their disbelief in order to care about the characters.

That Derrida explicitly problematised what we call biography makes the need for these caveats even more pressing. His analyses of proper names, the signature, hospitality, autobiography and, ultimately, the act of writing itself means that any declarative sentence is under suspicion, let alone any declarations about another human being. Access to the real is always already a 'representation', and all language is rhetorical rather than denotative.

The problem intensifies in an *intellectual* biography that, as part of its *raison d'être* seeks to identify and explicate the 'key concepts' or the 'fundamental ideas' of a particular thinker. Derrida's key concept or fundamental idea is to – and here one immediately searches verbs that are not emphatic – reject ('reject'), disorder ('disorder'), complicate ('complicate') or, to put it another way, to deconstruct ('deconstruct') what we mean by 'key concepts' and 'fundamental ideas'. As Derrida himself wrote, 'once quotation marks demand to appear, they don't know when to stop.'[2]

This can lead to a kind of panicked rush of obfuscation. Derrida's insistence on the equivocal, the ambiguous and the conditional renders unequivocal, unambiguous and unconditional statements instantly suspicious. The temptation to mimic

Derrida's own gnomic, allusive and elusive language can be overwhelming.

To 'do' deconstruction is indeed to start from the position that
any emphatic statement carries within it a cultural, lexical and
political history that reinforces (engenders, instigates, propagates)
what Derrida called the metaphysics of presence, the existence of
the transcendental signifier into which we can plant our flag of
meaning. It is a genuine problem, a genuine insight – but obeying
its demands can also lead to genuine rubbish.

Indeed part of the difficulty of approaching Derrida for the
first time can be reading the secondary texts that cluster around
him, worrying out the implications of his thought in a sort of
hermeneutic magic circle. Many of these texts end up talking
to themselves in a sub-Derridean word salad – full of puns,
neologisms, scare quotes, parentheses, footnotes and clubbable
jokes, none of which Derrida was averse to himself (he was just
better at it).

So a choice must be made between speaking, as it were, in the
voice of Derrida's thought, or not. Neither option will necessarily
result in a 'truer' version of Derrida or his thought. And neither
option will, necessarily, get closer to the man named 'Jacques
Derrida' and the concepts he sought to elucidate and interrogate.
One option will, however, be easier to read. As Derrida himself
put it, in one of his more laconic utterances, 'ordinary language
is probably right.'[3]

This biography aims to set out the intellectual development of
Jacques Derrida; to situate it in events both private and public;
and to argue for its importance as an event in the history of
philosophy and of thought more generally. It will argue that
Derrida is one of the great philosophers of this or any age; that
his thinking is a crucial component of any future philosophy; that
his thinking is immediately – always already – applicable to the
world as we find it; and that this application has political heft.

In doing so, I approach Derrida *as philosopher*. The Anglophone world has tended to elide this fundamental fact about his
thinking. Whatever form his writings took, whichever discipline
took him up or he took up himself, he was a philosopher first

and foremost. Thus the first half of the book concentrates on his development and the development of his ideas – from the student and junior teacher from Algeria with his interest in Sartre, Joyce and Camus (among others); to the philosophy student carrying out an intense reading of Husserl, Heidegger and Lévinas; and then on to the newly published lecturer at the École normale supérieure who felt, tentatively, and then with a growing sense of excitement and nervousness, that he had found an aporia – a break, an unresolvable contradiction – in Husserl. And that this aporia, this unresolvable contradiction was not Husserl's, but belonged to the whole history of Western metaphysics, an insight about the nature of all of philosophy from Plato to the present day.

Deconstruction is, as we shall see, born with Derrida's analysis of Husserl's 'now' – that originary moment, that imaginary vantage point, where one can carry out a phenomenological description of the world as though time does not exist (nor, therefore, history). Husserl relies on this 'now' to generate his philosophy and to set its limits, but the concept 'now' is itself assumed, unquestioned. For Derrida this is an example, par excellence, of the 'metaphysics of presence' – the unexamined assumption and therefore privileging of the notion that consciousness is fully present, that the world is fully present, and that we can analyse it with concepts which are fully present and that, in some sense, exist as things. Metaphysics privileges presence over absence. This is one of the binary oppositions which sustain metaphysics, and metaphysics is

> the enterprise of returning 'strategically', 'ideally', to an origin or to a priority thought to be simple, intact, normal, pure, standard, self-identical, in order then to think in terms of derivation, complication, deterioration, accident, etc. All metaphysicians, from Plato to Rousseau, Descartes to Husserl, have proceeded in this way, conceiving good to be before evil, the positive before the negative, the pure before the impure, the simple before the complex, the essential before the accidental, the imitated before the imitation, etc. And this is not just one metaphysical gesture

among others, it is the metaphysical exigency, that which has been the most constant, most profound and most potent.[4]

The task of deconstruction is to examine these binary opposi-tions in which the first term is privileged – good/evil, positive/ negative, pure/impure, simple/complex, essential/accidental, imitated/imitation (as well as speech/writing, man/woman, light/ darkness, white/non-white, Western/Oriental) – to problematise them, uncover their fabrication, and analyse the violence that this initiates and sustains.

Derrida argues that

> an opposition of metaphysical concepts (speech/writing, pres-ence/absence, etc.) is never the face-to-face of two terms, but a hierarchy and an order of subordination. Deconstruction cannot limit itself or proceed immediately to neutralisation: it must, by means of a double gesture, a double science, a double writing, practise an overturning of the classical opposition, and a general displacement of the system. It is on that condition alone that deconstruction will provide the means of intervening in the field of oppositions it criticises.[5]

To do our own sort of justice to this position requires a patient and in some sense radical reading – the coherence of Derrida's thinking, from his earliest works through to his last is remark-able. It requires that our attention be directed towards the foundational texts, Husserl, Heidegger, Nietzsche, Hegel. While structuralism furnished Derrida with an immediate field of enquiry, any philosophical theory would have done so.

Far from being the slippery and slick operator that his detrac-tors have attempted to paint him as, Derrida doggedly explored the implications of his fundamental insight across disciplines – literature, feminism, (post-)colonialism, law, psychoanalysis, politics, film theory, theology, even architecture, friendship, gift-giving and hospitality – and did so with rigour and logic. From his first writings on religious mysteries to his final works on animals and animality, Derrida displays a meticulous consistency of thought and method. While this leads him into areas presumably unthought of by the nascent phenomenologist he started as, bugged by a small section on writing in Husserl's *Origin of Geometry*, it seldom led him to contradict himself or recant. As he himself wrote, 'Whether it's my luck or my naiveté, I don't think I have ever repudiated anything.'[6]

That his writings are abstruse is an effect of his philosophy. His thought generates his style just as Wittgenstein's generated aphorisms, Spinoza's numbered propositions, Heidegger's compound neologisms and Plato's dialogue. There is nothing fake here. As Geoffrey Bennington puts it, 'Derrida's work has often been received as a virtuoso and sophisticated manipulation of paradoxes and puns, which takes an evil pleasure in mocking a whole metaphysical tradition, leading to a nihilism which paralyses thought and action or, at best, to an "artistic" practice of philosophy and literary aestheticism'[7] as opposed to analytic philosophy which 'asks and resolves serious problems in short, clear and clean articles without getting lost in these quotations and commentaries, and it can pride itself in real understanding without making a fuss about it.'[8] But the style of analytic philosophy, privileging clarity as though it was a transparent deliverer or meaning, is itself, as Derrida would argue, a style.

When I studied philosophy in the 1990s, in what one might call an outpost of the mainstream of Western metaphysics, Melbourne, Australia, the two main universities differed in their emphasis between 'analytical' and 'continental' philosophy. The latter was the domain of the moody, dreamlike Heideggerians, whose idea of a good time was to screen the film *The Ister* at lunchtime and think about Hölderlin, and then gather with the purple-haired overall-wearing Merleau-Ponty brigade (with their 'chiasms', 'folds' and long meditations on what it means when a hand touches another hand) and the Foucauldians, sniffing out power everywhere and generally messing up student politics. All of which was much more interesting, I felt, rightly or wrongly, than having the *Principia Mathematica* explained to me by a professor telling the same jokes as he had, by his own admission, been telling on the day of the moon landing.

But this either/or was not just a consumer choice between fla-
vours of philosophy. It was, for one side at least, a war, and it
was a conflict affecting all of Western philosophy. In May 1992,
eighteen academics drawn from Mannheim to Florence, Los
Angeles to Cracow wrote an open letter to *The Times* against
the proposal that Derrida receive an honorary degree at Cambridge University, arguing that while Derrida 'describes himself as
a philosopher, and his writings do indeed bear some of the marks
of that discipline', his work 'does not meet accepted standards of
quality and rigour' and that 'M. Derrida ... seems to us to have
come close to making a career out of what we regard as translating into the academic sphere tricks and gimmicks similar to those
of the Dadaists or the concrete poets'.[9] One of the signatories,
the philosopher David Hugh Mellor, later pro-vice-chancellor of
Cambridge, was moved to say, 'I'm sure Derrida himself doesn't
believe most of the nonsense he is famous for, but if you filter that
out, the rest doesn't add up to anything worthy of an honorary
degree.'[10]

The disdain did not dissipate even on his death. While the
French president Jacques Chirac was eulogising 'one of the major
figures of intellectual life of our time,' the *New York Times* obituary, under the headline 'Jacques Derrida, Abstruse Theorist,
Dies at 74' described deconstruction, of which Derrida was 'the
father' (a designation which would have amused him no end) as
'murky' and 'undermining many of the traditional standards of
classical education', and his prose as being 'turgid and baffling'. It
quoted lovingly from a number of Derrida's detractors, including
Malcolm Bradbury's bon mot that 'Literature, the deconstruc-
tionists frequently proved, had been written by entirely the wrong
people for entirely the wrong reasons.'

More recently Derrida has been lumped in with postmodernists in a discourse where 'postmodernist' means those who argue
that there is no such thing as truth and who, in the more extreme
versions, are responsible for the collapse of society, owing to
their espousal of radical indeterminism (a word that does not
exist in Derrida's corpus, except where he rejects accusations of
it), which has led either to a liberalism that cannot accept any

grand narratives or an authoritarianism that feels no obligation towards any fundamental truths, and which therefore can appeal, straight-faced, to alternative facts.

In this post-truth world, thinkers such as Derrida are seen as anticipating this dangerous relativism or even actually causing it. As astute a political writer as Matthew d'Ancona, in his 2017 book *Post Truth*, was moved to write that postmodernists, 'incomprehensible in [their] terminology and intellectual skittishness', had 'corroded our concept of truth'. It is, he writes, 'an arresting reflection that, etched into the long Parisian paragraphs of convoluted, post-modern prose, so often dismissed as indulgent nonsense, was a bleak omen of the political future'.[11]

Similarly, the cultural critic Michiko Kakutani, author of *The Death of Truth*, blames 'academics promoting the gospel of postmodernism' for the rise of Donald Trump. Meanwhile the philosopher and cognitive scientist Daniel Dennett, interviewed in the *Guardian* in 2017, stated baldly, 'I think what the postmodernists did was truly evil.'[12] More alarmingly, the 1,500-page manifesto *A European Declaration of Independence*, written by the Norwegian mass killer Anders Behring Breivik, cites 'Derridean deconstruction' as a tool used by cultural critics to 'remove traditional meaning and replace it with a new meaning ... indoctrinating this new generation in feminist interpretation, Marxist philosophy and the so-called "queer theory".'

Derrida himself parodied his antagonists in *Monolingualism of the Other*:

So you ask yourself questions about truth. Well, to that very extent, you do not as yet believe in truth; you are contesting the possibility of truth. That being the case, how do you expect your statements to be taken seriously when they lay a claim to some truth, beginning with your so-called questions? What you are saying is not true because you are questioning truth. Come on! you are a sceptic, a relativist, a nihilist; you are not a serious philosopher! If you continue, you will be placed in a department of rhetoric or literature ... You do not believe what you are saying; you want to mislead us.[13]

Derrida's defenders and advocates have not always been especially helpful either – tending to concentrate their efforts on what
might be called the more carnivalesque aspects of his thinking,
his disruptive potential, while again ignoring the rigour of his
philosophical project. In a sense this is fair enough. One of the
more daunting aspects of a diligent reading of Derrida is that
his work often appears to assume a thorough working knowledge of most of the history of Western philosophy, as well as vast
tranches of non-Western philosophy, Western non-philosophy
and non-Western non-philosophy too. For instance the opening
section 'Exergue' of his influential essay 'White Mythologies',
which takes as its jumping-off point an obscure chapter in the
obscure Anatole France book *The Garden of Epicurus*, then
assures us that to understand the argument requires an 'examination of the texts of Renan and Nietzsche ... as well as those
of Freud, Bergson and Lenin ... and one should reread the
entirety of Mallarmé's texts on linguistics, aesthetics and political economy'.[14] The footnotes to this paragraph also list Lacan,
Jakobson, Benveniste, Althusser, Hegel, Balibar, Marx and Jean-
Joseph Goux.

Thus Derrida was no gadfly. He read deeply and intensely,
scouring each text for the sorts of inconsistencies, hidden assumptions and breaks in logic which would become the target of
deconstruction. It was a way of working he was able to joke
about, as when, being interviewed in his extensive and chaotic
home library for the 2002 documentary *Derrida*, he tells the
interviewer, 'I haven't read all the books that are here ... Maybe
three or four. But I read those three or four really, really well.'

He also attempted to write really, really well. Having called
into question the binary opposition philosophy/literature (also
true/false, real/fictional, logical/rhetorical) his work often aspires
to the condition of art, and employs many of its strategies,
including irony, juxtaposition and hyperbole. While the latter
in Derrida does not carry the strategic prominence that it does
in, for instance, Nietzsche, Derrida confesses he is 'an incorrigi-
ble hyperbolite. A generalized hyperbolite. In short, I exaggerate.
I always exaggerate ... hyperbolism [has] invaded my life and

work. Everything that proceeds under the name of "deconstruction" arises from it, of course.'[15]

Here, then, was a new way of doing philosophy, in a new
language. One that, rather than wishing to expel the poets from
the polis – as philosophers had from Plato to J. L. Austin – had
as part of its grounding notion the position that not only are
the barriers between poetic speech and other utterances vague
and sometimes meaningless, but that, arguably, poetic speech
has a greater access to the particular 'truth' at which philosophy
has aimed in its narrative. It was, and is, exhilarating stuff. For
example, 'White Mythologies' opens with:

> From philosophy, rhetoric. That is here, to make a volume,
> approximately, more or less, a flower, to extract a flower, to
> mount it, or rather to have it mount itself, bring itself to light –
> and turning away, as if from itself, come round again, such a
> flower engraves – learning to cultivate, by means of a lapidary's
> reckoning, patience.[16]

While his seminal early essay 'Violence and Metaphysics' opens
like an incantation:

> That philosophy died yesterday, since Hegel or Marx, Nietzsche,
> or Heidegger – and philosophy should still wander towards the
> meaning of its death – or that it has always lived knowing itself
> to be dying (as is silently confessed in the shadow of the very
> discourse which *declared philosophia perennis*); that philosophy
> died *one day*, *within* history, or that it has always fed on its own
> agony, on the violent way it opens history by opposing itself to
> nonphilosophy, which is its past and its concern, its death and
> wellspring; that beyond the death, or dying nature, of philoso-
> phy, perhaps even because of it, thought still has a future, or
> even, as is said today, is still entirely to come because of what
> philosophy has held in store; or, more strangely still, that the
> future itself has a future – all these things are unanswerable ques-
> tions. By right of birth, for one time at least, these are problems
> put to philosophy as problems philosophy cannot resolve.[17]

If philosophy is 'wandering toward the meaning of its death', Derrida is teasing out its implications, in a sense of praying over it.

For many outside France, Derrida arrived, as it were, fully formed. Here was an *enfant terrible* who had declared, notoriously, 'there is nothing outside the text' (*il n'y a pas de hors-texte*). This was a sentence destined to be ripped from its context by both supporters and antagonists and reduced to a slogan, often held up as proof positive of either the calumnies or daring of postmodern thought. Derrida and 'that lot' had declared the author dead, and argued that all is text, that all truth is conditional and that the great narratives should be treated, at best with suspicion, at worst with contempt. To which Derrida would have answered: *well, perhaps*.

Also, reflecting a bias towards language and logic, most Anglophone introductions to Derrida have tended to start their analyses via linguistics and semiotics. In this version, Saussure's *Course in General Linguistics* establishes the arbitrary nature of the relationship between the signifier and the signified, the word and that which it denotes, and Derrida simply represents what happens when this argument is taken to its logical conclusion – *viz* all signifiers float free of their putative signifieds such that no transcendental signified can guarantee meaning. We become trapped in a mesh of language (*il n'y a pas de hors-texte*), where all is relative, contingent, tending towards chaos.

This reading does two things. First, it situates Derrida as simply a logical endpoint to language's dominance of philosophy in the twentieth century. Someone had to take the thought of Saussure to its logical conclusion, so it may as well be Derrida. The uniqueness and richness of his thought is effaced – anyone could have thought of that. But it also pulls him away from the philosophical discourses that, positively and negatively, were touchstones for a certain generation of French philosophers. These include Nietzsche, Marx and Freud, but also the phenomenology of Husserl and Sartre, Alexandre Kojève's revolutionary 1933 lectures on Hegel, the battles against and within existentialism as represented by Sartre and Heidegger, debates around communism and Algeria, as well as the influence of thinkers who are less well known outside of France – Georges Canguilhem, Jean Cavaillès and Gabriel Marcel.

The 'Derrida' who became something of a cause célèbre in the 1980s had in fact won his 'fundamental concepts' through exhaustive philosophical work. For obvious pop cultural reasons, as well as philosophical reasons, this has generally been ignored. In fairness, Derrida played to this crowd. Intellectually demanding French philosophers who at the age of thirty-seven are still slaving away unrecognised on obscure passages of Edmund Husserl concerning the origin of geometry, and of Rousseau's use of the word 'supplement', don't tend to find themselves, fifteen years later, smoking pipes and being sexy and incomprehensible in major feature films, so why not enjoy?

The Derridean writings of the mid-1970s and early '80s are his most experimental (again sexy) and autobiographical. While both of these moves are philosophically justifiable in terms of his 'project', neither harmed his growing reputation outside the academy. That his work was difficult also, perhaps, helped. It saved the bother of reading him. To be for or against Derrida could thus be a stance, and that position could be projected back onto him by both those who gloried in him and those who excoriated him.

This ambivalence often fed his work. Unlike that other 'literary philosopher', Nietzsche, he did not turn his back on the academy, whatever the academy's attempts to turn its back on him. 'I hope,' he wrote, 'this mingling of respect and disrespect for the academic heritage and tradition in general is legible in everything I do.'[18]

For the word 'academic', substitute 'philosophical'. As Husserl had argued 'to the things themselves', Derrida's battle cry might have been 'to the texts themselves'. Derrida's achievement is one of reading as much as of writing and, as he puts it, his 'desire to be faithful to the themes and audacities of a thinking'.[19] His 'deconstruction' of the great and sometimes less great works of philosophy, was a form of close reading, as rigorous as that of the New Critics, with whose work his own has parallels. He comes to bury and to praise simultaneously. 'I love very much everything that I deconstruct,' he wrote, 'the texts I want to read from a deconstructive point of view are texts I love.'[20]

For Derrida, this close reading involved taking philosophers at their word, and looking for where this operation leads to inconsistencies and internal contradictions, not due to the infelicities of the writers themselves, but as an inbuilt feature of language, the impossibility of its coherence. It also involved finding in the work of philosophers the points where it broke down or repressed certain notions in order to frame their position. Thus while the master of the spatial, Husserl, is analysed by the metaphor of the temporal, the great materialist Marx is confronted with the ethereal presence of 'spirit' in his work.

By identifying these inconsistencies and contradictions, we are led to explore how the text in question is, indeed, constructed. In part this is a political operation – we 'analyse historically the formation and layers of its concepts', 'carry out a genealogical analysis of a trajectory through which its concepts have been built, used and legitimized' and 'analyse the hidden assumptions.'[21] Deconstruction – which Derrida himself described as 'an ugly and difficult word' – is not a method or a tool imposed from outside the text, rather, 'there is always already deconstruction at work in works.' Here we can identify, for instance, where power lies, who is signing the cheques. In the Derridean sense, we also uncover logocentrism, phallogocentrism, ethnocentrism, among others.

But it is, crucially, also to seek out that term, or terms, which give the text the illusion of stability, a centre that holds the text in place. The history of Western metaphysics, Derrida argues, is a history of these 'centres'. He listed such terms in the paper he delivered at Baltimore, as '*eidos* [which he defines as form, essence, type, species], *arche* [beginning, origin, source], *telos* [end, purpose, goal], *energia* [energy, at-work-ness], *ousia* [essence, existence, substance, subject], *alethia* [truth], transcendentality, consciousness, God, man, and so forth,' each taken up by different eras, different philosophers, different systems.

Add to that another 'centre' that later became crucial to Derrida: justice. Our system of law is predicated on the existence

of justice, as our systems of theology are predicated on the existence of God, and yet neither justice nor God occur within the
systems, nor can their existence be guaranteed. They are both,
argues Derrida 'to come'. But this does not refute the system,
rather it is the engine of both its survival and its need to adapt.
Law will cease to have a function on the arrival of justice, as
theology will be made redundant by the arrival of God, and philosophy on the arrival of Truth.

Until such time, there will be deconstruction.

The unknown thirty-six-year-old who rose to speak at Baltimore
in 1966 was not yet the father of deconstruction. The boy who
grew up in Algeria had thus far failed twice to get into the École
normale supérieure, failed the oral examination once there, failed
to hand in a thesis, spent a year at Harvard not making any progress, then two years back teaching high school in Algeria as part
of his military service, and was lecturing at the ENS under the
tutelage of his old teacher Louis Althusser. Married, with one
child, his only book consisted of an introduction to Husserl's
On the Origin of Geometry, published five years earlier. While
a number of the essays which were to make up his first major
contribution, *Writing and Difference,* had been published, they
had received only moderate attention. His lecture series, including 'Heidegger and the question of Being and history' and 'The
theory of meaning in [Husserl's] *Logical Investigations* and
Ideas I', though esteemed at the academy, were out of step with
a philosophy department where bright young Marxist things
such as Étienne Balibar, Jacques Rancière and Pierre Macherey
were caught up in the heady excitement surrounding Althusser's
For Marx and the collective *Reading Capital*, far away from
Derrida's obscure concerns with phenomenology. Both Marxism
and structuralism, broadly speaking, regarded phenomenology
as theoretically regressive, centred as it was on the 'subject',
which both discourses were working to overcome.

At the time, Derrida felt he was making little progress, and
later described his 'solitude' and 'reclusiveness'.[22] 'I have the
impression', he wrote to Althusser, 'that I can see pearls out of

reach, like a fisherman afraid of the water even though he's a connoisseur of pearls.'[23] And yet ... in part Derrida's reticence – his fear even – was because he knew he was doing something new.

In 1965 two small articles of his were published in *Cahiers pour l'analyse* (one of the copious short-lived reviews generated at the time), one on Lévi-Strauss, and one on the *Essay on the Origin of Languages* by Rousseau. In the same letter to Althusser, he mentioned 'this little text on writing' he was working on, which would become 'Writing before the letter', which did indeed cause something of a stir on publication in two parts in *Critique*. This would become the first section in *Of Grammatology*, and the two smaller pieces were the germ for the rest of the book.

None of this added up to the sort of influence which would even get him invited to a colloquy such as the Baltimore one, let alone point to the possibility that he would overturn the entire philosophy it presumed to celebrate. And yet in less than an hour this is precisely what he did, and the obscure teaching assistant from Algeria was the most talked about philosopher in the world.

Something had just happened. An event, perhaps?

1

The Kid

The child who comes remains unforeseeable, it speaks, all by itself, as at the origin of another world, or at the other origin of this one...

— Echographies of Television

I have only one language and it is not my own.

— Monolingualism of the Other

His name was not even Jacques Derrida.

I am looking for his grave. The cemetery at Ris-Orangis, the Paris outer suburb where Derrida spent much of his adult life with his wife, the psychoanalyst Marguerite Aucouturier, is as nondescript as the suburb itself. Windswept and heterodox, there are sections for Christians, for Muslims, for Jews, but they flow into one another, placed according to chronology and available space. The rows are Jewish, Christian, Christian, Muslim, Jewish, Christian, Jewish, Jewish, Muslim. I am not sure where to look.

Ris-Orangis is an hour's drive south of Paris, snaking away from the Seine and back to it. There is a preschool here named after Derrida and one, incongruously, after Pablo Picasso. At the cemetery, two men in hi-vis jackets are blowing leaves and watch me striding up and down the rows, Christian, Muslim,

Jewish, Jewish, Jewish, Muslim. I nod at them and do another
lap, searching for Jacques Derrida.

One of the leaf blowers turns off his machine and approaches
me, 'Puis-je vous aider, Monsieur?' 'Oui,' I say, 'connaissez-vous
Jacques Derrida?' He looks puzzled, repeats theatrically, baffled
by my Anglophone pronunciation. '*Jacques* Derrida? Jacques
Derrida? Jacques Derrida?' Then realisation. 'Ah,' he says, throwing his arms wide and switching to English. 'Yes, Jacques Derrida!
The poet!'

The grave is not in any specific section. Facing a wooden fence
is a simple slab of marble on which his name is chiselled. He is
Derrida, yes, but the first name is the one he was born with, and
it is written too far away from his surname, as though it was a
last-minute decision not to write Jacques, with its fat q and u.
On his grave, as on his birth certificate, and as to his friends,
he is not Jacques. He is Jackie. Born Algiers 1930. Died Ris-
Orangis 2004.

It is not known in which of the cinemas in Algiers Haïm Aaron
Prosper (Aimé) Derrida, a wine merchant like his own father,
Abraham, and Georgette Sultana Esther Safar, daughter of
Moïse Safar and Fortunée Temime, saw Charlie's Chaplin's first
full-length feature film, *The Kid*, or even if they saw it together,
although the release date of 1921, the six to eighteen months
it took films to transfer from Paris to Algiers, and their marriage in 1923 make it tempting to believe that they did. There
were between fifteen and twenty cinemas in Algiers at the time,
most of them named – in a way that was to haunt Aimé and
Georgette's third son – after their equivalents in Paris, including Le Vox, Le Majestic, Le Splendid, Le Cameo, Le Regent, Le
Cinéma Musset, L'Empire, Le Bijou, L'Alhambra and Le Colisée.

Chaplin was a superstar in Algiers, as he was throughout the
world. While most films that transferred from Paris to Algiers,
such as *The Blue Angel*, *All Quiet on the Western Front* and *The
Threepenny Opera*, played for a week – plenty of time for as
many of the city's 400,000 people to see them if they wanted to –
Chaplin's 1931 film *City Lights* played for six weeks in the spring

of 1932. For many Algerians – then as now – the Little Tramp represented the common man fighting against the oppressors.

Chaplin himself visited Algiers in April 1931, but was forced to cancel all of the excursions his hosts had planned – to the Tomb of the Christian Woman, and the funerary monument to the Berber King Juba II and Queen Cleopatra Selene II, daughter of Cleopatra and Mark Antony – as the crowds that followed him everywhere, crying 'Charlot, long live Charlot!' were too large. As he wrote in his travelogue *A Comedian Sees the World*, 'With all his Omar Khayyam philosophy, the Arab is an enthusiastic film fan, for when we arrived thousands were lined along the road all the way to the hotel.'[1] In private he was less charitable, saying to his travelling companion, the actress May Reeves, 'What an unbearable race. Every cobbler takes himself for a sheik, although he is less than nothing! Enough of Arabs and these beastly Algerians, let's go back to France.'[2]

It is unlikely that Chaplin, mostly trapped in his hotel, passed down the propitiously named rue Saint-Augustin. Had he, the adoring fans may have included Aimé and Georgette, their eldest son René Abraham and their babe in arms, less than one year old in 1931, a boy they named after Jackie Coogan, the star of Chaplin's *The Kid*.

Jackie was born at daybreak on 15 July 1930. His mother was 'playing poker (already, always!) at my birth,' he wrote. Georgette was a week short of her thirtieth birthday (Aimé five years older), and her passion for poker lasted all her life. And yet it may be that the game was a way of distracting herself; only ten months earlier she had lost her second child, Paul, at three months old. The Derridas had, it would seem, chosen a quick, but risky, way to assuage their mourning.

This older brother haunted Jackie throughout his life. In his 'Circumfession' (written between visits to his mother, dying in hospital, he would call the book 'a kind of vigil, a wake') he described himself as existing 'in the place of another'. The death of Paul, it is impossible not to speculate, was responsible for the birth of Jackie.

Jackie's relationship with his mother was particularly intense. He was a boy who 'up until puberty cried out "Mummy I'm scared" every night', until, in an echo of the narrator in Proust, his parents allowed him to sleep each night on a divan beside their bed.[3] Georgette, he would later write, was not a very demonstrative or affectionate mother. She did not just keep her poker face for the card table.

The Algeria into which he was born was, in 1930, in the midst of an ambiguous celebration. Ten days before his birth was Le Centenaire de l'Algérie française, the hundredth anniversary of French colonial rule. There had been six months of celebrations, artistic, cultural and sporting.

The French president, Gaston Doumergue, unveiled a metre monument on the beach at Sidi Ferruch, 30 kilometres west of Algiers, the spot where 34,000 French soldiers commenced their invasion in 1830. The monument featured two entwined female figures, one representing France, looking maternal and protective, and the other representing Algeria, seeking guidance and protection. In his speech Doumergue said, 'The celebration of the centenary will show in a decisive fashion the human, peaceful, just and beneficial character of the French colonization methods and of the work of civilization she is pursuing.' The new Musée des Beaux Arts was opened in Algiers, as was an exhibition in Oran – each pavilion on its five hectares allowing people to tour all of Greater France in a day. Even Charlie Chaplin had, it was rumoured, been invited, but could not attend as he was shooting *City Lights*. The commissioner general of the Centenary, Gustave Mercier, saluted 'another France, barely a hundred years old, already strong, full of life and future, uniting in its happy formula Latin races and indigenous races, in order to make them all French races.'[4]

Eighty thousand tourists visited Algeria in the course of the year, attending its old and new attractions, indulging in the Orientalist thrill. As James McDougall writes in *The History of Algeria*, settlers 'saw their security of livelihood, home and person as dependent on the continued subjugation of Algerians, the "native peril" whom they saw through a confused combination of racial and religious stereotypes, exotic fantasies, imagined paternal benevolence and, from time to time, hysterical terror.'[5]

Frantz Fanon, the Martiniquais psychiatrist and political philosopher who would chronicle the Algerian independence struggle, would go further, noting it is always the coloniser who is seen to make history: 'His life is an epic, an odyssey. He is the absolute beginning. A compartmentalized Manichean and immobile world, a world of statues: the statue of the general who conquered the country, the statue of the engineer who built the bridge.'⁶ By contrast, the natives were part of the landscape, and thus dehumanised.

The question of where the Juifs d'Algérie, the community into which Jackie was born, fitted into Algerian society was, inevitably, a complex one. Derrida's family were Sephardic, and claimed roots from Toledo in Spain. In 1870, Algerian Jews were granted French citizenship by the Crémieux Decree, which brought their rights in line with the rest of the pied-noir (black-foot, i.e. wearing shoes) population of Algeria. The majority Muslim population had no such rights, and were subject to the Code de l'indigénat, which gave them, at best, second-class status before the law. Although tensions had not reached the scale that would lead to and accompany the Algerian War, they were already present. At the same cinemas where Aimé and Georgette had watched Chaplin, Algerians 'clapped and cheered when the hero made stirring speeches about Swiss independence in *William Tell* and when the Foreign Legionnaire heroes in *Le Hommes Sans Nom* (*The Men with No Name*) were shot by Moroccan insurgents.'⁷

In addition, the Jewish population's relationship with the rest of the pied-noir population often mirrored tensions present in France: as one account puts it, for European settlers, 'anti-Semitism tapped into [...] perceptions of themselves as ordinary, hard-working people. Jews were held up as a rich and exploitative breed intent on dominating French Algeria.'⁸ Derrida's grandmother, for instance, had to marry 'clandestinely in the back courtyard of a town hall in Algeria, because of the pogroms (this was in the middle of the Dreyfus affair).'⁹ Despite the clandestine wedding, Jackie's grandmother was part of an 'extraordinary transformation of French Judaism in Algeria'. Where the generation before had been close to the Arab population in language

and customs, she was 'already raising her daughters like bourgeois Parisian girls (16th Arrondissement good manners, piano
lessons, and so on)'.[10] Then, writes Derrida,

> came my parents' generation: few intellectuals, mostly shopkeep-
> ers, some of modest means and some not, and some who were
> already exploiting a colonial situation by becoming the exclu-
> sive representatives of major metropolitan brands: with a tiny
> little office and no secretary, one could, for example, become
> the sole distributor of all the 'Marseille soap' in Northern Africa
> (I'm of course simplifying a bit). Then came my generation (a
> majority of intellectuals: liberal professions, teaching, medicine,
> law, etc.).[11]

This gradual assimilation – and, indeed, *embourgoisement* – of
the Jewish population into Algerian French life saw forenames
gallicised and Jewish religious sites and practices Christianised:
'an insidious Christian contamination', Derrida later called it.
The synagogue was called the temple, bar-mitzvah called first
communion and circumcision called baptism. Derrida later
spoke of a quasi-subgroup, 'indigenous Jews', who could identify neither with the 'models, norms or values' of the French
population, nor those of the Arab.[12]

This 'disorder of identity' could be staggering in its complexity.
'In the milieu where I lived,' Derrida wrote, 'we called all non-
Jewish French people "Catholics", even if they were sometimes
Protestants, or perhaps even Orthodox: "Catholic" meant anyone
who was neither a Jew, a Berber nor an Arab.' At the same time,
settler anti-Semitism in Algeria fed anti-Semitism in France –
Algerian Jews were seen as part of the 'native peril' – 'Arabs of
the Jewish faith.'[13]

It is, of course, biographically reductive to see in this mélange
of identities, politics of naming, contested languages, contested
selves and overlapping boundaries the origin of deconstruction – leaving aside Derrida's problematising of 'origin'. Asked
in 1983 'where it all began', Derrida responded, 'Ay, you want
me to say things like "I-was-born-in-El-Biar-on-the-outskirts-of-

Algiers-in-a-petty-bourgeois-family-of-assimilated-Jews-but ..."
Is that really necessary? I can't do it.'[14]

But he himself recognised precisely this question, writing in
Monolingualism of the Other; or, The Prosthesis of Origin, 'A
Judeo-Franco-Maghrebian genealogy does not clarify everything,
far from it. But could I explain anything without it, ever? No,
nothing.'[15] Just as with every birth, the element of chance remains
irreducible, so 'a series of contingencies have made of me a French
Jew from Algeria born in the generation before the "war of independence": so many singularities, even among Jews, and even
among the Jews of Algeria.'[16] Identity, Derrida noted, 'is never
given, received or attained: only the interminable and indefinitely
phantasmatic process of identification endures.'

Derrida would write that his 'selfhood' was thrice dissociated,
fractured by three 'interdicts':

> (1) First of all, it was cut off from both Arabic or Berber (more
> properly Maghrebian) language and culture. (2) It was also
> cut off from French, and even European language and culture,
> which, from its viewpoint, only constituted a distanced pole or
> metropole, heterogeneous to its history. (3) It was cut off, finally,
> or to begin with, from Jewish memory, and from the history and
> language that one must presume to be their own, but which, at
> a certain point, no longer was. At least not in a typical way for
> the majority of its members, and not in a sufficiently 'lively' and
> internal way.[17]

Life was elsewhere, and

> elsewhere ... meant in the Metropole. In the Capital-City-
> Mother-Fatherland. Sometimes, we would say 'France,' but
> mostly 'the Metropole,' at least in the official language, in the
> imposed rhetoric of discourses, newspapers, and school. As
> for my family, and almost always elsewhere, we used to say
> 'France' among ourselves. ('Those people can afford vaca-
> tions in France'; 'that person is going to study in France'; 'he
> is going to take the waters in France, generally at Vichy'; 'this

teacher is from France'; 'this cheese is from France.') ... A place of fantasy, therefore, at an ungraspable distance. As a model of good speech and good writing, it represented the language of the master.[18]

And not the language of his neighbours 'the Arabs', their language being 'a strange kind of alien language as the language of the other ... a hidden frontier, at once invisible and impassable: the segregation was as efficacious as it was subtle',[19] so that they were 'very near and infinitely far away, such was the distance that experience instilled in us, so to speak. Unforgettable and generalizable.'[20]

Derrida did not forget, and throughout his life generalised about this hidden frontier, finding it in politics, ethics, language, sentences, words. 'The splitting of the ego in me at least,' he writes in 'Circumfession', 'is no transcendental claptrap.'[21] The right to self-possession and the ability to make meaning from a position of dominance, security and strength were, from childhood, disputed. He was, as he put it in one of his last interviews, 'a sort of child in the margins of Europe, a child of the Mediterranean, who was not simply French nor simply African, and who passed his time traveling between one culture and the other feeding questions he asked himself out of that instability'.[22] Analysing himself, Derrida wrote that 'The absence of a stable model of identification for an ego – in all its dimensions, linguistic, cultural and so on – give rise to impulses that are always on the brink of collapse ... under the guise of radical destructuring.'[23]

In 1934, shortly before the birth of Jackie's sister, Janine, the Derridas moved from rue Saint-Augustin to 13 rue d'Aurelle-de-Paladines in the district of El-Biar (the Well), an affluent suburb on the outskirts of Algiers. The house was located 'on the edge of an Arab district and a Catholic cemetery' and remained the Derridas' home until they fled to France in 1962, having only just managed to pay it off. The four-year-old Jackie Derrida was, by all accounts, a charming boy, who wore a boater and sang Maurice Chevalier songs, in a house dominated by his maternal grandmother.[24]

This idyll ended when Jackie went to school, where racial tensions manifested themselves physically in violence and the threat of violence, including 'anti-Arab racism, anti-Semitic, anti-Italian, anti-Spanish racism'. School also meant separation from his mother, who would take him in and then leave him with his teachers – 'monsters of abstraction' as he would call them.

> The first years of nursery school were a tragedy. I cried every single day in school. Before nursery school it was absolutely traumatic for me. It was like a repeated trauma every day for me. I remember it, it was absolutely terrible. And I have to say in a certain way it never ended. Throughout my life, even to today, I've never liked school.[25]

At school he learned the history of France, of which he was assured he was a citizen, yet not a word about Algeria.[26] Algeria existed as a land of homologues – streets named rue Michelet and avenue Georges-Clemenceau, regions named Burgundy and Bordeaux, while the academic year was the French one. 'Deep down, I wonder whether one of my first and imposing figures of spectrality, of spectrality itself, was not France; I mean everything that bore its name.'[27]

This immersion in the 'overthere', as Derrida later referred to France, started, inevitably, with language. While students did have the option of learning Arabic, 'French was a language supposed to be maternal,' but this was a mother tongue 'whose source, norms, rules, and law were situated elsewhere'. The one language that young Jackie possessed – or which possessed him – was not his own, it was the language of the coloniser.[28]

It was nonetheless the language he would come to love. 'I think', he wrote, 'that if I love this language like I love my life, and sometimes more than certain native French do, it is because I love it as a foreigner who has been welcomed, and who has appropriated this language for himself as the only possible language for him.'[29] This Oedipal, ambivalent love explained 'why there is in my writing a certain, I wouldn't say perverse but somewhat violent, way of treating this language. Out of love. Love in general passes

by way of the love of language ... You don't just go and do anything with language; it pre-exists us and it survives us.[30]

And yet the original scar still worked within it throughout his
life and work:

> My attachment to the French language takes forms that I some-
> times consider 'neurotic'. I feel lost outside the French language.
> The other languages which, more or less clumsily, I read, decode,
> or sometimes speak, are languages I shall never inhabit ... Not
> only am I lost, fallen, and condemned outside the French lan-
> guage, I have the feeling of honoring or serving all idioms, in
> a word, of writing the 'most' and the 'best' when I sharpen the
> resistance of my French, the secret 'purity' of my French, the one
> I was speaking about earlier on, hence its resistance, its relentless
> resistance to translation; translation into all languages, including
> another such French.[31]

But while the French language 'provided a model, a uniform
and a uniformity, a habitus, and one had to conform to it', its
sovereignty was not absolute – Derrida recalls that he and his
classmates made fun of a teacher who actually came 'from the
Metropole' – finding his accent ridiculous.

Here, in the complex relationship Jackie had with language,
we see the performative space in which the philosopher Jacques
Derrida carried out his task, problematising terms such as habitus,
home, the gift, the promise, hospitality, writing and speech.
'Deconstruction', he wrote, 'is always deeply concerned with the
"other" of language ... The critique of logocentrism is above all
else the search for the "other" and the "other of language".'[32] If he
was forced into the French language, so he would become the one
to make 'said language come to him, forcing the language then to
speak itself by itself, in another way, in his language.'[33]

If school was a tragedy, worse was to follow. In March 1940,
his younger brother, Norbert, died of tubercular meningitis. Jackie
now had dead brothers on either side. Then his beloved cousin,
Jean-Pierre, one year older than him, also died, hit by a car, the

shock magnified as he was initially told it was his oldest brother who had died. These events would always haunt Derrida. It was not until many years after the birth of his sons that suddenly he recognised the significance of his naming them Pierre and Jean. The place of ghosts in his philosophy is not inexplicable.

Despite the war having little initial impact in Algeria, anti-Semitism found fertile ground in the Maghreb, with the National Revolution called for by Pétain's Vichy government being embraced with fervour by local leaders. Soon after the German annexation of France, Jews were forbidden from practising certain jobs, quotas were introduced for the civil service and 'liberal professions' and the press threatened that synagogues would be subjected to 'sulphur, pitch, and if possible the fires of hell' to drive the Jews out 'like rabid dogs'.[34] In spite of finishing top of the class, which should have won him the honour of raising the flag at morning assembly, ten-year-old Jackie was replaced by a non-Jewish student.[35]

On 7 October 1940, the Crémieux Decree, and therefore French citizenship, was revoked, resulting in some 120,00 Jews of Algeria becoming non-citizens. This was not a decision imposed by the National Socialists, as Derrida was always at pains to point out: 'The withdrawal of French citizenship from the Jews of Algeria, with everything that followed, was the deed of the French alone. They decided that all by themselves, in their heads; they must have been dreaming about it all along; they implemented it all by themselves.'[36]

In September 1941, quotas were also introduced into schools: only 14 per cent of children could be Jewish, a system not implemented in France proper. Then in October 1942 the quota was reduced from 14 to 7 per cent. Jackie – 'a little black, very Arab Jew' – was summoned into the office of 'the only school official whose name I remember today,' who said to him, 'You are going home, my little friend, your parents will get a note.'[37] For Derrida this was 'an earthquake', 'a natural catastrophe for which there was no explanation'.[38] The decision reflected the virulence of Algerian/Vichy anti-Semitism. 'The wound', wrote Derrida, 'was of another order, and it never healed: the daily insults from the children, my classmates, the kids in the street, and sometimes the threats or blows aimed at the "dirty Jew", which, I might say, I came to see myself as.'[39]

It is, as Fanon argued, 'the racist who creates his inferior';[40] or, more specifically, in the words of Sartre, 'The Jew is one whom other men consider a Jew, that is the simple truth from which we must start ... it is the anti-Semite who makes the Jew.'[41] Before his expulsion Derrida's identification with Judaism had been, one might say, sufficient but not necessary. Made a 'Jew', and unmade from being French, Derrida was suddenly forced to study at an exclusively Jewish school, set up by Jewish teachers who had themselves been forced out of their teaching positions by the quotas. From day one, he hated it.

> Immediately I felt uneasy about belonging, about being part of this Jewish, closed and communitarian identity. I was twelve at the time, I was twelve, and at the same time I rejected, of course, the antisemitic and racist environment and I rejected in some way, in some interior and subtle way, rejected the Jewish community.[42]

His resistance in having to identify by fiat as Jewish was further complicated by his feeling that a clandestine part of his self was being handed over. 'I have', he wrote,

> often presented myself, barely playing, like a Marrano, one of those Jews converted by force in Spain and Portugal, who cultivated their Judaism in secret, at times to the extent of not knowing what it consisted in. This theme has also interested me from a political point of view. When a State does not respect the right to the secret, it becomes threatening: police violence, inquisition, totalitarianism.[43]

Or, more pithily, 'Belonging – the fact of avowing one's belonging, of putting in common – be it family, nation, tongue – spells the loss of a secret.'[44]

The idea of the 'secret' is important in Derrida's later explorations of identity, individual and collective, in works such as *The*

Gift of Death, with its meditations on Abraham and Isaac. As a philosopher, Derrida was no atheist, and Jewish themes and questions were central to the fabric of his work. This is overt in works such as *A Silkworm of One's Own*, in which he teases out his emotional and metaphorical relationship to the tallith, the prayer shawl which his maternal grandfather gave him, and crucially it informs his discourse around Judaism disrupting Greek thought in such key works as 'Violence and Metaphysics'. His work is also full of terms that carry with them Jewish connotations: the veil, Messianism and destinerrance – that roaming which is part of language, part of life, where the destination is never reached so the roaming becomes the destination – which echoes the story of the Wandering Jew. And, as his translator and collaborator Geoffrey Bennington notes dryly, 'Certain readers have noticed a stylistic family resemblance between Derrida's writings and the interminable commentaries of the Talmudists.'[45]

Jackie's expulsion lasted less than a year. On 8 November 1942, Allied Forces landed on the coast near Algiers and, in coordination with the Géo Gras Group, a mainly Jewish arm of Algeria's French Resistance, retook Algeria as part of their annexing of West Africa as a launching point for offensives in Southern Europe. Jackie celebrated their arrival, the return of their films, all the things that 'made them powerful (including as a dream) music, dance, cigarettes.'[46]

Algiers became, virtually overnight, the capital of Free France. But the Jewish population had to wait until October 1943 for the Crémieux Decree to be reinstated, an act Derrida again found disconcerting.

> Then, one day, 'one fine day', without, once again, my asking for anything, and still too young to know it in a properly political way, I found the aforementioned citizenship again. The state, to which I never spoke, had given it back to me. The state, which was no longer Pétain's 'French State', was recognizing me anew. That was, I think, in 1943; I had still never gone 'to France'; I had never been there.[47]

Citizenship – its meaning, limits, and the power of states and nations to grant or revoke it – would remain a crucial question in Derrida's philosophy and politics, and his later interventions in, for instance, Israel and Palestine, his passionate engagement with South Africa in the struggle against apartheid, and with any 'group that finds itself one day deprived, as a group, of its citizenship by a state that, with the brutality of a unilateral decision, withdraws it without asking for their opinion, and without the said group gaining back any other citizenship.'[48]

The other anti-Semitic laws were overturned on 14 March 1943, and in April Jackie was allowed to return to the Lycée Ben Aknoun. It was now also a military hospital and POW camp for Italians, so classes were conducted in huts elsewhere in the school grounds. Jackie, who had regularly bunked off from the Jewish school, became by his own admission a bad student, spending his time playing sport, chasing girls and visiting the cinema. 'For a sedentary little kid from Algiers, cinema offered an extraordinary boon of travel.'[49]

But if Jackie was not passionate about school, he was soon passionate about reading. He encountered as a teenager many of the writers who were to inform his life's work – Gide, Proust, Rousseau, Valéry, Camus, and Artaud. He identified particularly with the latter, finding himself in sympathy 'with that man who said that he had nothing to say ... while at the same time he was inhabited by the passion and the drive to write.' But these writers still described the world of 'overthere' – 'the discovery of French literature, the access to this so unique mode of writing that is called "French-literature" was the experience of a world without any tangible continuity with the one in which we lived, with almost nothing in common with our natural or social landscapes'.[50]

In the febrile atmosphere of wartime Algeria, literature provided Jackie with a medium which, by its very nature, disrupted power.

> Literature seemed to me, in a confused way, to be the institution which allows one to *say everything*, in *every way*. The law of literature tends, in principle, to defy or lift the law. It therefore

allows one to think the essence of the law in the experience of this 'everything to say'. It is an institution which tends to overflow the institution.[51]

Operating within a matrix of laws contested from above and below, which, as the revocation and reinstatement of his citizenship had shown, were often arbitrary, literature subverted this matrix, and opened a space for resistance. 'As an adolescent, I no doubt had the feeling that I was living in conditions where it was both difficult and therefore necessary, urgent, to say things that were not allowed.'[52]

The overthrow of Vichy France in September 1944 did little to ease tension within Algeria as 'French liberation' was, again, partial – *les indigents* gained little from it. The Derridas again found themselves as both the oppressors and the oppressed. 'Racism was everywhere at the time. Being Jewish and a victim of anti-Semitism didn't spare one the anti-Arab racism I felt everywhere around me, in manifest or latent form.'[53] On 8 May 1945, Arab nationalists in the town of Sétif held a demonstration marking France's liberation from Germany. Someone fired a shot and protesters murdered more than one hundred French residents. In response, during five days of violence more than 15,000 Arabs and Berbers were killed. In addition, 4,500 arrests were made and 99 death penalties handed down.

In 1947 Jackie failed the first part of his baccalaureate, which, his older brother René noted, finally jolted him out of his complacency.[54] This was also when Jackie discovered philosophy, reading Bergson, Nietzsche and, intensely, Sartre. He found himself 'in a certain ecstatic bedazzlement' as he read the latter's *Nausea*, a book he would continue to admire throughout his life. He also immersed himself in *Being and Nothingness*, reading it at the local Algiers library. Despite his later criticisms of Sartre ('not a very powerful philosopher, not a very good writer'), he always recognised his debt to this initial encounter.[55]

Sartrean existentialism, with its appeal to the real issues of everyday life, its focus on individual responsibility and authenticity, and its atheism, was, in a world emerging from war, very much in vogue, and Derrida's surviving teenage essays in philosophy are awash with Sartrean language – '*pour-soi*', '*en-soi*', '*angoisse*' – as he grappled with such things as the difference between existence and essence. His earliest surviving essay is called 'Moral Experience', a thoroughly Sartrean title and field of investigation. As late as his first year at the Lycée Louis-le-Grand, he was being advised 'not to imitate existentialist language too slavishly'.[56]

Sartre also represented the possibility of allying philosophy and literature at a time when the seventeen-year-old Jackie found himself torn between the two. He later joked that his choice of the former was a pragmatic one – the money was better.[57] For all that, his corpus, by his own admission, combined them. 'I'm amused by the idea that my adolescent desire – let's call it that – should have directed me toward something in writing which was neither one nor the other.'[58]

Passing his baccalaureate on the second attempt, Jackie – in a moment straight out of a bad movie – was still undecided as to what to do next when he happened to hear a programme on Radio Algiers offering career advice. The programme mentioned a place that was 'overthere' – the École normale supérieure (ENS) in Paris. Jackie decided immediately that it was what he wanted.

Enrolling in a *hypokhâgne* – essentially a crammer's course – at the Lycée Bugeaud, where Camus had also studied, he took philosophy under Jan Czarnecki, who, despite his dry method, as he guided his students from the pre-Socratics to the modern day, Derrida later called 'remarkable'.[59]

Derrida immediately joined the Cogito Club, an after-school philosophy group, where students presented papers on subjects they themselves found interesting. It was here that he first became acquainted with three philosophers who shaped his life: Hegel, Heidegger and, crucially, Edmund Husserl, whose *Cartesian Meditations* had been translated into French by Emmanuel Lévinas in 1931. Despite the philosophical intimacy Derrida later shared with Husserl, he initially found his work 'frigid', preferring Heidegger, whose *What Is Metaphysics?* he devoured, noting that 'The question of anguish, of the experience of nothingness prior to negation suited my personal sense of pathos.'[60]

Two of Derrida's essays from the Club survive. The first is on Sartre's critique of Husserl's intentionality and the 'natural attitude' – which, as we shall see, are precisely the contested points that later generated Derrida's own philosophical work. The second is on Heidegger, whom Derrida accuses of using:

> Noisy, pretentious and heavy dialect ... [a] crowd of neologisms of which a good part are superfluous, this reverse precocity, consists in deadening and complicating his language, as if for fun, and in giving the most everyday, the simplest of faults an air of profundity.[61]

Derrida's prejudices against this sort of writing were, one might point out, not ongoing.

Jackie excelled at his *hypokhâgne* – but life remained elsewhere. For his second year – the *khâgne* – Derrida knew he had to leave Algeria and cross the Mediterranean to Paris. He applied for, and won a place at the Lycée Louis-le-Grand, alma mater of Sartre, Merleau-Ponty, Verlaine, Diderot, as well as Robespierre and de Sade, Chirac and Pompidou.

Jackie was to be boarder 424, and he would be utterly miserable.

'From Algiers, the white city, I arrived in Paris, the black city.'[62] Black, and grey – Paris in September 1949 was far from the city of the nineteen-year-old Jackie's dreams. While suffering less bomb damage than many other Allied cities, Paris was run down and exhausted only four years after the occupation, and thirteen years before the then culture minister André Malraux's introduction of laws to maintain and restore its historical buildings.

The trip from Algiers to Marseilles – the first time Jackie had left Algeria, the first time he had set foot in France – was traumatic. He was seasick, and spent the entire passage vomiting. For all that he was later to theorise the disputed nature of boundaries, the symbolism of moving across this one could not have been more starkly represented.

At Lycée Louis-le-Grand the boys boarded in dormitories, washed in cold water and ate food so bad that some students went on hunger strikes. Unlike the day boys, the boarders wore grey smocks from morning to night, and their movements were subject to strict surveillance. The boys slept in large dormitories without curtains between the beds.[63]

Despite the privations, Jackie continued to excel in philosophy. His teacher, Etienne Borne, while more traditional in his philosophical interests than Czarnecki, was not untouched by the existentialism of the time. Nonetheless, as a Christian Democrat and one of the founders of the Christian-democratic Mouvement républicain populaire, he attempted to overcome existentialism's atheism in works such as *The Problem of Evil*, and the emphatically named *God Is Not Dead*.

Borne's religious concerns opened new areas of thinking for Jackie. His essays of the time seek to push back against the nihilism that is arguably implicit in existentialism – the position that life is absurd and therefore meaningless. For Jackie, if philosophy tended to this conclusion, it was a fault in philosophy or, more precisely, it was a 'characteristic' of philosophy. Life itself does not tend to this nihilistic conclusion, unless, for instance, the waters are muddied by philosophy. Analysing the most nihilistic of actions, suicide, Jackie argued that, in assuming the divine power to choose between life and death, I assert my own value. What appears most nihilistic therefore is not nihilistic. Man, wrote Jackie, is condemned to be an optimist. Consciously or not, his argument echoes that of Camus' *Myth of Sisyphus*, with its opening line, 'There is but one truly serious philosophical problem and that is suicide', and its conclusion, 'One must imagine Sisyphus happy.' This was also Derrida's first foray into regarding philosophy as a narrative, where its very form implies its conclusions.[64]

Two other thinkers were of particular importance to Jackie at this point. The first was the Christian existentialist Gabriel Marcel, whose two-volume *The Mystery of Being* attempted to distinguish between a 'problem', which exists independently of any individual and can be solved, and a 'mystery', which is one's own, and cannot. Life for Marcel is not a problem to be solved but a mystery to be lived.

The other was Simone Weil, whose Christian mysticism, in the strongest sense of that term, seemed to move him profoundly – he often gave *Gravity and Grace* as a present to friends.[65] Weil argued, if that is the right term given her numinous, aphoristic style, that human life is marked by 'gravity' and it is only by receiving God's gift – grace – that we can be redeemed and life's questions, which are beyond our understanding, can be answered.

Weil was one of the first women to attend the ENS, famously finishing first in her entrance exam ahead of second-placed Simone de Beauvoir. After experiencing a revelation while reading George Herbert's 'Love III' ('Love bade me welcome, yet my soul drew back'), she converted from Judaism to Catholicism – although she was never baptised, in part because she believed herself unworthy, in part in solidarity with the 'lost souls in hell'. She was extreme in how she lived her philosophy, which contributed to her early death at the age of thirty-four – despite her physical frailty she worked in an auto factory to understand the debilitating effects of factory work; and while living in the United States she starved herself during the war in solidarity with those left in France.

Jackie took up Weil's notion that we are powerless to save ourselves, writing that a way was needed beyond philosophy – with its tendency towards nihilism – but which did not, unlike Weil's position, reject philosophy outright but surpassed it in a way that 'would also be a return to existence enriched and purified by reflection'. This existence was in Sartrean terms 'être-pour-soi', or 'being-for-itself'. Jackie again equated this with the idea of a 'secret' – not one that we choose to keep, but one which we cannot communicate.[66] While these are the sophomore essays of a nineteen-year-old, again the consistency of Jackie's stance is remarkable. Already some of the main themes of his mature work are present – the idea of philosophy as one narrative among others, with its own characteristics and structural requirements unrelated to the object of its enquiry, a fealty to religious ways of thinking, and a fascination with aporias, those irresolvable internal contradictions which, to Derrida, raise questions of their own about the premises of our argument.

The essays also contain a certain optimism that continued to mark his work whatever his personal circumstances, which even he himself was surprised by

> the obscure chance, my good fortune, a gift for which thanks should be given to goodness knows what archaic power, is that it was always easier for me to bless this destiny. Much easier, more often than not, and even now, to bless than to curse it. The day I would get to know to whom gratitude must be rendered for it, I would know everything, and I would be able to die in peace.[67]

At the Lycée Louis-le-Grand this optimism continued to be sorely tested. He wrote to his friend Michel Monory that he was 'not able to produce anything other than tears ... I'm almost at the end of my tether, Michel, pray for me.' His reading remained resolutely melancholy, including Alain-Fournier's *Le Grand Meaulnes* and Gide's *Strait Is the Gate*.[68]

He again sought solace in the cinema, which acted as 'a drug, entertainment par excellence, uneducated escape, the right to wildness'. For Jackie, as for the man he would become, 'the movies are a hidden, secret, avid, gluttonous joy – in other words, an infantile pleasure'. While cinema never became 'a form of knowledge, or even a real memory', he saw parallels between filmic style and deconstructive writing – both adopting 'all the possibilities of montage, that is, of plays with the rhythms, of grafts of quotations, insertions, changes in tone, changes in language, crossings between "disciplines" and the rules of art, the arts.'[69]

The cinema was also a place of spectrality, phantoms, and, as he later punned on ontology, 'hauntology'. Film lets one see 'new specters appear while remembering (and then projecting them in turn onto the screen) the ghosts haunting films already seen ... Let's say that cinema needed to be invented to fulfil a certain desire for relation to ghosts.'[70] And film shares what we might call a certain consanguinity with psychoanalysis.

If his struggles in France were not enough, Jackie found his trips back to Algeria in the holidays 'gloomy and impossible.' For all its terrors, the stimulation of Paris left Algeria 'a real drag, terribly monotonous' and the people he knew to be 'of no interest'. The political situation remained tense – while the 1947 Statute of Algeria had granted French citizenship to all Algerian men, the creation of the Algerian Assembly, split into a house for the minority Europeans and 'meritorious' Arabs, and a house for the remaining eight million Muslims, did nothing to appease those who rose up in 1954.

While Jackie's brilliance at philosophy already provoked the sort of reactions his later work garnered – 'I confess I find this really difficult to follow,' wrote one teacher, 'remember the reader' – in other subjects he showed little talent.[71] He was okay at French and History-Geography but appalling at languages – English, German and Latin – scoring just 2.5/20 in the latter. His difficulties with languages were to last his whole life, a perpetual embarrassment, particularly once he had achieved worldwide fame with a philosophy that put language and its translation at centre stage.

Jackie failed his written examinations at the end of his first year. This was not unusual at the *khâgne*, but his marks were so low that he was not even eligible for the oral exams that followed (where one of the examiners would have been Merleau-Ponty). He was not only undone by weakness in certain subjects. He was also resorting to that great staple of students over the years, amphetamines bought over the counter, which disturbed his sleep to the extent that he kept nodding off during the exams. In his second year he repeated the same mistakes, this time being forced to abandon the first paper, handing in a blank sheet.

Jackie then had a new philosophy teacher, Maurice Savin, whose lectures were peppered with allusions to Proust, Freud and Bachelard. While recognising Jackie's natural ability, Savin was open about his frustration with Jackie's increasingly dense style. 'There is undeniably a philosopher lurking in there somewhere,' he wrote, 'despite your over-specialised, hermetic language.'[72] One examiner was even more blunt: 'The answers are brilliant in the very same way that they are obscure ... [he] can come back when he's prepared to accept the rules and not invent.'[73] Again the child would be father to the man.

In his third year, Jackie moved off site. While still anxious, and still taking amphetamines (albeit fewer), he worked harder, bringing his other subjects up to an acceptable level, and reaching new levels in philosophy. 'Reliably brilliant results; a definite philosophical personality; you must succeed,' Borne wrote.[74] He passed his written exams, and finally undertook the dreaded oral, where he was asked to speak on a page of Diderot's *Encyclopae-dia*. 'I deployed all my resources to uncover a range of meanings fanning out from each sentence, each word,' he wrote. 'I invented a Diderot who was a virtuoso of litotes, a maverick of literature, a resistance fighter from the word go.'[75] He scraped through, but he fell back ten places from his position after the written exams. In the exasperated words of one of the examiners, 'Look, this text is quite simple, you've simply made it more complicated and laden with meaning, by adding ideas of your own.'[76]

Jackie passed. At twenty-two he was to enter the École normale supérieure. It was to be his home, off and on, for the next thirty years.

2

Husserl et al.

It was Husserl who taught me a technique, a method, a discipline, and who has never left me. Even in moments where I had to question certain presuppositions of Husserl, I tried to do so while keeping to phenomenological discipline.

— *Sur parole*

In everything I've published there are always touchstones announcing what I would like to write about later on — even ten or twenty years later on.

— *I Have a Taste for the Secret*

There will be established in Paris an École normale, where, from all the parts of the Republic, citizens already educated in the useful sciences shall be called upon to learn, from the best professors in all the disciplines, the art of teaching.

So read the 1794 decree that founded the École normale supérieure. Exclusive, often cultish, the ENS remains a breeding ground for France's cultural elite, boasting thirteen Nobel Prizes (eight in physics), twelve Fields Medals for mathematics, and two Nobel Prizes in Literature — the awardees, Henri Bergson and the ubiquitous Sartre, taking their place at the ENS in a philosophical roll-call that includes Simone Weil, Raymond Aron, Jean Hyppolite, Étienne Balibar, Alain Badiou, Jacques

Rancière, Michel Foucault and Louis Althusser. The latter two, like Derrida, ended up on the teaching staff. Sociologists Émile Durkheim and Pierre Bourdieu, the novelist and filmmaker Assia Djebar and the economist Thomas Piketty are among the ENS alumni, while Samuel Beckett and Paul Celan taught there, as did Jacques Lacan.

Despite its influence, or perhaps contributing to it, the student body was small. In the 1950s, when Jackie attended, he was one of only around 200 students, all men. He was one of only six philosophy students accepted that year, along with Michel Serres, later an 'immortal' at the Académie française.

Then as now, for the students, known as *normaliens*, there are no set classes, no programme of study, no reading list. Students study for four years, the third year being taken up with the *agrégation* for the civil service (*normaliens* are trainee civil servants) and the final year being spent on a dissertation. Classes are sought outside of the university, the results brought back. Adding to the sense of a cloistered existence was the fact that many members of the teaching staff were themselves ex-*normaliens*.

It was to one such student-turned-teacher that Jackie Derrida had to report on his first day: Louis Althusser, *caïman* of the university – the professor responsible for preparing students for the *agrégation*. Derrida later remembered

> his face, Louis's so very handsome face, that high forehead, his smile, everything that, in him, during the moments of peace – and there were moments of peace, as many of you here know – radiated kindness, the need for love and the giving of love in return, displaying an incomparable attentiveness to the youth of what is coming, curiously on the lookout from daybreak on for the signs of things still waiting to be understood, everything that upsets order, programs, facile connections, and predictability.[1]

Twelve years older than Derrida, unknown and unpublished, the thirty-four-year-old Althusser was also born in Algeria, but to a prosperous Catholic family. His father had been a lieutenant in the French army and later the director of a bank, his mother a schoolteacher, and his childhood had been by his own admission a happy one. He was very much a petit-bourgeois product of French colonial culture. He was accepted into the ENS in July 1939. However, before the school year began, he was drafted into the army and, in June 1940, was captured at Vannes in north-western France and sent to a POW camp in Schleswig-Holstein. Here he spent the remaining five years of the war, initially carrying out hard labour before an illness saw him confined to the infirmary.

The shattering experience of the war had two decisive effects on Althusser. The first, as alluded to by Derrida, was lifelong bouts of mental instability and depression. From the 1950s onwards he required constant medical supervision, undergoing hospitalisation, narcotherapy, electroconvulsive treatment and analysis. Once they became colleagues, Derrida was often required to take on some of Althusser's teaching load when he was undergoing what Élisabeth Roudinesco has called 'the saga of confinement.'[2]

The second was his introduction to Marxism. As documented in his prison writings, *Journal de captivité, Stalag XA 1940–1945*, the combination of a sense of solidarity, a sense of community and a sense of the urgency of political action opened this child of the bourgeoisie to the idea of communism. 'It was in prison camp that I first heard Marxism discussed by a Parisian lawyer in transit and that I actually met a communist,'[3] he wrote in his memoir, *The Future Lasts a Long Time*. Moreover, 'Communism was in the air in 1945, after the German defeat, the victory at Stalingrad, and the hopes and lessons of the Resistance.'[4] The future primary author of the ground-breaking *Reading Capital* spent the first few years after his internment doing just that.

Returning to the ENS in 1945, Althusser obtained his diploma for the paper 'On Content in the Thought of G.W.F. Hegel'. Graduating in 1948 – first in his year – he was immediately offered the post at the university, a position that he held for thirty-five years. In the same year he joined the PCF, the French Communist Party, and attempted to synthesise his new worldview, Marxism, with his old, Catholicism, in articles with such exemplary titles as 'Is the good news preached to the men today?', which discussed the relationship between Catholicism and the labour movement.

If Althusser's attempts at synthesis were very much the *Geist* of the times, the eventual choice of one faith over the other was inevitable. A 1949 papal decree excommunicated, en masse, all members of communist parties. In France, the left-wing journal *Jeunesse de l'Eglise* – 'faithful to the Church while resisting' – was censored and forced to close. Meanwhile communism in France, as elsewhere, was itself striving for a greater level of ideological purity. One could not back both horses.

Both of these two great messianic, teleological faiths were competing to explain the calamity of the Second World War and to point to a final transformation into an ideal society. The effects of their battle were felt throughout France, and the ENS found itself at the intellectual cutting edge. The student body divided itself into the Talas (the Catholics) and the Stals (the Stalinists), the latter, as Derrida later noted, dominating 'in a very tyrannical manner', which included forcing the entire school to observe a minute's silence upon the death of Stalin.[5]

For young Jackie, pressured to join the Stals, the situation was complicated, politically, philosophically and temperamentally. The concerns of the Stals at the time were generally internationalist. The 'overtheres' of Hungary, Indochina, the Tito rebellion and such things were considered to represent parochial battles between Soviet and Western forms of not only politics but also philosophical and scientific knowledge. Worldviews were clashing, and they were fundamental to human subjectivity. To join the Party was to take a particular stance.

In addition, Algerian Jackie, without the buffer of wealth that the young Althusser had enjoyed, had seen at close hand the practicalities of a certain kind of class warfare. At seventeen he had 'belonged to groups that took a stance ... Without being for Algerian independence, we were against the harsh policies of France.'[6]

Notoriously, the PCF's position on Algeria was for the colonisers and against the colonised. The attacks of 1 November 1954, Toussaint Rouge (Red All-Saints Day), generally regarded as the starting date of the Algerian War, were written off as acts of individual terrorism. And in March 1956 the Party voted with the government of Prime Minister Guy Mollet to impose special powers on the Algerian situation, in order not to 'divide the republic', a decision fellow traveller Sartre called 'spineless'. While Jackie's position was not pro-independence, to have followed the Party line on this would have been a betrayal of Algeria and his political instincts. 'I was anti-Stalinist. I already had an image of the French Communist Party, and especially the Soviet Union, that seemed incompatible with, let's say, the democratic Left to which I have always wished to remain loyal.'[7]

In part, one can also cite Derrida's resistance to being affiliated to any sort of faction, his intense disinclination to have – as we saw in his response to his Jewish schooling – an identity imposed, with all of the approximations, lacunas and falsehoods that entails. But it goes deeper than that. Here, as during May 1968, Derrida's temperamental resistance was of a piece with his, at this point, nascent philosophy. Crucial to his thinking, and indeed later his deconstruction, was a radical questioning of 'the decision' and the violence of any gesture that pretends (assumes, supposes, presupposes) to know, whether it be in politics, philosophy or language. Thus his engagement was of a piece with his engagement with Western metaphysics: to contextualise, to seek out hidden assumptions and to reveal the violence of any dichotomy.

At the time Jackie found himself 'walled in by a sort of tormented silence' in an institution where 'there was, let's say, a sort of theoretical intimidation: to formulate questions in a style that appeared, shall we say, phenomenological, transcendental or ontological was immediately considered suspicious, backward, idealistic, even reactionary.'[8] Reflecting on Althusser's decision to join the Party and his own decision not to, he argued:

> each 'subject' (individual subject or subject trapped in a collective field) evaluates the best strategy possible from his place, from the 'interpellation' that situates him. For a thousand reasons that should be analyzed, my place was other. My personal history, my

analytical abilities, etc. made it so that I could not be a Communist
Party member... I had been plugged into another type of reading,
questioning, and style that seemed to me just as necessary.[9]

And what was this reading, this questioning and style? As
Derrida said in the same interview, it was to examine the work
of the philosopher he found most important, Edmund Husserl.

Derrida's taking up of Husserl was not absolutely *philosophy
ex nihilo* at the ENS in the early 1950s. Sartre's existentialism
was on the wane. Where both Husserl and Heidegger had previously been read through the existentialist lens, they were now,
as they were gradually translated into French, being read in the
original and Sartre's reading of Heidegger was more and more
being regarded as a misreading. Heidegger's thinking, however,
was problematic. 'Hitler's philosopher', as Althusser called him,
was not popular with the Communists, although Derrida would
later argue that his thought remained unavoidable and that 'the
avoidance of making any of this explicit annoyed me in a way,
especially since Althusser was always fascinated with Husserl
and Heidegger without his having ever given any public sign for
this fascination.'[10] Those who openly read Heidegger did so in
what Derrida would refer to as an 'occult atmosphere.'[11]

    Husserl, on the other hand, had no such associations. More-
over, his grounding in science, and his attempts to found a
philosophical one, ran closer to the concerns of the *normaliens*
than did the mysticism of Heidegger. As Derrida put it in 1980,
'In the fifties ... Husserlian phenomenology seemed to some
young philosophers to be inescapable. I still see it today as a discipline of incomparable rigour.' Jackie took to it wholesale, such
that as early as 1954, Althusser was warning him not write so
obsessively about his 'master'. It was advice he did not take – his
'master' was to dominate his thinking for over a decade. Jackie's dissertation for his *diplôme d'etudes superieures* (roughly
equivalent to a master's degree) tackled 'The Problem of Genesis
in Husserl's Philosophy', and is a wild, passionate piece of work,
overflowing with ideas.

Husserl was born in Prostějov in 1859, the son of non-Orthodox Jews, and studied physics, mathematics and astronomy at the University of Leipzig. It is to the sciences that he remained devoted: 'My mission,' he wrote, 'is science alone.'[12] After attaining his PhD in mathematics, in 1884 he attended the philosophy lectures of Franz Brentano (whose other students included Sigmund Freud and Rudolf Steiner). In 1887 he married Malvine Steinschneider, shortly after they had converted to Lutheranism.

Husserl's initial goal and lifelong obsession was to find a way of grounding mathematics. How can we know that mathematics is true? His decision to dedicate himself to philosophy was a means to this end, and phenomenology an accident of his pursuit. As a system of epistemology – How do we know stuff? How do we know the stuff we know is right? – it was to grow into one of the major philosophical movements of the twentieth century, but Husserl never lost sight of the original stuff he wanted to know: mathematical truth and our justification for our confidence in it.

His first book, *Philosophy of Arithmetic*, was published in 1891. In it, Husserl attempted to secure a foundation for mathematics by examining the concept of number, in particular the concept of multiplicity. How do we have the concept of a multiplicity, say the number seven? Husserl argued that we do by reflecting on a set of objects, connected by the conjunction 'and'. That is 'one and one and one', such that each object is identical with itself and different from the other objects. One then 'abstracts' a number from this multiplicity. This is a psychological answer – the work is done by the human mind.[13]

There are a number of objections to this. Where does one object end and another begin? How do we separate object x from the field of everything? And does our ability to make this judgement already rely on a concept of number (can I see seven things if I don't already have the concept of seven)? Also how, if we obtain numbers from counting, do we explain 0 and 1? Husserl argued that we get to them by 'taking away', but as the mathematician Gottlob Frege was to argue in his review of the work, when I see 'one moon', it is implausible to assert I have carried out a subtraction from two.

Frege's harsh review was of crucial importance to Husserl's development. Husserl's work, noted Frege, had a fundamental problem: psychologism. If numbers derive simply from a subject's experience, numbers then become subjective. So how can objectivity be certain? Couldn't the subject be wrong? Couldn't we all be wrong? Far from being a foundation for mathematics, this leads to radical subjectivity; we need to be confident that 2 + 2 = 4 whether or not there is a human mind in which that concept adheres. Husserl's book had thus failed in its mission. (In his dissertation, Jackie cheekily called it 'the book of a disappointed mathematician'.)[14]

Husserl was himself becoming aware of these problems, as a letter to Frege makes clear. As he put it:

> I was a novice, without a correct understanding of philosophical problems ... And while laboring over projects concerning the logic of mathematical thought ... I was tormented by those incredibly strange realms: the world of the purely logical and the world of actual consciousness – or, as I would say now, that of the phenomenological and also the psychological. I had no idea how to unite them; and yet they had to interrelate and form an intrinsic unity?[15]

Trying to unite these 'incredibly strange realms' constituted his life's work, which he performed with varying degrees of success, always attempting to answer what was for him the fundamental question of how the mind can transcend its own experiences and gain a foothold in objectivity and what accounts for validity of knowledge. This began with his next work, *The Logical Investigations*, published in 1900–1. These investigations were, as he put it, 'born of distress, of unspeakable mental distress, of a complete collapse'.[16]

Vast and unwieldy in its original form, with considerable slippage in the defining of its technical terms, it is for all that crucial in establishing Husserl's 'new science', phenomenology. It is in this work, as Jackie writes in his dissertation, that 'the phenomenological level is reached', introducing its key concepts, including intentionality, the distinction between noema and noesis, the intuition of essences and mereology (the study of wholes and parts, a philosophical field of its own).

For Husserl, the first of these, intentionality, became the 'indispensable fundamental concept of phenomenology',[17] and the key to any attempt to unite the incredibly strange realms. Descartes had argued *cogito ergo sum*, 'I think therefore I am.' But what is it to think? Consciousness does not simply 'think', it *'thinks about'* – about trees, or what to have for lunch, or the problem of the concept of number. An ego alone in the universe, thinking, with no objects of consciousness, bears no relation to our own. In order to describe consciousness – and therefore do philosophy – one has to acknowledge and incorporate an 'intentionality', a directedness to our thinking.

By interrogating consciousness in this form – by describing how it is for consciousness to be in the world – we can attempt to establish and understand this concord between consciousness and the outer world. Husserl's revolutionary insight is that this analysis does not require an investigation of one of the major questions that had dogged philosophy, overtly and covertly, since its inception: the question of the actual existence of the world. What is important is not, for instance, whether or not the tree I am experiencing actually exists, the important thing is my experience of it, as a first-person phenomenon. I am to describe this phenomenon and analyse it. This task of description and analysis is the task of phenomenology.

These ideas were elaborated on and interrogated further in the 1913 work, *Ideas Pertaining to a Pure Phenomenology and to a Phenomenological Philosophy*, generally known as *Ideas I*. Husserl introduced the concept of the 'epoché', – from the ancient Greek, meaning 'suspension of judgement' or 'withholding of assent' – whereby the question whether the world exists is 'bracketed' out of the analysis. Whether there is a world or not is moot; consciousness is to be studied precisely as it is experienced, and objects are to be studied only as they are given to experience, as, therefore, phenomena:

Let us suppose that in a garden we regard with pleasure a blossoming apple tree, the freshly green grass of the lawn, etc. It is
obvious that the perception and the accompanying liking are
not, at the same time, what is perceived and liked. In the natural
attitude, the apple tree is for us something existing in the transcendent realm of spatial actuality, and the perception, as well as
the liking, is for us a psychical state belonging to real people.
Between the one and the other real things, between the real
person or the real perception, and the real apple tree, there exist
real relations. In such situations characterizing mental processes,
it may be in certain cases that perception is 'mere hallucination', the perceived, this apple tree before us, does not exist in
'actual' reality. Now the real relation, previously meant as actually existing, is destroyed. Only the perception remains, but there
is nothing actual there to which it is related.[18]

This 'bracketing' was, importantly, not tactical; in no sense was
Husserl simply putting the question to one side. On the contrary, he was attempting to access how the world actually *is* to
consciousness in everyday life in the 'natural attitude'. As in the
above example, unless we make a conscious decision to question
the existence of the apple tree (or the entire world) – when doing
philosophy for instance, or as an intellectual game – we have
an absolute confidence it is there, its existence is self-evident, to
question it is unnatural. As he notes, in the epoché

the real world is not 're-interpreted' or even denied, but an
absurd interpretation of it, that is, an interpretation [such as
philosophy] which contradicts the proper sense of reality as it
is rendered self-evident, is removed. This interpretation is the
product of a philosophical hypostatization of the world, which
is completely alien to the natural view of the world.[19]

In other words, the world of human experience is the only world
there is – 'my world is the opening through which all experience occurs.' In any situation into which we are thrown, we, as
phenomenologists, must describe what it is like, and in absolute

detail, using the 'incomparable rigour' to which Derrida alluded. Intentionality here becomes paramount, as the 'existence of our consciousness is indubitably certain; existence of the natural world is phenomenal and doubtful; thus consciousness may exist without the material world, but the material world relies on consciousness.'[20]

The world becomes an intentional correlate of consciousness. This means it is absurd to posit, as Kant did, a realm of 'things in themselves', somehow existing 'behind' what I perceive – a real apple tree behind the apple tree I perceive, inaccessible to me and all human perception, always and forever. In fact, the apple tree exists 'for consciousness' and 'beyond that is nothing'.[21]

Husserl is thus trying to get to what he would term our pre-predicative (also called antepredicative) experience of the world. This is an originary moment where we are in the world, experiencing it before categories, before classifications, certainly before philosophical speculation. Hence his battle cry, 'to the things themselves', unmediated by conceptual baggage: immediate presence, timeless, uncontaminated by history.

Jackie spent the summer of 1953, back in El-Biar, immersed in a Paul Ricoeur translation of *Ideas I*. Then in January 1954 he was granted access to the Husserl Archives in Louvain, Belgium, where he studied Husserl's vast corpus of unpublished manuscripts, smuggled out of Nazi Germany in 1938. This included more than 45,000 shorthand pages, his complete research library and 10,000 pages of typescripts. It was during this visit that Jackie encountered the short text *The Origin of Geometry*, the translation of which would be his first book.

The weeks that Jackie spent at the Husserl Archive deepened his fascination with the thinker. While he was glad to return to Paris, the trip had had a decisive effect, and he threw himself immediately into his dissertation, 'The Problem of Genesis in Husserl's Philosophy', churning out in only a few months some 300 pages of dense, confident, interrogative prose.

In his introduction to the text, published thirty-seven years later, Derrida was astonished, as many other readers have been,

to find that in style, voice and concerns, the mature thinker was
more than recognisable in the twenty-four-year-old writing his
first sustained work of philosophy. He noted 'an originary com-
plication of the origin... an initial contamination of the simple.'
The dissertation 'even in its literal formation' determined everything he had written since.[22]

Jackie's main concern in the dissertation is to do, as the title suggests, with the idea of 'origin'. This is not 'the beginning' (although
it is that too), but the moment of apprehension on which Husserl's phenomenology depends. It is this moment of apprehension
which phenomenology sets out to describe. To describe it, we must
in some sense make time stand still. This is okay as a thought
experiment. But time does not stand still. Every moment contains
a temporal as well as a spatial thingness – a genesis. Suspend it
if you like, but don't then say that what you are presenting is a
true description. Derrida's dissertation essentially works through
Husserl's corpus identifying moments where it collapses under
the weight of this tension between the spatial and the temporal.

Derrida's insight was not completely original, although where
he went with it was. In fact, it was a fellow alumnus of the ENS
who had first identified a similar problem, the impossibility of
a pre-conceptual originary moment, secured against time and
history. Tran Duc Thao was born in French Indochina, in 1917.
Studying under Maurice Merleau-Ponty at the ENS, he later
became an anticolonialist, and was jailed in 1945 by the French
government. In 1951, at the invitation of the new communist
government, he returned to what was now Vietnam, becoming dean of History in the country's first national university. By
1956 Thao had fallen out with the ruling party, criticising the
land reforms that had led to large numbers of deaths. Forced to
publish two self-criticisms in the official newspaper of the Party,
he was stripped of his deanship. Spending the next thirty years
in the provinces translating philosophy texts into Vietnamese, he
eventually returned to France in the 1980s, dying in poverty in
an apartment in the Vietnamese Embassy in 1993.

In 1951 he had published *Phenomenology and Dialectical
Materialism*, a work of sustained brilliance which was hugely

influential at the ENS – around half the papers that year which mentioned Husserl referenced Thao, 'unheard of for the author of a secondary work.'[23] Thao regarded the Husserlian method as a decisive step in Western philosophy. However, as with Derrida, he was troubled by the pre-predicative state to which phenomenology appealed as the basis of its knowledge.

'Phenomenology,' he wrote, 'wants to go back to the origin of the world, in order to account for all worldly knowledge in general.'[24] But there is a problem here. How, in what Thao refers to as the 'rhapsody of sensations', can we experience an 'originary' moment, and form, for instance, an apple tree? How can we take this undifferentiated unity and extract the apple tree, without already having a sense of this determination itself? Transcendental subjectivity presupposes the very thing it is supposed to produce. Or, as Thao put it:

> It is all too clear that the genesis of antepredicative experience, the masterpiece of the Weltkonstitution [world constitution], was posited in reality on a ground incompatible with the philosophical framework on which it had been conceived.[25]

Husserl had maintained that the reduction required a suspension of the normal belief in the world, and yet required that the essential component of the perceptual act is a conviction in the existence of objects and their transcendental constitution as objects. On top of this, Husserl was forced to argue for what he called 'apperception'. If I see the front of an apple tree, I somehow intuit the rest of it. Again, I must already have the concept of the apple tree, or each new apple tree, otherwise it and any other object I encounter for the first time would be baffling in ways that new objects don't tend to be in reality.

Derrida did not adopt all of Thao's thinking – he felt that the second half of the book, which attempted to overcome the contradiction through dialectical materialism, was a 'dead end' – but he enthusiastically took up the question of pre-predicative experience, of origin and of the idea of genesis, with which Husserl himself had battled.

Derrida notes that it is much more difficult to identify, describe and analyse a particular moment in time than it is to do so with a particular point in space – standing in front of our apple tree for instance. It is a problem Husserl was aware of – in his 1907 lecture series, 'The Idea of Phenomenology', he noted that 'as soon as we even make the attempt to undertake the analysis of pure subjective time-consciousness we are involved in the most extraordinary difficulties, contradictions and entanglements'.[26] These were difficulties which, at various times, Husserl grappled with, elided, glossed over and – as Derrida was to identify and deconstruct – unconsciously ignored.

In two of his most memorable phrases, Husserl described life in *Ideas I* as 'the flowing thisness', such that 'incessantly the world of physical things, and, in it, our body, are perceptually there.'[27] All experience entails a temporal horizon, with time-consciousness at the basis of all intentional acts, as we experience all spatial acts, whether the object is stationary or not, as temporal, but not all temporal acts as spatial (speaking a sentence is an example of a temporal act that is not spatial). Time-consciousness is, as Husserl noted, the most 'important and difficult of all phenomenological problems.'

Immersed in the flowing thisness, we stand again before our apple tree. If time-consciousness was merely succession, one thing constantly being replaced by another, we would never be able to create the tree out of our successive impressions, which we obviously do. Again, how? For Husserl the answer was as synthesis – we take these successive impressions and synthesise them into a unity:

> Perception is a process of streaming from phase to phase; in its own way each of the phases is a perception, but these phases are continuously harmonized in the unity of a synthesis, in the unity of a consciousness of one and the same perceptual object that is constituted here originally. In each phase we have primordial impression, retention and protention ... it is a unity of continual concordance.[28]

Retention and protention are not, simply, memory and anticipation. They are structurally embedded in, and constituent of, any 'present'. A *now* is 'always essentially an edge-point in an interval of time'.[29] To use Husserl's favoured example:

> When, for example a melody sounds, the individual notes do not completely disappear when the stimulus or the action of the nerve excited by them comes to an end. When the new note sounds, the one just preceding it does not disappear without a trace; otherwise we should be incapable of observing the relations between the notes which follow one another ... On the other hand, it is not merely a matter of presentations of the tones simply persisting in consciousness. Were they to remain unmodified, then instead of a melody we should have a chord of simultaneous notes or rather a disharmonious jumble of sounds.[30]

A note in a melody is not heard in isolation, an originary point in the flux of time cannot, as Husserl hopes to argue, be pre-predicative. It always already requires categories and structures, in the same way that Thao had identified with concepts.

Husserl, notes Derrida, 'takes the demand for absolute beginning and the temporality of the lived experience as the ultimate philosophical reference.'[31] Genesis, which one might call the originary moment under the effects of time – each moment being a moment of 'becoming' – is problematic precisely as it occurs in time and thus requires the synthesis of protention and retention.

Jackie's dissertation homed in on this contradiction – this *aporia*, a word he was to use for the first time in this work, and which remained a key to this thought. From the Greek *a-* (without) and *poros* (passage), the word appears frequently in Plato. In fact, one of the goals of Socrates' dialogues is to force his interlocutor into an aporia by interrogating a concept (e.g. virtue) until the interlocutor is forced to admit he does not know its meaning. But where for Socrates the goal was to resolve the aporia in some sense, for Derrida, as we shall see, the goal was to keep an aporia in suspension, to, in Gabriel Marcus's terms, prevent a mystery being reduced to a problem.

In a move worthy of his later deconstructive texts, Jackie notes that, despite constantly asserting that he wishes to analyse the pre-predicative temporal, and that he regards this as having primacy over the spatial, Husserl only ever uses spatial examples when carrying out his analyses. 'In spite of frequent allusions at no time does time intervene in a decisive fashion.'[32]

Examples of this spatial bias abound in *Ideas I*: 'Lying in front of me is a piece of paper ...' (69); 'Constantly seeing this table and meanwhile walking around it ...' (86); 'we walk through the Gallery in Dresden ...' (250); 'This is black, an inkpot, this black inkpot is not white is, if white, not black ...'; and even in the realm of the imaginary, 'Let us generate optional intuitions in phantasy of physical things, such as free intuitions of winged horses, white ravens, golden mountains and the like...' (356). Again and again Husserl, notes Derrida, 'stops at becoming, turning it into eidos'.[33] Where Husserl had written, in his 1905 *The Phenomenology of Internal Time-Consciousness*, 'Naturally we all know what time is; it is that which is most familiar,' it had revealed itself as that which, if familiar, remained most uncanny, and which threw doubt on his whole philosophical project. As Jackie noted, *The Phenomenology of Internal Time-Consciousness* was never finished, never published as a completed work. The subject had proved too difficult.

There exists only one piece of footage of Husserl. Shot by James L. Adams when the philosopher was seventy-seven years old, two years before he died in 1938, it shows Husserl with his wife, Malvine, walking in an unidentified garden in summer. Husserl performs for the camera the part of the peripatetic philosopher. Suited, wearing sunglasses, he carries in his left hand his hat, and gestures emphatically with his right, to a nodding Malvine. Twice the camera zooms in to show him from the waist up; he stops speaking and returns the gaze of the camera as one would if being photographed. He stops talking, blinks at the camera, resumes. His image slides and wobbles, extends and shrinks back, as if viewed through bent plastic. It is pixelated into large square blocks; we are seeing and not seeing Husserl. The camera draws back and Malvine performs asking a question, to which Husserl performs replying. The footage ends with another close-up, or perhaps this is the same one.

At the time he was captured on film in the sunny garden Husserl was working on his last great work, *The Crisis of European Sciences and Transcendental Phenomenology*, which would remain unfinished. He was writing it in the shadow of catastrophe. In 1936 Europe was sick, as Husserl wrote in his Vienna lecture, 'The Crisis of European Humanity', and the human sciences were incapable of effecting a cure.

Three years earlier, in April 1933, he had been first suspended from his professorship at Freiburg University for being a Jew, despite that fact that both he and Malvine had converted to Lutheranism almost fifty years earlier. Both their sons had served in the German army in the First World War – the younger one losing his life – and his daughter had served as a field nurse. Two weeks later he had all his academic privileges terminated in accordance with the National Reich law of April 28, relegated, as he put it, to 'the non-Aryan dung heap'.[34]

Between these two events, on 21 April, his former student Martin Heidegger, who had dedicated his *Being and Time* to Husserl, had been appointed as rector of the University. In May, shortly after joining the Nazi Party, Heidegger gave his notorious rectorship address, 'The Self-Assertion of the German University', in which he – partially or fully, consciously or unconsciously, tactically or venally, the debate rages on – aligned the goals of the university, its 'historical mission' no less, with those of the Third Reich. Heidegger remained a member of the Nazi Party until the end of the Second World War.

Supporters of Heidegger have sometimes parsed his actions to the point where black is white, and where his extolling of the Führer Principle is 'an occurrence of unveiling, a fate-laden happening upon thought'.[35] They have pointed out, for instance, that the decision to suspend Husserl was taken by Heidegger's predecessor, and that the decision to terminate his academic privileges was simply the law. But Husserl himself was less sanguine. In a letter to another former student, Dietrich Mahnke, he wrote:

The perfect conclusion to this supposed bosom friendship of two philosophers was his very public, very theatrical entrance into the Nazi Party on May 1. Prior to that there was his self-initiated break in relations with me – in fact, soon after his appointment at Freiburg – and, over the last few years, his anti-Semitism, which he came to express with increasing vigor – even against the coterie of his most enthusiastic students, as well as around the department.[36]

This, he believed, was simply part of a wider cataclysm, which philosophy seemed incapable of explaining or preventing. For Husserl, this slide into barbarity, which had seen him lose most of his German students and in 1937 saw him lose his house, was intertwined with the deeply melancholy realisation that 'philosophy as a science, as a serious, rigorous, indeed apodictically rigorous science – the dream is over.'[37]

In *The Crisis* Husserl grapples with intersubjectivity and what he would call 'the life-world' – the 'coherent universe of existing objects … valid for our consciousness as existing precisely through living together' – which he recognised complicated his phenomenological project. But Husserl grappling with complications is, in a sense, Husserl par excellence. Few thinkers in the history of philosophy have tussled so unremittingly with their own ideas as he did, each book taking on the last, refining it, refuting it – one might cheekily say, deconstructing it. And in 1936, for Husserl the philosopher the difficulty had become, as it had become for Husserl the man, history and other people. How was one to find, in all this time and all these other beings – a point of origin from which to describe being?

Time – and history – which he hoped to hold at bay, kept asserting themselves, as problems that could not be bracketed off. Derrida's dissertation concludes, melodramatically but effectively, with Husserl's words to his sister during his final illness.

Just when I am getting to the end and when everything is finished for me, I know that I must start everything again from the beginning.[38]

❧

On reading the published edition of *The Problem of Genesis in Husserl's Philosophy* in 1990, the philosopher Jean-Luc Nancy wrote to Derrida that the incredible thing about the work was that 'you can't find the young Derrida in it ... the genesis of Derrida, yes, but not the young Derrida. He's already completely there, fully armed and helmeted like Athena.'[39] This was not simply a question of style, voice and concerns. In the dissertation we see, in utero, concepts that would remain central to Derrida's thought – the aporia, the decision, undecidability and, in that suspension of judgement, that retaining of a contradiction without privileging one term or the other, the idea he would come to call *différance*. And in its method – analysing the originary moment as it appeared in Husserl's work, book by book – it met the criteria he set for deconstruction in a lecture at Oxford thirty years later, 'a genealogical analysis of the trajectory through which the concept has been built, used, legitimized.'[40]

When Derrida submitted it, Althusser said, 'I can't grade this, it's too difficult, too obscure ...'[41] He decided to pass it on to a friend, an assistant professor at Lille who occasionally lectured at the ENS – Michel Foucault. Derrida had previously attended some of these lectures by this 'charismatic' young man, only four years older than himself. These included taking the students to a psychiatric hospital to watch patients being examined. He found it 'really upsetting'.[42] After reading the dissertation Foucault said to him, 'Well, it's either an F or an A+.'

For all his brilliance, Derrida continued to struggle at the ENS. In part the problem was his Husserl obsession, and, more crucially, the strain of creating the voice and the concepts that later both exhilarated and frustrated readers within academia and beyond. Althusser, marking one essay, noted that his work would only meet the approval of examiners 'if you perform a radical overhaul, in the exposition and the expression. Your current difficulties are the price you're paying for a year devoted to reading and thinking about Husserl, who as I have to tell you again, isn't a familiar thinker for the jury.'[43]

His problems at the ENS also arose from the same anxiety that had plagued him at the lycée. Again he resorted to amphetamines, again he fled part of the written exams, again he finished last in the orals. Failure at the *agrégation* was not unheard of – Sartre had likewise failed. But Derrida's failure condemned him to another year of work at the ENS. In the end, he passed, with results that were mediocre compared to his abilities. Althusser wrote to congratulate him, noting that 'quite simply your friendship has been for me one of the most fine and valuable things about these last two years at the Ecole.'[44]

If the seeds of deconstruction were present in 1954, it would be another ten years before they bore any sort of fruit. Before they did, Derrida had to look outwards, to move from an analysis of a single subject to the analysis of an intersubjective community. He would have to examine language and writing, and, like Husserl, the problem of the other.

3

Problems of Origin

Language is for the other, coming from the other, the coming of the other.

– Monolingualism of the Other

As soon as there is language, generality has entered the scene.

– 'There Is No One Narcissism'

Graduation from the ENS involved Derrida in a new set of problems. The most pressing of which was the necessity of submitting to two years of military service, a prospect he dreaded. To forestall this, Jean Prigent, the deputy director of the ENS, supported him in an application to be part of a student exchange with Harvard University, on the 'somewhat fictitious pretext of consulting microfilms of unpublished work by Husserl.'[1]

He would not be going alone. In 1952 he had met Marguerite Aucouturier, the sister of one of his classmates at Louis-le-Grand, on a skiing trip. Her father had been a student at the Normale Sup, and the family had lived in Prague, Belgrade, Cairo and Moscow, where she learned Russian before moving to Paris for school. This was a union that lasted the whole of Derrida's life, through various ups and downs. She always believed he was the greatest philosopher of his generation, and so cleared the space for him to do his work. But she was no mere facilitator – as a psychoanalyst after 1974, she translated the work of Melanie Klein, Maxim Gorky and Roman Jakobson.

Before leaving for America, Derrida spent August 1956 with his parents. Writing to Althusser he called Algeria a 'terrible, paralysed country', with 'daily attacks, deaths to which you get used, and which people talk about as if they were an unwelcome shower of rain.'[2] In March the French government had invoked the 'special powers' that unofficially sanctioned the use of torture, which became synonymous with the Algerian War. Meanwhile, the FLN – Algeria's National Liberation Front – had started recruiting female operatives who would famously plant time bombs in the heart of Algiers. Two FLN prisoners had been executed by guillotine in June, and the military chief of the Autonomous Zone of Algiers, Saadi Yacef, ordered his fighters to 'shoot down any European, from 18 to 54. No women, no children, no elder.'[3] By 1957 the French army was in charge, and January and February saw the Battle of Algiers. Derrida's aversion to military duty was not unreasonable.

At Harvard, Derrida – who could not afford the trip from the East Coast to the West that Althusser had suggested – spent much of his time at the Widener Library, reading Joyce. *Ulysses* and *Finnegans Wake* swiftly became crucial books for Derrida. They were examples of the sort of meta-discursive texts which his own work set out not only to deconstruct, but to generate and emulate – 'the potential memory of mankind'.[4] This 'most Hegelian of modern novelists', as he put it at the end of his 1964 essay 'Violence and Metaphysics', had 'read all of us – and plundered us'. Derrida's 1980 work, *The Post Card*, is in his words 'haunted by Joyce'.[5] Invited to deliver the opening address at the Ninth International James Joyce Symposium in Frankfurt in 1984, for which he wrote 'Ulysses Gramophone', he noted Joyce's continuing importance:

> Just as I was jotting down these titles, an American tourist of the most typical variety leaned over my shoulder and sighed: 'So many books! What is the definitive one? Is there any?' I almost replied, 'Yes, there are two of them, *Ulysses* and *Finnegans Wake*,'

but I kept this yes to myself and smiled inanely like someone who does not understand the language.[6]

But while Joyce demanded his concentration, it was Husserl who remained at the forefront of his thought. He was still thinking about the late and obscure work he had read at Louvain, *The Origin of Geometry*, little more than an appendix to *The Crisis*. As was so often the case with Derrida, it was the arcane, the ephemeral, the – to use a phrase that would dominate works such as *Of Grammatology* – supplementary, which attracted him and fired his philosophical imagination. And within the text itself it was not Husserl's main argument that attracted him, but a small section in which Husserl wrote about writing.

> Straight after the agrégation, I remember going to see Jean Hyppolite [then director of the ENS] and telling him: 'I want to translate *The Origin of Geometry* and work on that text' – because there was a brief elliptical remark on writing, on the necessity for communities of scientists and scholars to constitute communicable ideal objects on the basis of intuitions of the mathematical object. Husserl said that writing alone could give those ideal objects their final ideality, that it alone could enable them to enter history, their historicity came from writing. Husserl's remark was ambiguous and obscure, so I have been trying to articulate a concept of writing that would allow me simultaneously to account for what was happening in Husserl and ... also tackle the question that continued to interest me, that of literary inscription. What is an inscription? When and in what conditions does an inscription become literary?[7]

Hyppolite agreed to supervise it, calling it an 'excellent idea'. He had already read Derrida's dissertation and encouraged the young philosopher to attempt to publish it, an idea that fell by the wayside during the terrors of the *agrégation*.

But if he now had a project, he still faced the problem of military service, possibly on the frontline in Algeria. It was his father who came to his rescue. Aimé's wine deliveries took him to a little town near Algiers called Koléa, and the school was looking for a teacher for the children of soldiers. This counted as military service. So, after he and Marguerite married in America to be able to stay together, they rented a villa in Koléa. The teaching was monotonous but paid their way, and the couple travelled weekly to Jackie's parents for the Sabbath meal. Initially offended by the wedding to which they had not been invited, the Derridas quickly warmed to their new daughter-in-law.

Meanwhile Algeria itself was descending into chaos. Jackie wrote of living 'with rage in our hearts and more alone than ever, in prey to the surrounding stupidity, the most abject and malevolent imaginable, a real nightmare.'[8] The undeclared but obvious French policy of torture, and the FLN's guerrilla attacks, made the atmosphere unbearable. On top of it all, Derrida's dark complexion meant that the French often took him for an Arab, while the Arabs regarded him as both Jewish and French. Once again he found himself identified by all sides as the enemy.

In 1958, in an attempt to defuse the crisis, General Charles de Gaulle came out of retirement and established by referendum the Fifth Republic. De Gaulle had some prestige with Algeria's Jewish population; it was he who had re-established the Crémieux Decree in 1943. One of his first acts as president was a famous speech for the Arab population in Algiers on 4 June 1959, known as the speech of '*je vous ai compris*' – 'I have understood you.' There was to be, to the horror and disgust of the pied-noirs, a referendum on Algerian independence.

All the while Derrida was working on his translation of *The Origin of Geometry*. When his two years in Koléa were up, it seemed briefly that with the assistance of Althusser and Hyppolite he had secured a teaching place at the Sorbonne. But academic manoeuvrings saw the job disappear, and he was forced to take up a teaching post in Le Mans, starting in 1960.

His year in Le Mans was horrible. Derrida was now thirty and having to work with 'bloody idiots' who 'got on his nerves'. On one occasion, he was invited – forced – to give the speech on prize-giving day, a 'ridiculous secular homily'. He was bored, irritable, suffering from what he later called his 'big depression'.

Students recall his anger that they had not, at seventeen, read Kant's *Critique of Pure Reason*. He saw a psychiatrist and was prescribed the antidepressant Anafranil, which gave him tremors and hot flushes.[9]

Still he continued to write about an obscure passage in an obscure text. It took a great deal of intellectual courage to continue to plough a furrow in the face of bafflement and incomprehension (and it presumably took a lot of patience on the part of Marguerite). There are, of course, many thirty-year-olds convinced of their own genius. The vast majority are wrong. Given everything that followed, however, Jackie had a fair point. But sitting in staff meetings in Le Mans, success seemed a long way off. It would also require an engagement with another thinker whose work would become central to his own.

Some time in 1943, at a prisoner-of-war camp in Hanover, Emmanuel Lévinas and seventy fellow captives were returning from a day of manual labour, when they had an encounter which was to shape Lévinas's thinking forever. In three years of their internment, the prisoners had, Lévinas was later to write, been 'stripped of human skin ... we were subhuman, a gang of apes.' Not only the guards, but women and children who passed the camp had made them 'no longer part of the world ... beings without language'.

> And then, about halfway through our long captivity, for a few short weeks, before the sentinels chased him away, a wandering dog entered our lives. One day he came to meet this rabble as we returned under guard from work ... we called him Bobby, an exotic name, as one does with a cherished dog. He would appear at morning assembly and was waiting for us as we returned, jumping up and down and barking in delight. For him, there was no doubt that we were men.[10]

This dog, 'the last Kantian in Germany', not only guaranteed the prisoners' humanity, it returned it to them in an act of creation. For Lévinas, always, the encounter with another – the Other (*l'Autrui*) – was not a secondary aspect of being human, outside of subjectivity. Subjectivity is, rather, established on this encounter. We are not selves, radiating outwards, who happen to encounter other people. With no other people we would not be selves.

It was an insight he was to explore most fully in *Totality and Infinity*, published in 1961. The book, given to Derrida by Paul Ricoeur, for whom he was working as an assistant, had a profound and lasting effect on him, from his earliest works to his later turn to ethics.

Little known of before *Totality and Infinity*, Lévinas was born in Lithuania in 1906, into a middle-class Jewish family. Moving to Alsace in France at seventeen, he studied philosophy at the University of Strasbourg, where he met his lifelong friend Maurice Blanchot. In 1928 he arrived at Freiburg, and attended a lecture series by Edmund Husserl on the 'Phenomenology of Empathy'.

Husserl was sixty-nine years old, and it was to be his final year of teaching. The previous year, his brilliant student Heidegger had published *Being and Time*, dedicating it to his teacher 'in friendship and admiration'. On the copy he gave Husserl Heidegger had written, 'For me the greatest clarity was always the greatest beauty – Lessing.' The pair had spent much of the last year working together sporadically on the entry on phenomenology for the *Encyclopædia Britannica*.

But the tensions in their relationship were already beginning to develop. While not political at this stage (the Nazi Party receiving less than 3 per cent of the vote in the 1928 election), it was becoming more and more evident, to Husserl in particular, that the version of phenomenology he had inaugurated and continued to pursue was not Heidegger's, and that Heidegger's version was already gaining acolytes. It was not only Husserl who had noticed: 'I came to see Husserl,' wrote Lévinas, 'and what I saw was Heidegger.'[11]

For the Heidegger of *Being and Time*, the fundamental question of philosophy is the question of Being, which, in his analysis, has been forgotten. Philosophy, since Plato, has analysed *beings* – things – whether concrete or abstract, and not Being itself. To put it in linguistic terms, if I say 'the chair is red' or 'phenomenology is difficult' or 'Derrida is a man', philosophy deals in the subject (the chair, phenomenology, Derrida) and the predicate (red, difficult, man) and ignores, or covers over, the copula 'is'. What is 'is'?

What 'is' isn't, for Heidegger, is an abstract notion – there is only an 'is' where there is a thing, and someone for whom it exists (which is Heidegger sort of doing intentionality). Humans hold a privileged position as opposed to other beings (animals, vegetable, stones) in that the question of Being is a problem for them. And yet philosophy has generally treated human beings as just the same as other beings, a bunch of objects in the world, describable as such.

Where Husserl attempts to bracket the world, Heidegger's philosophy is that of immersion in it – being-in-the-world. The meaning of 'phenomenology', he argues, is there in its etymology, 'phenomena' and 'logos' – 'Letting that which shows itself be seen from itself in the very way in which it shows itself from itself.'[12] Husserl's concentration on consciousness, intentionality and subjectivity is replaced by a way of relating to the world that displaces consciousness. When we hammer in a nail, for instance, we do not, as we would in Husserl's description, have full cognisance of the hammer, the nail, our hand, and so on. Instead, we do it 'without thinking'. Only when we miss the nail and hit our finger do we become conscious of the objects around us, and even then not fully. Thus phenomenology is no longer a science of phenomena, but a method through which Being reveals itself in Dasein, Heidegger's neologism for 'being here' by which he refers to the human 'subject'. Human existence *reveals* itself. Phenomenology as a method uncovers that which is concealed.

Dasein, then, is a type of 'continuous incompletedness' (*eine ständige Unabgeschlossenheit*)[13] through which the truth of Being is (or can be) revealed, and is determined by what Heidegger calls 'existentia' – 'being-in-the-world', 'care', 'anxiety' and 'discourse'.

In the beginning Husserl was receptive to Heidegger's work. However, it gradually became clear that, whatever this was, it was not phenomenology as Husserl understood it. 'Genial unscientific philosophy', he later called it, and the marginal notes in his copy are soon reduced to interjections of 'nonsense' and 'absurd'. In fairness, it soon became evident to Heidegger that this was not 'phenomenology' in Husserl's sense either. And so he stopped using the term.

Both thinkers fascinated Lévinas. In 1929 he presented his doctoral thesis, 'The Theory of Intuition in Husserl's Phenomenology', and in 1931 he translated Husserl's Sorbonne lectures, *Cartesian Meditations*, into French, the first appearance of Husserl's work in that language. Throughout the 1930s he continued to publish studies on the thought of both, moving between the intellectualism of Husserl and the worldliness of Heidegger, embracing and repudiating each in turn.

In 1939 Lévinas became a French citizen, was mobilised soon after, and in 1940 was captured and taken to Hanover where he was assigned to a special barrack for Jewish prisoners; no religious practices were allowed. Here he spent his limited free time jotting in a notebook, notes that formed the basis of his first books, *Existence and Existents* and *Time and the Other*. Where Heidegger has Dasein, 'being here', Lévinas has *il y a*, 'there is'. His philosophy would be predicated on this outward turn, and on how what 'there is' would constitute Dasein. It was to have an abiding influence on Derrida.

Husserl in his final lectures was grappling with the problem of intersubjectivity. It is one of the enduring problems of philosophy – the 'Other Minds' problem. We can, perhaps, prove to our own satisfaction that we exist and are conscious. But how can we be sure that others do, and that they have similar mental attributes to our own? What justifies this belief?

In Husserl, the problem is rich and deep. If the world and meaning are generated by me – my 'sphere of ownness' or 'primordial sphere' – how am I to account for other beings who also generate meaning? How can they be objects in my world in the same way as the apple tree, but also subjects, in the same way as I experience myself? And how can I, who exist as an embodied self, and therefore as an object for others, be both object and subject? This is one of the deepest puzzles of his transcendental philosophy. By giving primacy to the ego, Husserl risked solipsism, as he was well aware.

What was at stake for Husserl, as ever, was the validity of the objective, scientific world. If this world is not congruent for all subjects – whatever, ultimately, 'congruent' means – then the status of science is fatally undermined. Scientific 'truths' lose their validity as they become purely subjective – just 'what I reckon'.

Husserl's attempt at a solution, beginning with his fifth *Cartesian Meditation* of 1931 – the Sorbonne lectures that Lévinas translated – was to invoke the act of *empathy*, which has a phenomenological meaning more or less congruent with its everyday use. When confronted with a being that acts, speaks, and looks like us, we, by analogy, ascribe to that being intentionality and transcendent subjectivity, and assume (unreflectively) that they do likewise.

The other assumption we make in the natural attitude, argues Husserl, is that the spatiotemporal world that these other beings 'encounter' – that is given to them by their intentionality – coincides with our own to a large extent. When I see an apple tree, my neighbour-being does too; when I eat the apple, it tastes more or less the same to them. In fact, Husserl argues, this is precisely how we build the 'objective' spatiotemporal world (and thus give objects an objective and therefore potentially scientific status) – we presuppose that, if my neighbour-being and I have a roughly coincident objective reality there must be, presumably, a world which exists independently of my own subjective perception of it.

Extrapolating from this, Husserl builds what he calls the life-world (*lebenswelt*).

> In whatever way we may be conscious of the world as universal horizon, as coherent universe of existing objects, we, each 'I-the-man' and all of us together, belong to the world as living with one another in the world; and the world is our world, valid for our consciousness as existing precisely through this 'living together.' ... Obviously this is true not only for me, the individual ego; rather we, in living together, have the world pre-given in this together, belong, the world as world for all ... The we-subjectivity ... [is] constantly functioning.[14]

Lévinas found Husserl's account of intersubjectivity inadequate – phenomenologically. Phenomenology asks us to describe the world as it is experienced – is this how we experience other humans? Simply as mere confirmers or refuters of our perception regarding our lifeworld? When we encounter another human being, is it more or less like encountering a chair, except we always already ascribe to it intentionality?

Lévinas had long found Husserl's constituting ego problematic, in part due to the more worldly phenomenological arguments of Heidegger: hammers, nails and so forth. The primacy of consciousness in defining subjectivity in Husserl (and much of Western philosophy) seemed, post-Heidegger (and post-Nietzsche, Freud and Marx) increasingly problematic, increasingly inadequate and increasingly false. Husserl's 'new science' seemed to generate many of the same problems as Descartes' cogito. To merely regard 'the world' as a production of consciousness – or consciousnesses – was to generate a world with no guarantee of truth.

The problem is, again, particularly acute when it comes to other humans: the neighbour-beings, or alter egos to use the Husserlian term. If we derive their existence from the interiority of self-consciousness, we cannot eliminate the possibility they are a subjective projection of our own, and we certainly can't call upon them as a guarantor of the objective world or of scientific truth.

In questioning Husserl's phenomenological interpretation of intersubjectivity, Lévinas analysed phenomenologically how it is we actually encounter 'the Other' (*l'Autrui*). This is not, he argued, as simple a relationship as the Husserlian version: the other as an object in the world with which we empathise and thus ascribe a subjectivity like our own. The Other resists phenomenological grasping in a way that the apple tree doesn't. We do not encounter other humans as we encounter other objects. Our relationship to them is always already different, and radically so. The key term for Lévinas, proposed and explored in *Totality and Infinity*, is 'face'. For Lévinas, the term 'face' is broader than our usual everyday use of it. It represents precisely our encounter with the Other.

When we perform the thought experiment that sees us alone in the universe, as the last human, or the only human, we generally imagine we are just like ourselves now, but without other people. Our ego remains intact. But had our ego never encountered another ego – another face – how would it be constituted? Would it even be constituted? Would we have language? If not, how would we think – in the sense that we think in words?

Lévinas wished to turn Husserlian intersubjectivity 'about face'. It is not, he argued, my constituting ego that produces the Other. Rather, it is the Other who constitutes, and guarantees, my subjectivity. My ego is produced by the encounter with the Other. It is only because there is the Other that an ego is required. The Other – sometimes even a dog in a concentration camp – constructs or restores my sense of subjectivity, of human 'being'.

Lévinas referred to this relation of the self to the Other as 'epiphanic', from the Greek, 'to reveal', but also, further back, from the word for light. Phenomenology shares the same root, but Lévinas wished to emphasise the sense of a rupture, a revelation. The face of the Other calls to me, it demands responsibility. For Lévinas this relationship is an ethical one. Ethics is therefore the 'first philosophy', and it is a concept Husserl's intersubjectivity is unsuccessful in generating or explaining. As we shall see, Lévinas's ethics were crucial in Derrida's, exploring similar terrain with the ideas of the gift, hospitality and friendship. But more immediately it was the question of language which called to Derrida. For Lévinas,

> the original function of speech consists not in designating an object in order to communicate with the other in a game with no consequences, but in assuming toward someone a responsibility on behalf of someone else.[15]

Thus the origin of language is always 'response' – responding to the Other, to their summons. The face 'interrupts' us, demands fraternity and discourse, which is what generates speech. And it is here that we can start to build an objective world – objectivity is impossible without the Other, as it is only by detaching an object from my own subjective point of view and encountering it in the sphere of the Other that it becomes an object (whether material or not). This is achieved through discourse. Prior to any encounter with the Other, a chair cannot become a chair.

Later – not much later – Derrida famously questioned this primacy of speech over writing. At the same time that Lévinas was writing *Totality and Infinity*, Derrida was writing his introduction to *The Origin of Geometry*. Their respective texts had their own dialogue for many years. Speaking at Lévinas's funeral some thirty years later, Derrida noted, 'I will never stop beginning or beginning anew to think with them on the basis of the new beginning they give me, and I will begin again and again to rediscover them on just about any subject.'[16] For now, however, the subject was Husserl.

The translation of *The Origin of Geometry* is an astonishing work. Husserl's text runs to little more than 30 pages; the introduction to the book takes up more than 150. Again, the nascent ideas of deconstruction are present, but lacking their familiar names the text is forced to strain at the very limits of language to make its points. It is, if such a thing were possible, an even denser version of Derrida than his later works.

The ostensible purpose of Husserl's text is to attempt again, as the name suggests, to find an origin – in this case 'the submerged original beginnings of geometry as they necessarily must have been in their "primally establishing" function'.[17] This is not to seek the first geometer in the historical or biographical sense; rather it is an enquiry back into 'the most original sense in which geometry once arose'.[18] Kant, for instance, saw the origin of geometry as being one of revelation. Geometry had existed before human subjectivity apprehended it, and would have continued to exist had human subjectivity not done so. Then one day, someone noticed (and could possibly not have). For Husserl, rather – for whom, as we saw, Kant's 'things in themselves' are redundant – geometry is a human creation, and continues to be a 'creation': something to be achieved continually.

As Derrida notes in his introduction, Husserl privileges the mathematical object – an isosceles triangle, a mathematical formula, the idea of refraction – as 'its being is thoroughly transparent and exhausted by phenomenality'.[19] It is an object, therefore, for pure consciousness. This is important for Husserl, as we need to establish certain indisputable truths. A mathematical object such as a triangle is an object for all, as it 'is accessible to all men, first of all to the actual and possible mathematicians of all peoples, all ages; and this is true of all its particular forms'.[20]

We have all encountered mathematical objects, from isosceles triangles to $e = mc^2$ – they have been handed down to us (it is unlikely that many humans have deduced isosceles triangles themselves, let alone $e = mc^2$), modified over the course of their existence by 'an open chain of the generations of those who work for and with one another, researchers either known or unknown to one another who are accomplishing subjectivity of the whole science.'[21] The first geometer, for whom the isosceles triangle became what Husserl calls 'self-evident', initiated this open chain – had the knowledge stayed in his or her head it would not be with us now.

But how? The answer is mundane in a basic sense, of little interest to Husserl. But absolutely crucial to Derrida. He or she *told someone*.

Here language enters, to pun slightly, the equation. Language has, of course, always been one of philosophy's problems, but often as a separate discipline within philosophy or, as we shall see, a problem to be overcome in order to get to 'the truth'. As Lévinas had argued, language creates the objective world, as a response to the Other. This is not the stated Husserlian position, but Derrida catches Husserl out, proposing it without realising he is doing so.

'Living wakefully in the world,' Husserl writes, 'we are constantly conscious of the world, whether we pay attention to it or not, conscious of it as the horizon of our life, as a horizon of "things" (real objects), of our actual and possible interests and activities,'[22] and

> It is precisely to this horizon of civilization that common language belongs. One is conscious of civilization from the start

as an immediate and mediate linguistic community. Clearly it is only through language and its far-reaching documentations, as possible communications, that the horizon of civilization can be an open and endless one ... Language, for its part, as function and exercised capacity, is related correlatively to the world, the universe of objects which is linguistically expressible in its being and its being-such.[23]

This accords with Lévinas's position. But it is what follows that provoked Derrida's intervention; not in fact a 'brief elliptical remark on writing' as he had put it to Hyppolite, but several paragraphs which were to fire the task of deconstruction into being.

Let us assume for the moment that Husserl's analysis of the production of mathematical objects and, mutatis mutandis, the objective world is right, or at least adequate. The first geometer finds an object, such as an isosceles triangle, that is self-evident, and transfers this knowledge along the chain of geometers. It is still possible, in this schema, for any or every piece of knowledge to be forgotten. 'What is lacking', notes Husserl, 'is the persisting existence of the "ideal objects" even during periods in which the inventor and his fellows are no longer wakefully so related or even are no longer alive. What is lacking is their continuing-to-be even when no one has [consciously] realized them in self-evidence.'[24]

How is this achieved? *It is achieved by writing things down.* As Husserl notes, 'The important function of written, documenting linguistic expression is that it makes communications possible without immediate or mediate personal address; it is, so to speak, communication become virtual.'[25]

He had, in fact, touched on this as far back as the *Logical Investigations*, noting:

Science exists objectively only in its literature, only in written work has it a rich relational being limited to men and their intellectual activities: in this form it is propagated down the millennia, and survives individuals, generations and nations. It therefore represents a set of external arrangements, which, just as they arose out of the knowledge-acts of many individuals, can again pass over into just such acts of countless individuals, in a readily understandable manner, whose exact description would require much circumlocution.[26]

If the exact description required too much circumlocution for Husserl, it did not for Derrida. What he identified in *The Origin of Geometry* was not that Husserl required writing to guarantee the persistence of ideal objects, but that he actually required writing to guarantee that they *were* in fact ideal objects. And, as this fixing of the possibility of ideal objects is fundamental to the possibility of fixing the possibility of the objective world, writing becomes fundamental to that as well.

Speech, as Derrida notes, 'frees the object of individual subjectivity but leaves it bound to its beginning and to the synchrony of an exchange within the institutive community'; but *only*

> the possibility of writing will assure the traditionalization of the object, its absolute ideal Objectivity – i.e. the purity of its relation to a universal transcendental subjectivity. Writing will do this by emancipating sense from its actually present evidence for a real subject and from its present circulation within a determined community.[27]

Writing enables repetition or, as he would later term it, iteration. It also allows development. It thus allows an object to move beyond an individual ego. Without this, language would 'remain captive of the de facto and actual intentionality of a speaking subject or community of speaking subjects. By absolutely virtualising dialogue, writing creates a kind of autonomous transcendental field from which every present subject can be absent.'[28]

Derrida later explored the ways in which philosophy – from Plato, through Rousseau, to Husserl, to Austin – had privileged speech over writing. For deconstruction, it was one of the many binary oppositions that needed to be problematised: reason/passion, man/woman, inside/outside, presence/absence. Each of which, he would argue, is actually an arbitrary division, both porous and mutually definitional, but in privileging the first term over the latter performs a founding violence that is not unmotivated, consciously or not. But the relationship between speech/writing, in a biographical sense, was foundational for Derrida and would be explored most fully in *Of Grammatology*.

More immediately, it presents Husserl with an unrecognised problem which is, Derrida argues, indicative of one of the central unrecognised problems of philosophy. For Husserl, 'the model of language is the objective language of science.' In contrast, 'a poetic language, whose significations would not be objects, will never have any transcendental value for him.'[29] The first geometer and those who follow must be concerned about 'the univocity of linguistic expression and about securing, by a very careful coining of words, propositions, and complexes of propositions, the results which are to be univocally expressed.'[30] They must aim for 'clarity', for a language which matches the world. The 'free play of associative constructions' remains a 'constant danger'.[31]

And yet writing, in ways in which Derrida will explore more thoroughly later in works such as *Glas* and *The Post Card*, generates the equi-vocal. Meaning cannot be fixed – a sentence from *Finnegans Wake*, such as 'riverrun, past Eve and Adam's, from swerve of shore to bend of bay, brings us by a commodius vicus of recirculation back to Howth Castle and Environs', has no other absolute version lying behind it that could be ascertained by patient elimination of ambiguities. Similarly, 'And whowasit youwasit propped the pot in the yard and whatinthe nameofsen lukeareyou rubbinthe sideofthe flureofthe lobbywith Shite! will you have a plateful?' For it is Joyce whom Derrida invokes here, inserting him into his philosophical work with an audacity and strangeness that marks his corpus.

The endeavour of Joyce is

to repeat and take responsibility for all equivocation itself, utilizing a language that could equalize the greatest possible synchrony with the greatest potential for buried, accumulated, and interwoven intentions within each linguistic atom, each vocable, each word, each simple proposition, in all wordly cultures and their most ingenious forms (mythology, religion, sciences, arts, literature, politics, philosophy, and so forth).[32]

For Derrida, Joyce and Husserl are 'the two great models' on the 'relationship between language and history'. He returned to them in 'Ulysses Gramophone', noting:

Husserl proposes to render language as transparent as possible, univocal, limited to what, by being transmittable or able to be placed in tradition, thereby constitutes the only condition of a possible historicity ... The other great paradigm would be the Joyce of *Finnegans Wake*. He repeats and mobilizes and babe-lizes the asymptotic totality of the equivocal. He makes this both his theme and his operation. He tries to make outcrop, with the greatest possible synchrony, at great speed, the greatest power of the meanings buried in each syllabic fragment, subjecting each atom of writing to fission in order to overload the unconscious with the whole memory of man.[33]

And yet, here again, the binary opposition of univocal/equivocal displays all the tensions of any other binary pair that Derrida deconstructs. The danger of equivocality haunts the univocal and vice versa. Joyce's work cannot be absolutely equivocal, or we would not be able to understand it. Even *Finnegans Wake* adheres to various rules, language games as Wittgenstein might put it, grammatically, etymologically, narratively. It is, for instance, a novel, it tells a story.

In his 1873 essay, 'On Truth and Lies in a Nonmoral Sense', Nietzsche wrote of truth that it is:

A mobile army of metaphors, metonyms, and anthropomor-phisms – in short, a sum of human relations which have been enhanced, transposed, and embellished poetically and rhetorically, and which after long use seem firm, canonical, and obligatory to a people: truths are illusions about which one has forgotten that this is what they are; metaphors which are worn out and without sensuous power; coins which have lost their pictures and now matter only as metal, no longer as coins.[34]

Joyce, for Derrida, 'mobilises'. He also 'babelises'. In 1985, Derrida wrote his most influential work on translating, 'The Tower of Babel', noting that the biblical story 'recounts among other things, the origin of the confusion of tongues, the irreducible multiplicity of idioms, the necessary and impossible task of translation, its necessity as translation.'[35] This translation is not simply across languages, it happens within language, and within the very sorts of knowledge transmission which Husserl is attempting to base objectivity on. That is the idea that

a continuity from one person to another, from one time to another, must have been capable of being carried out. It is clear that the method of producing original idealities out of what is pre-scientifically given in the cultural world must have been written down and fixed in firm sentences prior to the existence of geometry; furthermore, the capacity for translating these sentences from vague linguistic understanding into the clarity of the reactivation of their self-evident meaning must have been, in its own way, handed down and ever capable of being handed down.[36]

In the penultimate paragraph of his Introduction to *The Origin of Geometry*, Derrida returns to his earlier problem with Husserl – in our pre-predicative grasping of the world, the impossibility of finding an absolute origin.

The impossibility of resting in the simple maintenance [nowness] of a Living Present, the sole and absolutely absolute origin of the De Facto and the De Jure, of Being and Sense, but always other in its self-identity; the inability to live enclosed in the innocent undividedness of the primordial Absolute, because the Absolute is present only in being deferred-delayed (différant) without respite, this impotence and this impossibility are given in a primordial and pure consciousness of Difference ... Difference would be transcendental. The pure and interminable disquietude of thought striving to 'reduce' Difference by going beyond factual infinity toward the infinity of its sense and value, i.e., while maintaining Difference – that disquietude would be transcendental.[37]

Capitalised as Difference, without its 'a', this is a first, furtive appearance of the concept of perhaps Derrida's most famous term – différance.

For anyone approaching Derrida for the first time, différance remains difficult to grasp. This is precisely because différance is not a concept – a 'thing', which 'exists' – thingness and existence are terms where, as Derrida might put it, a founding violence has already occurred. What is this 'founding violence'?

The naming of an object is to perform such an act of founding violence. By naming this object an 'apple tree' I perform a number of operations. First, I bring it into the world of nameable things and bring it into language. I place it in a category, an 'order of things' as Foucault put it. In fact, if I was feeling particularly Foucauldian, I might argue that I am exerting power over it. Like Adam naming the animals, I am wielding sovereignty over it, although the power here is arguably benign, unlike when we name something 'refugee', 'homosexual' or 'mad'.

I am also making a distinction which was not made before: it is different from other trees that are not apple trees. As part of a species that eats apples I am, perhaps, bringing it into the functional domain. The tree becomes a potential source of food in a way that a larch isn't, and this may affect my immediate plans for it, as well as my future plans, in that I might cultivate it. In making it functional I might also impose a temporal and qualitative dimension that I would not to an unfunctional tree – it is not blossoming, it is now blossoming, it has failed to blossom, it provided a good yield, it failed to do so (with various meteorological and agricultural conjectures to follow). And the same tree might have different names with different implications. For example, if one of its names is 'the tree that blocks my view' a new set of relationships is generated.

For Derrida this is true of all naming, including philosophical. Différance, therefore, is the moment before this founding act of violence, where we are held before the decision. It is the moment of aporia, before there is a road taken and a road not taken.

The word itself carries within it some of the philosophical heft Derrida wishes to assign it, playing on the fact that *différer* in French means both to differ and to defer. It is also a word that is, deliberately, only distinguishable from *différence* – French for difference – when written down (although it has become an unacknowledged commonplace in English to sound hyper-French when pronouncing it). It thus calls to be written, and on the question of writing. The replacing of the 'e' with an 'a' is inaudible: 'it remains silent, secret, and discreet, like a tomb'.[38]

Différance also anticipates the semiotic turn Derrida's thinking is beginning to take, in identifying the relationship between words. The meaning of a word is, as we shall see, generated by its difference to other words – 'apple tree' is not 'lemon tree', and it is also not 'applied tree' or 'Jacques Derrida'.

Generally, particularly in Anglophone introductions to Derrida, it has been traditional to explain différance exclusively through language, in particular through the work of the linguist Ferdinand de Saussure and his posthumous 1916 text *Course in General Linguistics*, with its positing of the sign, constructed from the signifier and the signified, and this definition remains crucial. It was a position Derrida himself had assumed by the time he wrote his 1968 essay 'Différance'. But it should not be considered as solely a linguistic question.

It is important to remember that Husserl's epoché derives from the idea of 'suspension of judgement' and, as Derrida argued, Husserl had attempted in his analyses to resist dogmatic thinking that would decide between two modes of description – the structural and the genetic, where the structural 'leads to a comprehensive description of a totality … organized according to an internal legality', and the genetic searches 'for the origin and foundation of the structure.'[39] In phenomenological description – and phenomenology, as Husserl had argued from the off, was always a mode of description – there are no 'choices' to be made, including between genesis and structure. The object perceived keeps itself open to continuous and inexhaustible description, and to 'decide' on one mode of description is to falsify the project.

Husserl's error, in his late works, is the result of privileging passive genesis over active when considering (again) intentionality. Passive genesis implies that consciousness does not constitute an object, but rather it unveils or receives it. Thus a prior genetic process must have already constituted the object – it has a prior existence, and a subsequent one, to being perceived. This history, once more, intercedes in apprehension. But what is important here for Derrida is that Husserl, in spite of himself, decides – in this case for genesis over structure. His suspension of judgement is suspended in the violence of a decision which, ultimately, has no greater claims, except perhaps that it is easier.

In July 1961, Derrida completed his introduction and submitted to Hyppolite, who wrote that he read 'with great interest' the way it 'followed the meanders of Husserl's thinking.' It was a less than glowing endorsement, and certainly failed to engage with the new ideas Derrida was worrying into being. Derrida also contacted Paul Ricoeur, then chair of General Philosophy at the Sorbonne, and whose translation of *Ideas I* had been Jackie's introduction to Husserl. Ricoeur was effusive, calling it 'scrupulous', 'profoundly intelligent', 'full of meaning and big with promise'.[40] This was high praise from one of Derrida's philosophical heroes.

Before publication, there were two significant developments in Derrida's life. First, he was able to leave Le Mans. He himself found work at the Sorbonne, as an 'assistant in general philosophy and logic'. Allowed to choose his own subjects he chose, gnomically: 'Irony, doubt and the question'; 'Thinking means saying no'; 'Evil is in the world like a slave who brings water up from the well – Claudel'; and 'The present (Heidegger, Aristotle, Kant, Hegel and Bergson)'. Despite their eccentric titles, or perhaps because of them, his lectures became so crowded he was forced to split his classes in two.

Shortly before that he was invited to give a paper at the 'Colloques de Cerisy', held each year at Cerisy-la-Salle, a gathering of 'phenomenologists, dialecticians (idealist and materialist), logicians and epistemologists, historians of the economy, art and language, ethnologists, biologists, etc.'[41] The theme was to be 'Genesis and Structure', referencing Hyppolite's 1947 text *Genesis and Structure of Hegel's Phenomenology of Spirit*.

Hegel's importance to Derrida is fundamental. In a later interview Derrida said, 'We will never be done with the reading and re-reading of Hegel, and in a certain way, I do nothing other than attempt to explain myself on this point.'[42] If Husserl was the foundation of Derrida's deconstructive impulses, it was Hegel whose spirit – *Geist* – moved through his works in the early 1960s.

Hyppolite had famously treated the *The Phenomenology of Spirit* as a sort of *Bildungsroman* – the protagonist, 'Spirit', travels through the history of consciousness from its primal beginnings to its final destination as Absolute Knowledge. This was a linear, teleological process, governed by rationality. The motor of this progress is, roughly, the Hegelian dialectic: thesis, antithesis, synthesis. An idea or state of the Spirit at a given moment (thesis) is challenged (antithesis) and then incorporates the challenge to rise to a higher level (synthesis). This schema – with its Eurocentric good-news story of Western progress – has rightly become more problematic as the philosophical landscape (for instance) has become more diverse, and more willing and able to challenge such master narratives.

It was not a problem to which Derrida was oblivious, and his later thinking on logocentrism and then phallogocentrism – his own neologism for the privileging of the masculine in the construction of meaning – called Hegel to account. In 1964–65, however, his central concern was the interaction between thesis and antithesis: Hegel's *Aufhebung*. Variously translated as 'to lift up', 'to abolish' and 'to transcend', it is a moment of suspension and contradiction, before the progress of *Geist* – before the moment of decision. Here again we are in the realm of différance. In fact, Derrida would argue that:

If there were a definition of différance, it would be precisely the limit, the interruption, the destruction of the Hegelian relève [aufhebung] wherever it operates. What is at stake here is enormous.[43]

Looking back, Derrida characterised his exploration of Hegel as seeking a 'kind of general strategy of deconstruction'. We must

traverse a phase of overturning. To do justice to this necessity is to recognize that in a classical philosophical opposition we are not dealing with the peaceful coexistence of a vis-à-vis, but rather with a violent hierarchy. One of the two terms governs the other (axiologically, logically, etc.), or has the upper hand. To deconstruct the opposition, first of all, is to overturn the hierarchy at a given moment.[44]

This became one of the central methodological strategies of deconstruction, and perhaps has had the greatest practical and theoretical impact outside the academy of any of Derrida's interventions. As we have seen, for Derrida the history of Western thought relies on the apparent 'logic' of binary oppositions, where the first term is privileged over the second. But, as Derrida points out, this is not a 'peaceful coexistence of two terms, it is a violent hierarchy'. The task of deconstruction is to suspend the hierarchy at this moment and analyse and criticise it, in a sort of productive ambivalence. As each of the terms has a constructed meaning, as all meaning is constructed, why does this opposition exist, why is one term privileged, whom does it serve, what does it fail to acknowledge, convey or understand? The answer may be political, cultural, philosophical and so on – each analysis may unearth more hidden assumptions – but the task of deconstruction is not then to efface the difference through synthesis, but to mark it, to note its undecidability and explore its complex interplay.

Derrida arrived at the conference in his 2CV and met such esteemed names as Jean Piaget, famous for his work on child development, and Ernst Bloch, the German Marxist. Gabriel

Marcel, who had argued for the distinction between a problem and a mystery, was also there.

Derrida delivered his paper on 31 July. It was titled '"Genesis and Structure" and Phenomenology', and again Husserl was the focus. Later to appear in the collection of essays *Writing and Difference*, it is notable for three main reasons. First, différance makes its first true appearance, in the form that would become familiar. Second, Derrida's problematising of voice begins to emerge, and with it the question of the metaphysics of presence. He notes, in terms which are now familiar:

> Reason, Husserl says, is the logos which is produced in history. It traverses Being with itself in sight, in sight of appearing to itself, that is, to state itself and hear itself as logos. It is speech as auto-affection: hearing oneself speak. It emerges from itself in order to take hold of itself within itself, in the 'living present' of its self-presence. In emerging from itself, hearing oneself speak constitutes itself as the history of reason through the detour of writing. Thus it differs from itself in order to reappropriate itself.[45]

Finally, the paper is significant for its signature. The boy from Algeria no longer presents himself as Jackie. For the first time he signs his name as Jacques Derrida.

4

Jacques Derrida

It is true that for me Husserl's work, and precisely the notion of the epoché, has been and still is a major indispensable gesture. In everything I try to say and write the epoché is implied. I would say that I constantly try to practise that whenever I am speaking or writing.

– 'In the Blink of an Eye'

Let us begin with the problem of signs and writing – since we are already in the midst of it.

– 'Différance'

To describe his years from 1962–67 as prolific is to perform one's own act of violence on the language. Jacques Derrida – this 'semi-pseudonym', as he called it, which allowed entry into the 'space of literary and philosophical legitimation' – was always prolific. His corpus runs to over eighty books, and he was not given to slim volumes. While some are collections of essays, he continued to generate longer texts throughout his life. This was absolutely congruent with his thought. For Derrida, a text was an event, and, aside from his planned works, he delighted in being set topics to analyse.

For Derrida 'it is necessary in each situation to create an appropriate mode of expression, to invent the law of the singular event, to take account of the presumed or desired addressee.'[1] He saw this as a responsibility – a response in the sense which Lévinas gave it. Thus his later work includes a number of interviews, collaborations and roundtables, forcing him, by choice, to engage with an interlocutor, another face, which he saw as the 'most fruitful' way of doing philosophy 'of our time'. Thinking, Derrida argues – for both collegiate and deeply philosophical reasons – is a mode of dialogue. Language that presumes itself fixed and proclaimed from the mountain is the sovereign right of God, not of humans.

But it was on the page, or later on the screen of his Macintosh, that Derrida did his most intense thinking, producing book after book of astonishing quality. This graphomania had a deeply personal motivation. 'Deep down,' he wrote, 'my desire to write is the desire for an exhaustive chronicle … what's going on in my head … a total diary.'[2] What was going on in Derrida's head seems, most of the time, to have been philosophy and literature.

But the years from his first publication in 1962 to the miracle year of 1967 were, even by his own standards, exceptional in the breadth of his achievement and the development of his thought. In that short time, the assistant in general philosophy and logic, and later *caïman* at the ENS, produced all of the essays that were collected as *Writing and Difference*, including some of the most notoriously difficult and (to his adherents) philosophically revolutionary texts of the twentieth or any century. These included: the paper given at Cerisy, '"Genesis and Structure" and Phenomenology'; what is generally regarded as the first truly deconstructive masterpiece, 'Violence and Metaphysics: An Essay on the Thought of Emmanuel Lévinas'; 'Freud and the Scene of Writing', in which his own nascent concept of grammatology emerges for the first time; his critical essay on Foucault, 'Cogito and the History of Madness'; 'From Restricted to General Economy: A Hegelianism Without Reserve', which uses Bataille's reading of Hegel to explore sovereignty; and two essays on Antonin Artaud, 'The Theatre of Cruelty and the Closure of Representation' and 'La Parole soufflée'. In addition, during this period he wrote the other two books of the big three, *Of*

Grammatology and *Speech and Phenomena: And Other Essays on Husserl's Theory of Signs*, which continues to explore Husserl and language.

But before all that, Derrida was to suffer a shock he knew was coming: Algerian independence. De Gaulle had called the referendum for 2 July 1962, and it was always clear which way the vote would go, and what would be the consequences for the pied-noir population. They were being offered, it was said, a choice between the 'coffin and the suitcase'. In May, the family of Derrida's sister arrived in Paris, and in June, Aimé, Georgette and the rest of his family. At one point the Derridas' flat slept seventeen family members.

Politically, Derrida's position remained similar to that of Albert Camus – he hoped for 'a political solution that would allow French Algerians to continue to live in that country'. Camus had famously said, 'People are now planting bombs in the tramways of Algiers. My mother might be on one of those tramways. If that is justice, then I prefer my mother.'³ But, for all its humanity, this moderate position, appealing to reason, is the privilege of the oppressor. As Frantz Fanon argued, 'colonialism is not a thinking machine, nor a body endowed with reasoning faculties. It is violence in its natural state, and it will only yield when confronted with greater violence.'⁴ Fanon was under no illusion that compromise was possible. Aside from his overtly political activities, his work with psychiatric patients had brought him into close contact with the victims of French torture. For Algerians, the struggle for independence was not an incremental accretion of rights – it was 'total war'.

Two weeks after the referendum – the result was 99.72 per cent in favour – Derrida returned to El-Biar to help pack the last of his parents' belongings. The house that Aimé and Georgette had bought at the limit of their means when Jackie was four years old, and had just finished paying for, became the property of the Algerian state. When he returned for the first time in 1971, the very street he grew up on had ceased to exist, as those French homonyms that had haunted his childhood were replaced by Arab names. He never got over what he came to call his 'nostalgeria' – his longing for the land of his birth, from which he was not only in exile, but which no longer existed.

Derrida's translation of *The Origin of Geometry* with its exorbitant introduction was well received by his peers, including Ricoeur, Jean Wahl (champion of Hegel and Kierkegaard) and Foucault, who was 'filled with admiration' for its 'regal honesty' and who identified a mutual obsession. 'The first philosophy for us ... is reading.'[5] It also won, alongside Roger Martin for his *Contemporary Logic and Formalisation*, the Prix Jean-Cavaillès, meaning that Derrida's first philosophical prize was one traditionally given for a work of scientific philosophy. The prize was named for Jean Cavaillès, a hero of the Resistance, whose most important text, *On the Logic and Theory of Science*, was written in prison in Montpellier in 1942. After escaping to London and meeting de Gaulle, Cavaillès was betrayed, arrested, tortured and shot on his return to France.

Cavaillès had a particular resonance for Derrida, as he had identified the same problem with Husserl as Tran Duc Thao. In Cavaillès's case it was logic that caused an aporia that muddied Husserl's intersubjective world – 'If transcendental logic really founds logic, there is no absolute logic ... if there is an absolute logic, it can draw authority only from itself, and then it is not transcendental.'[6] While Derrida would identify Thao as more influential, he was aware of Cavaillès's work too, mentioning him in the introduction to *The Origin of Geometry*.

New commissions soon flooded in – Derrida found himself writing about the poet Edmond Jabès, about Foucault, about Artaud. But perhaps the most important of this early work was his essay on Lévinas, 'Violence and Metaphysics'. Originally planned for publication in the journal *Critique*, the essay grew too large, running to over a hundred pages in its first draft. In the end it appeared across two issues of Jean Wahl's *Revue de métaphysique et de morale* in late 1964. It is in this essay that most of the great themes of Derrida's work are definitively announced. Leonard Lawlor in his *Derrida and Husserl* goes so far as to say that 'Derrida's own thinking begins with "Violence and Metaphysics" ... [it] has an unrivalled privilege in regard to the general development of Derrida's thought.'[7] The text drew on the suggestive elliptical pronouncements of thinkers as diverse as Nietzsche, Heidegger and Blanchot, as well as the subject of the essay, Lévinas.

'That philosophy died yesterday ... and philosophy should still wander toward the meaning of its death ...' – the opening, dense, poetic and allusive, struck a new note. Philosophy has died, and yet still wanders towards the meaning of its death. In this atmosphere of bereavement are we mourning a passing, or are we performing last rites?

It is not unusual, of course, as Alain Badiou reminds us, for the promulgators of 'new philosophies' to begin by declaring the death of philosophy itself, at least as it has been disseminated up till then.

> The best way to say 'I am a new philosopher' is probably to say with great emphasis: 'Philosophy is over, philosophy is dead! Therefore, I propose that with me there begins something entirely new. Not philosophy, but thinking! Not philosophy, but the force of life! Not philosophy, but a new rational language! In fact, not the old philosophy, but the new philosophy, which by some amazing chance happens to be mine.'[8]

But Derrida comes not to bury philosophy. The 'death of philosophy' is not a historical event, it is a structural one: philosophy has always lived in the shadow of its own death. As he had argued as far back as his first essays, nihilism is not a property of the world, but an aspect of philosophy, born from its language. For Derrida, language is not to be regarded as a medium behind which lies the truth, whatever philosophy's attempts to classify it as such. Language *is* the medium of philosophy, right up to and including the sense in which Husserl used it as a guarantor of objectivity. Philosophy is a narrative technique. Where Nietzsche situated himself in the twilight, anticipating sunset, Derrida places himself in what we might call the gloaming, with its double etymology of gloom and glow.

In the *Crisis*, Husserl had gone back to the founding of philosophy and noted that its origins made it a particularly Western (his term is 'European') phenomenon. Derrida takes up this theme. 'The founding concepts of philosophy,' he writes, 'are primarily Greek, and it would not be possible to philosophise, or speak philosophically, outside the medium.'[9] This is not to argue that other traditions cannot think their own problems, or that there is a clear demarcation, but it is saying that Western philosophy is Western philosophy, and its founding concepts, such as truth and being, are inaugurated, develop and are disputed within this tradition, for instance in Husserl, where Plato is seen to inaugurate the question of Being; or in Heidegger, where Plato is seen to cause the question of Being to be forgotten.

Derrida is explicit that philosophy has no special rights compared to other narratives.

> Philosophical language belongs to a system of language(s). Thereby, its nonspeculative ancestry always brings a certain equivocality into speculation. Since this equivocality is original and irreducible, perhaps philosophy must adopt it, think it and be thought in it, must accommodate duplicity and difference within speculation, within the very purity of philosophical meaning.[10]

'Adopting equivocality' is perhaps as close as Derrida gets to a call to arms.

Thus the essay begins with a wake for Husserl and Heidegger – like that of Finnegan it is both a mourning and a celebration. Then a characteristically Derridean non sequitur, as though an unruly guest has grabbed the microphone – 'It is at this level [the level of thinking of Being and its revelation or forgetting] that the thought of Emmanuel Levinas can make us tremble.'[11] We are suddenly thrown into the main body of the essay, which explores the thought of Lévinas.

As we have seen, for Lévinas it is the epiphany of the face of the Other that creates our subjectivity. Epiphany is from the Greek *epiphainein*, a revealing, a coming of the light. It is Derrida's interrogation of light in Lévinas around which the essay circles. If, as Borges has speculated, 'universal history, is but the history of several metaphors', might not philosophy be the same? And if so, what does it mean to speak of light in philosophy, from Plato to Lévinas?

The Greek ideal in its search for truth, Derrida notes, is 'a world of light and of unity, a philosophy of a world of light, a world without time. [A] heliopolitics ... which, turned toward the intelligible sun, toward the truth, experiences the other at his side and not face to face with him.'[12] As we have seen, Lévinas, while inhabiting the metaphor 'light', locates it in the face of the Other. He disrupts, here, the Greek metaphor, and therefore the philosophy. It puts into question philosophy's dream, since Plato, of being a science, as it presents ethics, concern for the other, as first philosophy instead of ontology.

'It would be frivolous to think that "Descartes", "Leibniz", "Rousseau", "Hegel", etc. are names of authors,' Derrida would write in *Of Grammatology*; rather 'they are the names of problems.'[13] The disruption of Western philosophy is, in Derridean terms, the problem given the name Lévinas. Lévinas intervenes in the progress of philosophy down from the Greeks, and his intervention is, in spirit and method, Jewish. The epigraph at the head of Derrida's essay is from the English poet Matthew Arnold's *Culture and Anarchy*:

> Hebraism and Hellenism – between these two points of influence our world moves. At one time it feels more powerfully the attraction of one of them, at another time of the other; and it ought to be, though never is, evenly and happily balanced between them.[14]

After the war Lévinas had immersed himself in the Talmud, and it affected both the method and content of his thinking. The Talmud is the vast oral counterpart to the Bible, which collects the work of rabbinic scholars up to the sixth century of the common era. While Lévinas had some acquaintance with it before the war it was not until 1945 that he began to study it intensively, after an encounter as strange and mythical as one of its own stories.

A close friend, Henri Nerson, told Lévinas about a mysterious individual known only as Chouchani – meaning 'person from Shushan' – who in the manner of mysterious individuals was repugnant to look at, but had great wisdom. For two years Lévinas refused to see him. Finally he relented, and spent the whole night talking with the strange wise man. In the morning he went to see Nerson and told him, 'I can not tell what he knows, all I can say is that all that I know, he knows.'[15]

It was from this moment that Lévinas immersed himself in the Talmud, studying with the mysterious *clochard* for five years, before Chouchani disappeared, legend has it to Israel and then South America, finally buried in Uruguay. The most obvious fruits of this engagement are the *Nine Talmudic Readings*, collected from his commentaries at annual Talmudic colloquia of a group of French Jewish intellectuals in Paris between 1963 and 1975.

For Lévinas, and later Derrida, the Talmud allowed for a new system of thought outside the Western philosophical tradition. 'It is certain that, when discussing the right to eat or not to eat an egg hatched on a holy day, or payments owed for damages caused by a wild ox the sages of the Talmud are discussing neither an egg nor an ox, but are arguing about fundamental ideas without appearing to do so,' Lévinas wrote.[16]

He argued that the translation of the Torah into Greek was necessary in order to express in Greek what Greece cannot express itself. The traditional privileging of the Self over the Other can be challenged, and concern for the Other ceases to be a merely rhetorical exercise, antedating ontology.

For Derrida the thought of Lévinas, 'which fundamentally no longer seeks to be a thought of being [Heidegger] and phenomenality [Husserl], makes us dream of an inconceivable process of dismantling and dispossession'.[17] This is also Derrida's dream – his questioning of Lévinas is 'anything but an objection'.[18] And the dismantling and dispossession was to be called deconstruction; and non-ontological thought was to be called hauntology.

Derrida has two problems with Lévinas's position. First, Lévinas emphasised the physical aspect of meeting the face of the Other. In Lévinas, the Self and the Other must actually be present to each other, face to face, to give birth to an ethics. Can I not, however, asks Derrida, encounter the Other through writing? 'Is it not possible to invert all of Lévinas's statements on this point? By showing, for example, that writing can assist itself, for it has time and freedom, escaping better than speech from empirical urgencies.'[19]

Second, in Derrida's argument, Lévinas is attempting to propose a 'non-violent language'. The only possible non-violent language is one that does not name, a language 'which would do without the verb to be, that is, without predication.'[20] To name the apple tree, again, is a founding violence. And the copula 'to be' – as in S *is* P – became central to Derrida's ongoing analyses of language and metaphor. For now, however, it was enough to say:

> Since the verb to be and the predicative act are implied in every other verb, and in every common noun, non-violent language, in the last analysis, would be the language of pure invocation, pure adoration, proffering only proper nouns in order to call the other from afar.[21]

In other words, the praising of God.

So, 'Are we Jews? Are we Greeks. We live in the difference between the Jew and the Greek, which is perhaps the unity of what is called history.' Derrida ends the essay by once again invoking Joyce with the question, 'What is the legitimacy, what is the meaning of the copula in this proposition from perhaps the most Hegelian of modern novelists: "Jewgreek is Greekjew. Extremes meet."[22]

At the ENS, Althusser was entering his own productive phase, but one accompanied by a series of breakdowns. He had shared the dream of getting Derrida back to the Normale Sup, and the growing reputation of the young philosopher made the proposition ever more attractive. Then, to the delight of both, in 1963–64 the opportunity arose for Derrida to teach forty-eight hours of classes over the course of the year while remaining at the Sorbonne; by 1964–65 he was a full *caïman*, a position he held for more than thirty years.

Althusser's fragile mental state was exacerbated by the suicide of his close friend Jacques Martin. It precipitated a crisis leading to institutionalisation, and Derrida, as he did frequently for the next fifteen years, took over where necessary. 'I bless you for existing and being my friend,' Althusser wrote to him; and despite their philosophical differences, they never crossed swords in print.

While happy to return to the ENS, Derrida was once again caught in political battles which were not close to his own concerns. In 1964–65, despite his troubles (and perhaps partially generating them), Althusser presented his groundbreaking seminar that would become the book *Reading Capital,* which, with 1965's *For Marx,* marked a dramatic shift in the French, and worldwide, reception and understanding of Marx. The passions of the students reflected this – where Derrida was hoping to analyse the foundations of metaphysics, the ENS was once again dividing into 'camps, strategic alliances, manoeuvres of circlement and exclusion.'[23]

Despite this, and the birth of his first child, Pierre, Derrida continued to produce work at an astonishing clip, especially considering its density. If anything, the obscurity of his concerns, and the growing conviction that he had opened if not a new field then the possibility of one, drove him on. Deconstruction and différance existed at this point only for him, and he was determined to explore the reach of their potential impact.

He had also found a way of writing. Aside from establishing many of Derrida's themes, part of the importance of 'Violence and Metaphysics' is that it also establishes his style. Dense, often gnomic, it expected the reader to have read everything in Western philosophy or to then go off and do so. Although he did not use the term until *Of Grammatology*, the opening is a sort of exergue, an inscription at the beginning of the book, which introduces themes which then play through the essay, either directly or not. It is a style aspiring to the literary in a way that perhaps no philosopher except Nietzsche had done before.

None of these are contingent aspects of Derrida's thinking. To take the literary style – if his argument was that a philosophical narrative has no privileged access to the truth compared to literature, then the tropes, strategies and styles of literature were valid in putting forward a philosophical argument. Thus, there is the playful but exhaustive teasing out of metaphors, sudden shifts, that evocative opening, the mysterious end.

As with his Introduction to *The Origin of Geometry*, and any number of subsequent works, there are footnotes by the yard. The footnotes too are performative. In his deconstruction of texts, Derrida analysed their instability, and the strategies deployed to mask it. Footnotes are exorbitant – from the Latin ex (out from), orbita (the track) – originally a legal term to describe going outside the law. The apparently natural coherence and unity of a text is called into question by these exorbitances – footnotes, prefaces, forewords, epigraphs. These 'supplementary' aspects of the text reveal unity as an artifice, a subterfuge that anyone who has ever written a text understands if not acknowledges.

For instance, in writing a text such as this, I make progress, I pause for months, I read more and change my emphasis, I worry at this moment that I have not written enough about Heidegger in the opening chapters (and so when writing about him in the next section wonder how much I need to say). Whereas in the book you now hold I may have returned and sorted out the problem. I fudge bits I don't understand so well or cadge other books' explanations (remembering to reword them) or – like a painter who can't do hands – hide them and hope no one notices; I start writing in one direction and realise I am going down the wrong track and so delete it; I make notes such as 'WIKIPEDIA DUMP, REWRITE'; move things up and down into and out of my own footnotes depending on emphasis or word count, and so on. I am edited and copy-edited. And yet the book you are reading is presented as coherent and of a piece, whether successful or otherwise, and is signed 'Peter Salmon', as though I sat down to write it, knowing everything I needed to know, and then said it in one breath.

No text can escape this – the problem is not simply practical but is embedded in the structure of 'the book', 'the sentence', 'writing'. And the conditional nature of the book is not simply in its generation – as noted, it is in the absolute nature of writing that it escapes from the writer. It can be passed around, read after my death, change meaning and emphasis, sound antiquated, be mistranslated (within the language or into another). And, as Derrida will later argue, the recipient cannot be guaranteed; like postcards, texts can arrive at the wrong address.

During this maelstrom of activity, Derrida had begun work on what he would later call the 'essay I value most'.[24] *La Voix et le Phénomène* was originally translated in 1973 as *Speech and Phenomena*, which is how it is generally known in English. However, as Leonard Lawlor has pointed out, translating *voix* as 'speech' implies that Derrida is investigating language only as it is spoken, where, crucially, it is 'voice' which is the subject of his analysis; as it is spoken, yes, but before it is spoken too. As it is in our heads. Lawlor himself re-translated it as *Voice and Phenomenon* in 2010 and it is this title I will use from here.

The essay's subtitle is 'An Introduction to the Problem of the Sign in Husserl's Phenomenology': it is Derrida's last great work on Husserl and, arguably, his first great work on the sign, and thus on language and writing. As such, it represents a transition from his analyses of phenomenology to his analysis of semiotics – questions of which had been hinted at, even haunted his work for the last decade. Many of the concerns remain the same, including the idea of the ideal object and its transmission from mind to mind.

About the same length as 'Violence and Metaphysics', *Voice and Phenomenon* returns to the *Logical Investigations*, where Husserl engages with the question of language. As Derrida notes in the opening paragraph, the philosophy of Husserl exhibits no radical breaks. He is always trying to understand how the 'strange realms' of subjectivity and objectivity interact. How – and here language intercedes – does one go from the indubitable concepts which our transcendental consciousness apprehends (what we experience is what we experience), via a repertoire of symbolic representations (including language), to arrive at a knowledge which is both objective and still indubitable?

Language is a system of signs. Things stand for other things – words for objects, for instance. The 'problem of the sign' in Derrida's subtitle points to an ambiguity in how this works. A sign, for Husserl, has a double sense. For him, it can be either an 'indication' (*Anzeichen*) or an 'expression' (*Ausdruck*). In the former, a sign indicates a state of affairs – a fever indicates an illness, a red-and-white spinning pole indicates a barber shop, a puff of white smoke indicates a new pope. As Husserl notes:

> In these we discover as a common circumstance the fact that certain objects or states of affairs of whose reality someone has actual knowledge indicate to him the reality of certain other objects or states of affairs, in the sense that his belief in the reality of the one is experienced (though not at all evidently) as motivating a belief or surmise in the reality of the other.[25]

Thus any mark on paper – a word, a nonsense word, a scribble, a drawing – is, in some sense, indicative.

Husserl wants to narrow down this vast field, to focus on signs that are meaningful in a certain way – he calls these 'expressions', where 'each instance or part of speech, as also each sign that is essentially of the same sort, shall count as an expression, whether or not such speech is actually uttered, or addressed with communicative intent to any persons or not'.[26]

If I 'express' something, I wish to communicate this thing to an interlocutor in a meaningful way. This can be, for example, an internal state of affairs that I wish that person to become aware of, as simple as *I am not feeling well* or as complex as, *Husserl wants to narrow down this vast field, to focus on signs that are meaningful in a certain way*. All expressions are also, therefore, indications, but not all indications are expressions, a situation Husserl accepts but Derrida needed to problematise.

As ever, for Husserl, it is the 'living present' that we must investigate and privilege as the basis of knowledge. As Derrida puts it, 'Presence has always been and will always be, to infinity, the form in which – we can say this apodictically – the infinite diversity of contents will be produced.'[27] Produced for consciousness where – in what may be the most Derridean sentence of all time – 'consciousness means nothing other than the possibility of the self-presence of the present in the living present.'[28]

This is the basis, notes Derrida, of Husserl's *metaphysics*, and we have already seen the ways in which he questions this desired purity of the living present. Now Derrida links this to the ways in which, as he argued in the introduction, ideal objects require language for their construction.

> Husserl no doubt did want to maintain, as we shall see, an originally silent, 'pre-expressive' [pre-predicative] stratum of experience. But since the possibility of constituting ideal objects belongs to the essence of consciousness, and since these ideal objects are historical products, only appearing thanks to acts of creation or intending, the element of consciousness and the element of language will be more and more difficult to discern.[29]

Derrida here lays down a challenge to himself. He wants to be a more thorough phenomenologist than Husserl, which involves a phenomenological investigation of areas which Husserl's hidden assumptions left unanalysed.

Derrida's focus is the voice. Speech is an extremely strange activity in which humans engage. When we consider talking, we tend to regard it, to use a Derridean term, as somehow 'supplementary' to what it is to be human. When we do thought experiments where we imagine not speaking, we tend to draw on our own experience of being silent, as though human beings would be much the same without speech. In identifying the birth of speech, we might imagine the moment where one of a group of cavemen, sitting around a fire, makes a grunting noise, and away we go. It may be that we call them human beings, and, indeed, this may be what happened, but the consciousness of a caveman would be so radically different to ours as to preclude philosophical investigation.

The pervasiveness of human language, human speech and the unthinkability of its absence, makes us, Husserl included, under-estimate this strangeness. We use language to order, to argue, to pray, to philosophise, to complain and to praise. We use it in poetry, fiction, legal documents, song. We use it directly, we use it obliquely, as in phatic speech, where 'How are you?' is a form of greeting and not a question about health. We use it to confess, to testify, as a guarantor of veracity: 'I swear to *tell* the truth and nothing but the truth.' We use it, in the distinction that J. L. Austin was to introduce, constantively (declarative sentences) and performatively. These include speech acts which, in their instantiation, perform an act: 'I name this ship the Queen Elizabeth' or 'I will' in response to 'Do you take this man …?' We tell jokes. We attempt to convince. We talk to dogs and babies as though they can understand. We talk to ourselves. We promise. We lie. We say goodbye.

What is remarkable about this – and again strange – is that within a linguistic community, while each utterance may be unique, we still use the same words, albeit in different configurations. Husserl himself noted this, without investigating further. For him, words are, in the same way that isosceles triangles are, ideal objects. Take, says Husserl, the word 'lion' (*Löwe* in German). The word 'lion' exists only once in English – using it does not exhaust it. It remains a unified idea no matter if it appears in print, in speech, in different accents, at different volumes. If I use it, or you use it, or hear it said across a room, it is the same word. It is, and this is the key to an ideal object, repeatable or, to use the term Derrida preferred, iterable. All words are. This is the fundamental property of ideal objects. Unlike actual existents, which are unique (and thus uniquely located in space and time, unrepeatable, uniterable) and can and will degrade, ideal objects are non-real, detached from the spatiotemporal.

Here Husserl has repeated the founding moment of all metaphysics, separating form and matter, the non-real and the real, as Plato did. Derrida's close analysis of language and, later in the book, of voice, should not blind us to the stakes. This is not simply a linguistic battle for Derrida – in fact there is no sense in which something can be simply linguistic. This is Derrida identifying, analysing and ultimately attempting the destruction of – the deconstruction of – what he would term the 'metaphysics of presence'.

Anyone who has studied philosophy, starting with Plato, will be familiar with the baffling moment of being told of the theory of forms. By definition there are no perfect circles in the world. However, to know that, we must have an idea of a perfect circle. How? Because they exist, argues Plato, as forms. Where? Somewhere else. We are, as he puts it in Book VII of *The Republic*, like prisoners in a cave, shackled to a wall with a fire burning behind us. Unable to turn our heads, we mistake the shadows we see in front of us with the real objects.

And not simply objects such as circles of course, but chairs, truth, the good and so on, 'beings beyond being', *epekeina tes ousias* as Plato refers to them. Their earthly versions are only a substandard representation of the perfect form, although they are also indicative of it, allowing us to speculate if not to turn to face them. As Joyce's Stephen Dedalus puts it in *Ulysses*, 'Horseness is the whatness of allhorse.'

For Derrida this original bafflement is a genuine and valid response. It is indeed strange that the strangeness of forms is not only elided where possible, but that they form one of the foundations of philosophy. They – and this will be crucial for his criticism of structuralism – exist outside the system (the world) and yet it is they that guarantee the system works. Or to put it in mathematical terms, they are outside a set, and yet the set relies on them to define and sustain itself.

Their non-reality is, of course, a major plank in Nietzsche's criticism of Western philosophy. 'God is dead' is not simply a theological statement. Rather, it seeks these terms outside the system (God, truth, the forms and so on – Derrida will add justice and democracy) and nullifies them (from the beginning, or from now on). For Nietzsche, this then meant an ethical reassessment. His concern was with values and the 're-evaluation' of all of them.

Derrida, while not dismissing this, is more interested in (at least) two other things. First – with Nietzsche, what is 'the world' like if we remove these exterior props? Second, and again Nietzsche's analysis was cleaved to morality, why do we have these props, and why do they persist? What is their function? Nietzsche expressed his exasperation in *Twilight of the Idols*: 'I am afraid we are not rid of God because we still have faith in grammar.'[30] Or, as Baudelaire had put it twenty years earlier, 'God is the only being who, in order to rule, does not even need to exist.'

It is one of the fundamental 'properties' of ideal objects that their interactions must be logical and formal. Their essence must be independent of any set or sets of circumstances. An isosceles triangle, a perfect circle, horseness cannot be affected by space or time, or they are not ideal. For Husserl, language as spoken is problematic. Elements of expression can only stay non-real because they take place in what he calls the 'sphere of solitary mental life' – self-consciousness, immediately and absolutely present to itself. This privileged sphere is abandoned, and its contents contaminated, when they enter the realm of the empirical, the real, circumstance – when they are said out loud.

For example, I may have a meaning-intention in my mind, but it cannot, by definition, be delivered in a pure state to my interlocutor (we will later see this problem re-emerge in Derrida's argument with the speech act theories of Searle). So Husserl proposes a perfect language in which meaning is absolute and absolutely transparent, and that happens 'in the blink of an eye'. This is the interior monologue. Thus, in what Derrida notes is a paradoxical move, Husserl attempts to fix the essence of expression (to press outward) in the unexpressed, in 'the voice that keeps silence'. 'Self-presence must be produced in the undivided unity of a temporal present so as to have nothing to reveal to itself by the agency of signs.'[31]

Two objections present themselves. First, as Derrida has argued, the guarantor of the ideality of language is, in fact, speech. Second, what is this 'in the blink of an eye'? Husserl is once again seeking a unit of time so small it no longer exists, the absolutely punctual in the flowing thisness of the temporal.

But Derrida is out-phenomenologising Husserl. Is what Husserl is describing what actually happens? Is the experience of absolutely self-present meaning true to our experience in any recognisable sense?

What happens when we speak, in all the ways outlined above, and including the voice in our head? Philosophy, alongside common sense, tends to argue that I have a thought of more or less absolute clarity; I then change it into words. I say these words. My interlocutor (in a perfect world) understands my words, and the thought I have communicated, transparently, enters their mind. The interlocutor may be myself; and ideally for Husserl, that is exactly who she or he is.

Each of these steps is highly problematic, Derrida resolved. Try having a thought without words. If such a thing is possible, how is that then turned into words? How lucky would humans have to be – if they are, say, an English speaker with an alphabet of twenty-six letters – that there are the words to carry out this operation and retain the true, full meaning of the thought? Every time. Next time you speak, is this schema recognisable? Do you always know what you are going to say, and then say it? Or is it the fact of saying it that makes the thought?

It is not, argues Derrida, that we have self-presence and the voice in our head (or out loud) expresses it; rather, the voice in our head (or out loud) gives us the illusion of self-presence. I hear myself speak, and the proximity of the sound appears to guarantee the contiguity of the words to thought. In contrast with, say, our seeing ourselves via the medium of a mirror, or touching ourselves where exterior surface meets exterior surface, this particular type of 'auto-affection', hearing oneself speak, is unmediated by the world. It is *pure* auto-affection, and we therefore tend to treat it, our voice, as our most intimate version of ourselves – or as ourselves completely.

We might even mistake it for our soul. In *Of Grammatology*, Derrida quotes Hegel, who also 'demonstrates very well the strange privilege of sound in idealization, the production of the concept and the self-presence of the subject.'[32] Writes Hegel:

> The ear ... perceives the result of that interior vibration of material substance without placing itself in a practical relation toward the objects, a result by means of which it is no longer a material form in its repose, but the first, more ideal activity of the soul itself which is manifested.[33]

It is this 'strange privilege' that sees philosophy, often with great belligerence, defend the purity of the spoken word against the contamination of the written. As we will see, from Plato to Rousseau, from Husserl to Saussure, this 'phonocentrism', as Derrida called it, has led philosophy astray. Instead of trying to capture pure presence, instead of attempting to make of it the foundation of our metaphysics, we must recognise that pure presence is, in a sense, a wager. It is not a science but a bet, a construction to give the illusion of coherence to a field of difference, or différance.

In September 1966, Derrida was exhausted. *Voice and Phenomena* was running two months late, while his ENS teaching load, supplemented by covering for Althusser, had left him in a period of 'nervous exhaustion not far removed from despair'. He was also typing up another book he had been working on, called *Of Grammatology*, while having to deal with a four-year-old son at home and with students who 'devour my liver'.[34]

So an invitation to speak at a conference on structuralism at Johns Hopkins University in October could not have come at a worse time. Still, Derrida broke off from his other work and, in the two weeks he had before the conference, sat down and wrote the lecture 'Structure, Sign, and Play in the Discourse of the Human Sciences'.

5

An Event, Perhaps

I am very mistrustful whenever people identify historical breaks or when they say, 'This begins there.' I have never done that, and I believe I have even set down here and there reservations with regard to this type of periodization and distribution.

— Ear of the Other

Why would one mourn for the centre? Is not the centre, the absence of play and difference another name for death?

— Ellipsis

The 1966 Baltimore colloquium was organised by Richard Macksey, then acting director of the newly instituted Humanities Center (now named the Department of Comparative Thought and Literature), and the literary critic Eugenio Donato. Macksey was a polymath whose huge personal library, some 70,000 volumes, dwarfed even Derrida's eventual collection. 'There's no topic in the world that bores him' noted a colleague, and he was famed for his overwhelming intellectual enthusiasm, for riding a Harley Davidson to work, and for living on 'three hours of sleep and pipe smoke.'[1] He was a revolutionary thinker in his own right, in that the Humanities Center was the first interdisciplinary department at an American university.

Macksey had organised the conference to introduce structuralism to American intellectual life; it was already the dominant theoretical discipline in France, having displaced the existentialism of Sartre, de Beauvoir and Camus. As Macksey noted in his opening address, structuralism called into question the notion of the 'subject' – the human being, however defined – as being central.

Structuralism was, in a sense, a reaction to a certain romanticising of the cogito by existentialism. It challenged the primacy of consciousness, and the individual, as the seat of meaning. Where a conscious human being existed within a structural field, it was not 'what that person reckoned', as a sovereign instigator of meaning. Rather, human culture – including human beings – need to be understood in terms of relationships to a broader conceptual grid. To understand an object – or indeed a subject insofar as that designation is allowed – one looks at its position in the grid, at how it differs or is similar to the things around it. Every system has a structure, and the position of each element within the structure is dictated by the structure – there is no surplus, the matrix is whole.

It was from two unexpected thinkers that the intellectual terrain of structuralism emerged, and a critique of each was central to Derrida's paper.

Ferdinand de Saussure and Claude Lévi-Strauss could not have been more different from each other, nor could they have imagined the impact their work would have outside their seemingly narrow disciplines of linguistics and anthropology, respectively. In fact Saussure published little in his lifetime, and much of what he did publish, such as his work on Lithuanian linguistics despite his inability to speak the language, is the source of some embarrassment. He was born in Geneva in 1857, and as a young linguistic teacher he cut his teeth studying such things as 'primitive vowel systems in Indo-European Languages', the topic of his first and only full-length book. He lived a mostly blameless life, lecturing on Gothic and High German in Paris, and Sanskrit and Indo-European at the University of Geneva, before becoming obsessed with the search for anagrams in Greek and Latin poems. He was fascinated for reasons known only to himself by the idea that poets encoded the name of certain gods in their poems; in the end, this obsession generated eight boxes of notebooks and sketches, and no publications.

In 1907 the sudden death of a colleague forced him to add to his teaching load a course in general linguistics for beginner students. The lectures, which he gave until 1911, caused little fuss at the time, and he was more than happy to return to his more niche concerns when they were discontinued. On his death in 1913 the lectures remained unpublished, as they remained until they were collected by his former students Charles Bally and Albert Sechehaye, and published in 1916, based on their notes and recollections.

Course in General Linguistics is one of the most influential books of the twentieth century, its impact spreading far beyond the field of linguistics and into philosophy, anthropology, the social sciences, semiotics, psychoanalysis and feminism. Russian formalism later incorporated its findings wholesale. Both structuralism and poststructuralism regard it as a fundamental text. When Saussure wrote in the *Course*, 'For the study of language to remain solely the business of a handful of specialists would be a quite unacceptable state of affairs. In practice, the study of language is in some degree or other the concern of everyone,'[2] he had no notion of how wide this set of 'everyone' might become, or how deep their concern.

His basic insight was, indeed, basic, but revolutionary. First, Saussure wished to distinguish between language as it is used, actual utterances, and the whole system of language, that which precedes speech and makes it possible. The former he termed *parole*, the latter *langue*. *Langue* is the *structure* of language that allows for meaningful utterances, *parole* is the utterances themselves. This structure operates as a system of signs, and signs are made up of two components, the signifier, which is the sound-image, such as 'apple tree' and the signified, the object to which the signifier refers, that thing over there made of wood and full of fruit.

Crucially, the relationship between the signifier and the signified is arbitrary. The signifier 'cat' does not embody 'cat-ness' – we could use any other signifier, as foreign languages show us, *chat* does the job in French, *paka* in Swahili. In French, for instance, *mouton* means both 'mutton', the cut of meat from an older animal, and a living 'sheep', while the English reserve it for the latter. Lamb works in the opposite way.

Saussure was not the first to identify the arbitrary nature of the relationship between signifier and signified. John Locke had previously drawn attention to the situation in his *Essay Concerning Human Understanding* (1689), while Aristotle had referred to the relationship as 'conventional', that is, a matter of convention rather than necessity.

But Saussure was the first to argue that not only are the signifiers arbitrary, but so are the signifieds.

Traditionally, the world had been seen as a world of objects. Language named these objects (things, ideas). As noted, an object may have a different name but the thing named still retained its discrete existence. But for Saussure, language is not simply a system of representation, of labelling. Rather, it is a system of 'articulation', in which the naming creates the object.

Saussure illustrates this by comparing words to money. If I want to know the meaning of a £5 note, I require two things. First, I need to know the number of things I can exchange for it (cartons of milk for instance). But second, I need to be able to compare it to other denominations (euros, dollars) and to other values in the same denomination (how does it compare to £10?). To understand a given signifier, 'one must compare it with similar values, with other words that stand in opposition to it.'[3]

These signifiers form a matrix: a conceptual grid that we impose on the world to make it make sense, and this conceptual grid creates the signifieds. What is key here is that each signifier gets its validity not from some quality of itself; rather, it gets it from how it differs from other signifiers. Cat is cat, and not cut, because it differs in one of its phonemes. *Language is a system of differences.*

And this is true of every word within language. There are no 'first words' that exist, and from which differences and relations emerge. Rather the 'things' emerge *from* the differences and relations, an emergence that has no end, and that can never be complete. As Saussure put it, language is a system of differences without positive terms. Derrida's *différance* attempts to capture this same idea: a difference without origin, without end, always delayed and deferred. To pin down a point of origin is not only false, but an act of violence. It may be a useful one, but it is invalid within the system presented. In the beginning isn't the Word. In the beginning is *différance*.

For Claude Lévi-Strauss, anthropology, the study of human behaviour and societies, was also an analysis of conceptual grids, of matrices of meaning. Born in Paris in 1908, the son of a portrait painter, Lévi-Strauss studied law and philosophy before, almost by accident, taking up a position at the University of São Paulo in Brazil, as a visiting professor in sociology. He and his then wife spent 1935–39 in anthropological fieldwork in Mato Grosso and the Amazonian rainforest. After passing the war years in the United States, Lévi-Strauss produced his first major work, *The Elementary Structures of Kinship*, published in 1949.

Instead of analysing human relationships by looking at their content, as previous anthropological theories had, Lévi-Strauss sought out the deep structures that underlay how the relationships came into being. He also studied what relationships were forbidden within a society. For Lévi-Strauss, the *ne plus ultra* of prohibition is the incest taboo, which occurs universally. Within a given society, by circumscribing the possibility of incest, members of the clan, men invariably, were forced to look outside the clan for a marriage partner. This prohibition thus functioned to, for instance, build alliances and widen the gene pool. (It also leads to the circulation of women; a point Derrida took up in later writings about the idea of reciprocity and the gift.) This is a structuralist notion of agency. Unlike, say, for Sartre, for whom the individual is the hero of his or her own story, here the individual's acts are dictated by a system outside of her or his own activity.

Lévi-Strauss's other structural 'gambit' was to explore the function and construction of myths, particularly in his four-volume work, *Mythologiques*, published between 1964 and 1971. Lévi-Strauss was fascinated by the fact that myths, which are completely open in what they can contain, from flying horses to wicked stepmothers, seem to exhibit similarities across cultures, and across time. He posited that this sameness was at the level of structure: thus the *parole* of a given myth is the story itself as it is recited (around a fire, in a book, through dance, in song); the *langue*, the underlying conceptual grid, remains as a narrative vehicle for universal meanings beyond history or news. It is put together according to certain rules, an act Lévi-Strauss refers to as bricolage: the taking of materials ready to hand and recombining them into something new.

In fact, the content of the myth is secondary and can change over time, but the underlying structure is primary, and retained. These 'bundles of relations' as he called them are fundamental, and cross cultures. Myths are good to think with, and, unlike poetry, do not suffer in translation.

Saussure and Lévi-Strauss's theories were to have an immediate effect on literary studies. Narratives were no longer (simply) the products of a freewheeling genius setting his or her words down, but have deep structures within which they function and which can be interpreted.

If Saussure was happy to potter with his anagrams, his index cards and his anonymity, Lévi-Strauss was a very different beast. His 1955 memoir, *Tristes Tropiques* is a work of both formidable scholarship and astonishing beauty, and established him as one of France's most prominent intellectuals, a role he was nowise uncomfortable with. The book is a lament for a lost world, the 'sad tropics' of the title, which he saw as dying at the hand of Western civilisation. In arguing that cultures exhibited structural similarities, regardless of the content of their endeavours, Lévi-Strauss was also arguing that no culture can claim to be better than another. The culture he grew up in and that of the Nambikwara, the indigenous Brazilian tribe he studied, were equally valid. That one culture was destroying the other had no justification.

Culture, then, is a system of symbolic communication, and a goal of structuralist analysis is to organise the given data from a society in the simplest possible way and to find the rules governing behaviour. 'Structuralism', wrote Lévi-Strauss, 'is the search for unsuspected harmonies. It is the discovery of a system of relations latent in a series of objects.'[4]

Derrida's argument with structuralism had begun, surreptitiously, in 1963. The review *Critique*, founded in 1946 by Georges Bataille and featuring an editorial committee of Michel Deguy, Foucault and Roland Barthes, had, on the back of the success of *The Origin of Geometry,* offered the young philosopher space in a forthcoming edition. He proposed a response to an essay by the literary critic Jean Rousset titled 'Form and Signification: An Essay on Literary Structures from Corneille to Claudel.' Rousset's essay is a work of structuralism par excellence, beetling away at finding schematic constructions which generate the works of literature, for instance Proust's *À la recherche du temps perdu.*

The article Derrida produced, 'Force and Signification', ran to over forty pages, and Deguy initially proposed running it across two issues. But the piece was of such quality he decided to publish the whole thing; this was unprecedented in the journal's history. It eventually became the first essay in *Writing and Difference* and thus the starting point for many readers of Derrida.

And it is hard to think of an opening gambit more Derridean than the first paragraph, perfectly designed to draw in the initiate and to send generations of philosophy students scampering back to analytic philosophy:

> If it recedes one day, leaving behind its works and signs on the shores of our civilization, the structuralist invasion might become a question for the historian of ideas, or perhaps even an object. But the historian would be deceived if he came to this pass: by the very act of considering the structuralist invasion as an object he would forget its meaning and forget that what is at stake, first of all is an adventure of vision, a conversion of the way of outing questions to any object posed before us, to historical objects – his own – in particular. And unexpectedly amongst these, the literary object.[5]

'If it recedes one day ...' Derrida's provocation is immediate. This way of philosophising, structuralism, will soon die, he is

saying. From the vantage point of history, any way of thinking can be analysed like this, but to do so in the very thick of it
is breathtakingly presumptuous. The essay then, with swagger-
ing confidence, ranges across Flaubert, Gide, Freud, Bachelard,
Kant, Blanchot, Eliot, Woolf, Proust, Buber and Merleau-Ponty.
God gets a look in, as do Jeremiah and Saint John Chrysostom.
And that's just the first half.

Derrida's criticism of structuralism (via Rousset) centres on
the privileging of 'form' over 'force'. Again, this is a question
about time, about the static compared to the genetic. Structuralist analysis of a literary object (and, mutatis mutandis, any
object of its investigations) by imposing a matrix on a particular
text 'becomes the object itself, the literary thing itself.'[6] In this
static reading, in this convocation of form, the object is forced to
conform to the reading. Sentence x does not just mean the words
of sentence x, it also gets its meaning from sentences y and z, and
this can be mapped.

So while a book, any book, is only encountered in 'successive fragments', the task of the (structuralist) critic is to make
the work 'simultaneously present', all its aspects presented as an
immediate, punctual, total whole (like a Husserlian moment).

Derrida uses Rousset's reading of Proust to draw out his point.
Proust, notes Derrida, is perfect for the sort of reading Rousset
wants to impose, in this case a circular one (Corneille is read in
the essay as performing a spiral). After all, Proust himself had
said that he wrote the opening and closing paragraphs of À la
recherche one after the other, and then just filled in the other
1.2 million words in the middle. The book, then, according to
Rousset, is a story where, in the final pages, 'the hero and narrator unite after a long march during which they each sought after
the other, sometimes very close to each other, sometimes very far
apart, they coincide at the moment of resolution, which is the
instant when the hero becomes the narrator, that is, the author
of his own story'.[7]

Against this, Derrida introduces 'force', which is a form of
motion and therefore temporal. 'Force', for Derrida, is a product
of language's power of signification. The signifier always means

more than it wants to, it escapes and exceeds the author's intention. Criticism, in privileging form over force, the static over the
genetic, freezes meaning. Structure can only ever be a spatial
term, and to investigate any object only spatially is, once again,
to exclude time. 'In this demand for the flat and the horizontal,'
writes Derrida, 'what is intolerable for structuralism is indeed
the richness implied by the volume, every element of signification that cannot be spread out into the simultaneity of a form.'[8]
So structuralism presents simultaneity as 'the myth of a total
reading or description, promoted to the status of a regulatory
ideal.'[9]

So here we are again. Derrida once again identifies the unacknowledged metaphysics behind a conventional reading. And
again, his analysis is not without phenomenological heft – this is
not how we encounter novels, nor is it how they work. Rousset
is forced, by his schema, to exclude anything that doesn't in
fact evoke the 'true Proust', where the author's words and his
own reading accord, and does what he can to forgive Proust's
mistakes – the false Proust – or to make them fit his overall
reading at any cost. And for a writer as digressive as Proust this
cost can be quite high. Of course, one might argue that digression is one of the structural components of the novel, but if that
is the case, it would be hard to argue what is not a structural
component.

Writing doesn't work like this. As Merleau-Ponty puts it, 'My
own words take me by surprise and teach me what I think,'
echoing Flannery O'Connor, who said, 'I write because I don't
know what I think until I read what I say.' While an author of
any sort can attempt to impose a form – Proust with his circular
configuration; Joyce in *Ulysses* with his chapters proscribed by
the use of certain colours, episodes from the *Odyssey*, parts of
the body; and Georges Perec with his 'knight's tour' organisation
of the narrative in *Life A User's Manual* – the work itself exceeds
these 'limitations' and generates meaning and formal elements
beyond the author's intention.

Derrida, in identifying the privileging of the static and spatial
over the genetic and temporal, is not arguing that this opposition

should be reversed, and the temporal given pre-eminence – this would simply repeat the error. Rather,

> our intention here is not, through the simple motions of balancing, equilibration or overturning, to oppose duration to space, quality to quantity, force to form, the depth of meaning or value to the surface of figures. Quite to the contrary ... we maintain that it is necessary to seek new concepts and new models, an economy escaping this system of metaphysical oppositions.[10]

That is, ante factum, deconstruction.

While the essay was highly praised, its fundamental takedown of structuralism was missed by most readers perhaps dazzled by its web of allusions, its playing with metaphors about light, and its final drawing of breath. Derrida quotes Nietzsche's *Thus Spake Zarathustra*: 'Behold, here is a new table, but where are my brethren who will carry it with me to the valley and into the hearts of flesh.'[11]

Derrida had not yet found his brethren, but he was about to create them in America.

In many ways 1966 was the apotheosis of structuralism. The year saw the publication of Foucault's *The Order of Things: An Archaeology of Human Sciences*, which analysed the way that structures change over time, either slowly or suddenly (generally the latter for Foucault), without throwing out the fact that they are structures. The book was a bestseller in France. In it, Foucault declared the 'death of man' – stating 'Man is probably no more than a rift in the order of things ... it is comforting, however, and a source of profound relief, to think that man is only a recent invention, a figure not yet two centuries old, a new wrinkle in our knowledge.'[12] The 'responsible subject', he opined, was a nineteenth-century invention, and modernity lay in rejecting the illusion of the Cartesian ego in its primacy.

The year also saw the publication of *Écrits*, the collected writings of Jacques Lacan. It was also a bestseller, although its 911 pages were daunting enough before even approaching its formidable content. For Lacan, broadly, humans experience three registers. First is the Imaginary, the realm of self-awareness and consciousness: what one imagines oneself to be, and others to be, and the world to be. These are illusions in the sense that they are constructed and not open to verification, but they are necessary illusions, integral to actual human reality as it is lived.

Second, there is the Symbolic: the structuralist realm par excellence in this context. This includes the customs, laws, regulations, traditions and so on of a culture in which we live. These are pre-existing and we are thrown into them and mediated by them, and for Lacan that mediation is as speaking subjects. The unconscious, as he famously put it, is structured like a language because it is in the Symbolic realm that we encounter the world.

Finally, there is the Real. Lacan's definition is slippery, but it has affinities with Kant's things-in-themselves, and if Lacan does not give these things ontological status in the way that Kant does, he nonetheless conjures them – it, the Real – as the limits of the Imaginary–Symbolic.

Always a controversial figure, Lacan had been excommunicated from the International Psycho-Analytical Association (founded in 1910 by Freud). Wounded by this betrayal he cancelled his teaching at the Hôpital Sainte-Anne for that year. It was Althusser who saved him, offering him a position at the ENS, and in 1963–64 he delivered his seminars *The Four Fundamental Concepts of Psychoanalysis*.

Despite teaching at the same institution, and being aware of each other's work, Lacan and Derrida had not met until they attended a dinner at the Belvedere Hotel in Baltimore. It was at an event hosted by the conference organisers, with Lacan holding, incongruously, a plate of coleslaw. According to one account by Lacan's biographer, Élisabeth Roudinesco, the pair immediately exchanged terse words on 'the Cartesian subject, substance and the signifier', with each claiming the primacy of his own position against the other's, chronologically and intellectually.

Derrida's own recollection is more mundane. Lacan was concerned with more prosaic matters. Éditions du Seuil had decided to bring *Écrits* out in a single volume and he was concerned that the binding might be insufficient, meaning that it could fall to pieces in the reader's hands. Lacan quizzed Derrida about what he knew of binding and glue. Derrida recalled the conversation – '"You'll see," he told me as he made a gesture with his hands, "it's not going to hold up."'[13] Derrida does not relate any advice he may have offered regarding adhesives.

The Baltimore conference was exemplary in presenting structuralism as it stood at that point, and many of the papers, like the title of the event itself, 'The Languages of Criticism and the Sciences of Man', have a pleasingly anachronistic feel to them. During the proceedings René Girard spoke on the daddy of structuralist myths, Oedipus, in 'Tiresias and the Critic'. Tzvetan Todorov gave a paper called, simply, 'Language and Literature', exploring the idea that 'Literature is, and can be nothing other than, a kind of extension and application of certain properties of Language.' And Jean-Pierre Vernant presented 'Greek Tragedy: Problems of Interpretation', again looking at the Oedipus myth.

Lacan's impact on the conference was baffling to most concerned. The seminars were structured to allow questions and answers at the end; most of the contributions collected in the volume *The Structuralist Controversy* feature Lacan's interventions, often bearing little relationship to the paper given. In addition, when his turn came, he insisted on giving his own paper – the snappily named 'Of Structure as an Inmixing of an Otherness Prerequisite to Any Subject Whatever' – in English, a language in which he had little ability, making his abstruse theories just that little bit more abstruse.

Attendees may have been excused for regarding the presentation of another potentially recondite Frenchman with a degree of trepidation.

Perhaps something has occurred in the history of the concept of structure that could be called an 'event', if this loaded word did not entail a meaning which it is precisely the function of structural – or structuralist – thought to reduce or to suspect. Let us speak of an event nevertheless, and let us use the quotation marks to serve as a precaution. What would this event be then? Its exterior form would be that of a rupture and a redoubling.[14]

If it was the British analytic philosopher Elizabeth Anscombe who first used the phrase 'scare quotes' in her 1956 essay 'Aristotle and the Sea Battle', it was the work of the final speaker on day three of the Baltimore conference, 'Monsieur Derrida', which popularised them. This was just one of the ways his work would permeate popular culture – from, for instance, 'deconstruction' becoming a buzzword for the far less methodical notion of taking apart ('the deconstruction of the administrative state' – Steve Bannon), to the idea of a statement appearing under erasure ('sorry, not sorry'), to advertisements that draw attention to their artificiality, their basic desire to sell you something. Anyone who has formed quotation marks in the air with their fingers to identify a word where its use and meaning are not absolutely cleaved has acknowledged the possibility of différance as posited by Derrida.

It is fitting that the paper that was to launch Derrida onto a global stage begins with both scare quotes and a 'perhaps'. Perhaps this is the case. Perhaps this is just a theory. Perhaps I am wrong. Perhaps an event. Sorry, not sorry.

The paper, with its faintly antediluvian title, 'Structure, Sign and Play in the Discourse of the Human Sciences', is short by Derridean standards: a mere eighteen pages. The arguments were familiar to those who had been following his work, of whom at the time there were very few. But the essay's emphasis on the idea of play, and on the notion of the 'centre' that undermines structuralism's pretensions, were a new departure.

Structure, notes Derrida, has always been 'neutralised or reduced' by a process of 'giving it a centre, or referring it to a point of presence, a fixed origin'.[15] This centre has been called many things in the history of metaphysics, including 'eidos [form, essence, type species], archè [origin], telos [aim], energia, ousia (essence, existence, substance, subject), aletheia [truth], transcendentality, consciousness, or conscience, God, man, and so forth.'[16] The history of metaphysics is 'the history of these metaphors and metonymies', this 'linked chain of determinations of the centre.'[17] Derrida uses the term 'the transcendental signified' as a catch-all that pointed to Saussure's linguistic schema. All the signifiers within language point to each other, relate to each other, differ from each other. Metaphysics attempts to nail down this mess by evoking a transcendental signified, fully present and meaningful, from which the other terms can derive their own meaning and place in the system.

But whatever the centre is called, the overall pattern remains similar across philosophies. What is curious here, notes Derrida, is that the centre, while presuming to anchor the structure, cannot be a part of it; it is the guarantor of a set, without belonging to the set. The centre has 'no natural site' it is not a 'fixed locus'. Rather, the centre becomes 'a sort of nonlocus in which an infinite number of sign-substitutions come into play'.[18] As much as the centre hopes to fix the matrix in place, the elements of it continue to chatter away to each other, to shift and dissemble, to play.

Derrida locates the calling into doubt of this metaphysical schema as a recent development – 'the Freudian critique of self-presence … the Heideggerian destruction of metaphysics'. In fact, from Heidegger he borrowed the notion of *Destruktion*. Like deconstruction, this is, argues Heidegger, never merely a negative concept:

> It has nothing to do with a vicious relativizing of ontological standpoints. But this destruction is just as far from having the negative sense of shaking off the ontological tradition. We must, on the contrary, stake out the positive possibilities of that tradition, and this means keeping it within its limits … to bury the past in nullity is not the purpose of this destruction; its aim is positive; its negative function remains unexpressed and indirect.[19]

However, both Freud and Heidegger, in Derrida's analysis, while attempting to overcome metaphysics (whatever they might call it), remain enmeshed within it, forced as they are to use its terms. Freud's replacement of the conscious as a source of meaning with the unconscious merely shifts the 'centre' without destroying the underlying pattern. One still has confidence that there is a discoverable, unified and transparent source of meaning (a childhood trauma for instance, and an explicable way to understand it and thus nullify it). That it may be too deeply hidden ever to emerge is a separate problem – what is sought is still seekable.

Those great destabilisers of presence, Nietzsche, Heidegger and Freud, still drag metaphysics along with them as

> all these destructive discourses and all their analogues are trapped in a sort of circle. This circle is unique. It describes the form of the relationship between the history of metaphysics and the destruction of the history of metaphysics ... there are many ways of being caught in this circle. They are all more or less naïve, more or less empirical, more or less systematic, more or less close to the formulation or even to the formalization of this circle.[20]

Derrida is not presuming to have escaped this circle; he too is using metaphysical terms to interrogate – to deconstruct – metaphysics. 'There is no sense in doing without the concepts of metaphysics in order to shake metaphysics. We have no language – no syntax and no lexicon – which is foreign to this history.'[21] We live in the death of metaphysics, we understand there is no anchor, God is dead, and yet metaphysics continues. The terms Plato set for philosophical enquiry abide.

Having set the general grounds for his enquiry, Derrida then shifts his focus to structuralism, in particular the work of Lévi-Strauss. Derrida quotes approvingly the following insight, from *The Raw and the Cooked*:

> In effect the study of myths poses a mythological problem by the fact that it cannot conform to the Cartesian principle of dividing the difficulty into as many parts as are necessary to resolve it. There exists no veritable end or term to mythical analysis, no secret unity which could be grasped at the end of the work in decomposition. The themes duplicate themselves to infinity ... Consequently the unity of the myth is never more than tendential

and projective and cannot reflect a state or a particular moment of the myth.[22]

There exists no veritable end or term to mythical analysis, no secret unity which could be grasped at the end of the work in decomposition. The themes duplicate themselves to infinity. This is the free play of signifiers, the chattering away of the elements within a system, and Lévi-Strauss recognises the impossibility of finding a centre or a point of origin. But this does not last: drawn by 'a sort of ethic of presence, an ethic of nostalgia for origins, an ethic of archaic and natural innocence, of a purity of presence and self-presence in speech,' Lévi-Strauss proposes a lost time where unity reigns. The sadness of *Tristes Tropiques* is a nostalgic yearning for pure nature that he sees as being destroyed by the accretions of culture, where 'culture' is the incursion of the West, with its divisions and its languages.

Derrida also takes Lévi-Strauss to task for his inability to explain historical changes within a system. Structuralism, with its conceptual basis being a spatial metaphor, always struggles to explain change; hence a tendency to posit 'epistemological breaks', 'paradigm shifts', the 'event'. Always, the before and after of a particular paradigm shift can presume to be shown, as can the meaning of the shift, but the actual transition cannot be captured.

Lévi-Strauss is always forced to ascribe change to an outside force coming in to disrupt. Again, the system, the structure, must look outside itself to explain itself.

> The appearance of a new structure, of an original system, always comes about [in Lévi-Strauss] by a rupture with its past, its origin, and its cause ... by omitting to posit the problem of the transition from one structure to another, by putting history between brackets.[23]

This 'bracketing' of history recalls Derrida's criticism of Husserl. Although not mentioned in the paper, Derrida is transferring the insights from his study of the phenomenologist directly to his critique of structuralism, and thus revealing their shared metaphysical assumptions. At the precise moment that Lévi-Strauss wishes to 'recapture the specificity of the structure' (ground the meaning of the phenomenological project), he must 'set aside all facts'.[24] In the case of Lévi-Strauss, he must 'always conceive of the origin of a new structure on the model of a catastrophe'.[25]

Here, suddenly, Derrida introduces his notion of play. 'Play', argues Derrida, 'is the disruption of presence.'[26] Indeed, 'play is always play of absence and presence' but 'if it is to be thought radically, play must be conceived before the alternative of absence and presence'.[27] Here, again, we are in the realm of différance, that which comes before the choice, but that which only provides the condition under which the choice is made (or not made). It is, in this essay, compared to the

> Nietzschean affirmation, that is, the joyous affirmation of the play of the world and of the innocence of becoming, the affirmation of the world of signs without fault, without truth, and without origin which is offered to an active interpretation. The affirmation then determines the noncentre otherwise than as loss of centre.[28]

In evoking this notion of play, Derrida reveals an important strand of his thought. What can be forgotten in the deep woods of philosophy, the often abstruse and opaque world of 'categorical imperatives', 'anarcho-primitivism', 'transcendental idealism', 'metaphysics of presence', is that philosophy seeks to encapsulate, in some sense, what it is like to be alive. If a philosophy fails to do this, it is the philosophy that must yield. When, as we shall see, a philosopher of language such as J. L. Austin says that words can only be taken seriously if said seriously, he excludes a whole realm of meaning that most people, in a fairly mundane sense, regard as meaningful. Derrida seems to be saying that something should not be inexplicable to philosophy that is explicable to humans.

Derrida, despite his own often abstruse and opaque style, is trying to capture life as it is lived. In truth much of it is done, meaningfully, without being 'offered to active interpretation'. It is odd, for instance, for analytic philosophy, that humans read novels – but humans do read novels. It is odd that humans pray and seek meaning in religion, that they find the words of religious works moving – and yet they do. It is eternally frustrating to Husserl that the strange realms of consciousness and the objective world interact, and yet they do.

Derrida's paper ends by offering two ways forward as of 21 October 1966. One is to continue to dream of 'deciphering a truth or an origin which escapes play and the order of the sign', or we can attempt to affirm play and 'pass beyond man and humanism, the name of man being the name of that being who, throughout the history of metaphysics or of ontotheology… has dreamed of full presence.'[29] And, never one to resist a rhetorical flourish he concludes with

> a glance toward those who, in a society from which I do not exclude myself, turn their eyes away when faced by the as yet unnamable which is proclaiming itself and which can do so, as is necessary whenever a birth is in the offing, only under the species of the nonspecies, in the formless, mute, infant, and terrifying form of a monstrosity.[30]

A rough beast is slouching towards Bethlehem to be born.

The response to Derrida's paper was almost immediate. As the literary critic Georges Poulet noted, 'Structure, Sign and Play' went against all his own theories, but was without doubt the most important paper given at the conference. 'Did we know what had happened?' Richard Macksey asked rhetorically in the *New York Times* obituary of Derrida. 'No, but there was a sense.' The last thing Macksey expected was that Derrida was going to be 'the Samson to tear down the temple of structuralism'.[31]

Derrida answered questions at the end of the session. Jean Hyppolite, who confessed he was not sure where Derrida was going ('I too was wondering whether I know where I am going,' Derrida replied), asked him to clarify the idea of the centre.

Derrida responded that 'it is a rule of the game which does not govern the game; it is a rule of the game which does not dominate the game,' and 'when the rule of the game is displaced by the game itself, we must find something other than the word rule.'[32] He did not, he clarified for the author and critical theorist Serge Doubrovsky, say there was 'no centre, that we could get along without a centre', rather 'the center is a function, not a being – a reality, but a function.'[33] And finally, in response to a question from the Marxist theorist Lucien Goldmann (who opened with 'Derrida, with whose conclusions I do not agree'), gave his first and perhaps still clearest definition of deconstruction:

> As to what Mr. Goldmann has said to me, I feel that he has iso-lated, in what I said, the aspect that he calls destructive. I believe, however, that I was quite explicit about the fact that nothing of what I said had a destructive meaning. Here or there I have used the word deconstruction, which has nothing to do with destruction. That is to say, it is simply a question of (and this is a necessity of criticism in the classical sense of the word) being alert to the implications, to the historical sedimentation of the language which we use – and that is not destruction.[34]

Looking back in 1989, Derrida acknowledged how influential the conference was. It was

> an event in which many things changed (it is on purpose that I leave these formulations somewhat vague) on the American scene – which is always more than the American scene. What is now called 'theory' in this country may even have an essential link with what is said to have happened there in 1966.[35]

In the four years since the publication of his Introduction to *The Origin of Geometry*, Derrida had built up a body of work for which the word impressive barely does justice. Ten of these essays, plus an 'Ellipsis', were to be published by Éditions du Seuil. The collection was *L'Écriture et la différence*, or *Writing and Difference* in its English translation. In addition to the essays mentioned here, it also contained two studies of the French dramatist Antonin Artaud, whose final years were spent in a psychiatric clinic. 'The Theatre of Cruelty and the Closure of Representation' and 'La Parole soufflée' resist attempts, however subtle or well meaning, to turn Artaud into a 'case' and his works into clinical exegeses, and return him to being 'the enigma of flesh which wanted properly to be called Antonin Artaud.' Also included was the essay 'Freud and the Scene of Writing', which invokes Freud as a possible ally in the work of deconstruction, while exploring the complicity between psychoanalysis and the metaphysics of presence, in ways that would be vital in his next great work.

Finally, the collection contains an essay that was to have long-lasting ramifications in Derrida's personal and professional life, 'Cogito and the History of Madness'. It was the text of the first ever paper Derrida had presented in Paris, and it was an analysis of Foucault's magisterial 1961 text *Folie et Déraison: Histoire de la folie à l'âge classique* or *Madness and Civilisation*. Foucault traces the evolution of the concept of 'madness' from the Renaissance to modern times, contending that with the age of reason (roughly the mid-seventeenth century) the notion that the mad had a sort of magical wisdom was overthrown, and madness was seen as something either to be cured or to be excluded from society, a process he called the Great Confinement. In doing so, society set out not only what madness meant, but therefore what reason meant. Rationality was precisely that which is not mad (and this definition being both constructed and malleable, allowed a juridical intervention, power).

Foucault attended Derrida's lecture on his work, which begins, after an epigram from *Ulysses*, by praising it, Mark Antony style, stating the author's feelings of intimidation in even approaching Foucault's work. However, with the 'interminable unhappiness of the disciple' he 'must break the mirror' of his 'infinite speculation on the master' and thus 'start to speak'.[36]

His point of departure might, he warns the audience, 'appear slight and artificial': three pages in a text that is 673 pages long. This is Derrida par excellence, seeking the telling detail in a mass of material, the glitch in the matrix. The question at issue relates to Descartes method of systematic doubt, which Foucault sees as a crucial expression of the construction of the rational/mad barrier. In his 'First Meditation', Descartes writes (writes Foucault):

> How can I doubt that these hands or this whole body are mine? To doubt such things I would have to liken myself to brain-damaged madmen who are convinced they are kings when really they are paupers, or say they are dressed in purple when they are naked, or that they are pumpkins, or made of glass. Such people are insane, and I would be thought equally mad if I modelled myself on them.[37]

'According to Foucault,' notes Derrida, 'Descartes, encountering madness alongside (the expression *alongside* is Foucault's) dreams and all forms of sensory error, refuses to accord them all the same treatment.'[38] Here Derrida, slowly and patiently, disagrees. Descartes does accord them the same treatment, and therefore Foucault's identification of this as 'the event' that excludes madness is false.

In fact, Derrida finds the whole project suspicious. Foucault presumes to 'write a history of madness *itself. Itself.* Of madness itself. That is by letting madness speak for itself.'[39] But isn't it a basic condition of madness that it cannot speak for itself? Foucault's task is at best incoherent, at worst impossible. As in his Artaud essays, Derrida fears that by categorising madness we tame it, or we are forced to exclude the very aspects of it that make it madness. Derrida concludes by stating his 'gratitude' that despite its 'naïve reading of the Meditations' this 'monumental' book at least warns us 'to what degree the philosophical act can no longer be in memory of Cartesianism.'[40] As ringing endorsements go, it isn't.

Looking on, Foucault obviously had not been as attentive as he might have been. He afterwards wrote to Derrida thanking him for the 'immense and marvellous attention' he had paid his words and the 'rectitude of your remarks, that went, unerringly, to the heart of what I wanted to do and beyond it'.[41]

It was not until 1972, by which time Derrida had acquired a huge level of fame, that Foucault revised his position. He did so publicly in an article called 'My Body, This Paper, This Fire', written for the Japanese review *Paideia*. As Derrida had done, he begins by praising his interlocutor for his analysis that was 'undoubtedly remarkable' in its 'philosophical depth.' But philosophy is now not Foucault's concern. Unfortunately, he writes, he had still been lured by it when writing his *History of Madness*, and thus felt he had to include the section on Descartes, which was, on mature reflection, 'the most expendable part of the book'. Any criticism of it is therefore, quod erat demonstrandum, redundant.

That said, Foucault still feels duty bound to refute Derrida's reading. He is scathing about what he regards as Derrida's 'omissions, displacements, interventions and substitutions,' without enumerating them to any great degree, and then dismisses deconstruction as 'a historically well-determined little pedagogy.' The essay ends with a quote by Descartes: 'As only the wise can distinguish what is clearly conceived from what only appears to be so, I am not surprised that this fellow can't tell the difference between them.'[42]

The pair would avoid each other for years. It was not until 1982 that they resumed relations, when Derrida spent a night in a Prague jail. On hearing of his arrest, Foucault appeared on radio demanding he be set free. Derrida extended his thanks, and shortly afterwards Foucault invited he and Marguerite for dinner, an occasion of considerable warmth. In 1991, on the thirtieth anniversary of the publication of *History of Madness*, seven years after the death of Foucault, Derrida presented the paper '"To Do Justice to Freud": The History of Madness in the Age of Psychoanalysis', in which he praises Foucault's book as 'an event whose repercussions were so intense and multiple that I will not even try to identify them, much less measure them, deep inside me.'[43] When 'a certain debate ensued' which 'obscured this friendship' it did not diminish his admiration.[44] Due to the 'overdetermined nature of it that saw texts continue to pile up discussing it', he does not wish to return to it, rather speculating on Freud and power in Foucault's later works. How would Foucault have responded to his analysis? 'I am still trying to imagine Foucault's response,' wrote Derrida. 'I can't quite do it. I would have so much liked for him to take it on himself.'[45]

L'Écriture et la différence was published in spring 1967 to great enthusiasm, Foucault calling it an 'amazing' book. In the autumn it was followed by *Voice and Phenomena*, which again garnered great praise. But throughout the writing of all this material, Derrida was working on a larger project, which would also appear in the autumn of 1967 and which remains the work most associated with his name. It is *Of Grammatology*.

6

Of Grammatology

One shouldn't complicate things for the pleasure of complicat-
ing, but one should also never simplify or pretend to be sure of
such simplicity where there is none. If things were simple, word
would have gotten around.

– Limited Inc

If this work seems so threatening, this is because it isn't simply
eccentric or strange, but competent, rigorously argued, and car-
rying conviction.

– Honoris Causa: 'This Is Also Very Funny'

O*f Grammatology* is a gloriously bonkers book, and the
founding text of deconstruction. It is also many other
things. It is the ur-text in the philosophy of writing – the 'grammatology' of its title. It is also a sustained reading of the works
of Rousseau and, through him, the history of language. It puzzles
over hieroglyphics. It analyses the Chinese alphabet. It ranges
across Lévi-Strauss, Heidegger, Leibniz, Condillac. The reference
list alone contains over one thousand titles, some obscure beyond
belief. Its most celebrated chapter occurs in quotation marks,
within an ellipsis '… That Dangerous Supplement …' It discusses
masturbation at some length, Rousseau's in particular, comparing it to the act of writing. It is exorbitant. It is hyperbolic. It

ploughs forward. It obfuscates. It bursts at the seams with the profusion of its ideas.

The book starts with a triple 'exergue', a word Derrida rescues from obscurity and offers up without explanation, certainly not revealing to the reader that it means 'a small space or inscription below the principal emblem on a coin or medal, usually on the reverse side', the first of which reads, 'The one who will shine in the science of writing will shine like the sun. A scribe (EP, p. 87)' and 'O Samas (sun-god), by your light you scan the totality of lands as if they were cuneiform signs (ibid.).'[1] No details are given of either the scribe or EP, which turns out to be *L'Ecriture et la psychologie des peuples: actes de colloque* (*The Writings and the Psychology of the People*) in which Derrida found these 'sayings of the ancients'.

The book ends with a quote from Rousseau:

> the dreams of a bad night are given to us as philosophy. You will say I too am a dreamer; I admit it, but I do what others fail to do, I give my dreams as dreams, and leave the reader to discover whether there is anything in them which may prove useful to those who are awake.[2]

In between, the reader is asked to absorb such concepts as différance, the trace, logocentrism, phonocentrism, arche-writing, the supplement and auto-affection. It is not so much a philosophical text as the sort of volume you might stumble across in a garden shed after the death of a mad neighbour who had been working in a new conception of the world for the last thirty years, complete with his own set of neologisms and archaisms. It is perhaps the *Key to All Mythologies* Edward Casaubon spent all of *Middlemarch* not finishing. To read it is exhausting, inspiring and infuriating, to write it nearly unimaginable. Derrida argued elsewhere that 'a book' is the imposition of coherence on the immoderation of writing and *Of Grammatology* performs this immoderation almost to its limits, its coherence almost at breaking point.

Interviewed for the 2002 documentary *Derrida*, he was explicit about the importance of *Of Grammatology* to him, personally and professionally:

> The feeling that I had when I wrote *Of Grammatology* – not the book but those first two articles in the summer of 1965 – I actually had the feeling that something very unique for me took place. I had the impression that an interpretive edge, a lever, appeared to me ... I felt as though something had happened to me. I don't want to give this a religious sensibility – it wasn't an apparition or an ecstasy, but that something had taken hold of me and happened not by me, but to me. Something that allowed me or put at my disposal an interpretive edge, a lever, that was very powerful. This was a lever for interpretation, for reading the tradition, when I say tradition, this Western philosophical tradition. I have the impression that – I use the word lever but I could call it a kind of machine, an apparatus, for thought and technique that allows me to formalize and economically decipher, not every text, but that which is dominant in our culture ... I remember very well that summer I wrote those two articles and sent them off to *Critique*, the long sixty-page articles – as we went as a family to Venice. I remember very well telling Marguerite, when we were on the vaporetto, I told her, 'You know Marguerite, I think that something has just happened.' And I remember well the strange feeling I had, of obviousness, that I'd never had before, and in a certain sense would never have again ...[3]

Of Grammatology – 'grammatology' is borrowed from the linguist Ignace Gelb, who coined it to refer to the science of scripts or writing systems – grew out of two articles 'put together somewhat artificially', as Derrida admitted. The first, 'Writing before the Letter', was published in *Critique* in the summer of 1965. It is Derrida's close reading of Saussure, and again uses the word 'deconstruction'. He had ruled out a straight transliteration of Heidegger's *Destruktion*, as 'in French the term destruction too obviously implied an annihilation'.[4] The second article was 'Nature, culture, writing', which engaged with a famous chapter in Lévi-Strauss's *Tristes Tropiques*, 'The Writing Lesson', in which the Brazilian Nambikwara people imitate the anthropologist's action of writing, which Lévi-Strauss then links to the appearance of a new violence within the tribe. To these essays, Derrida adds a long exploration of the work of Rousseau who, like Lévi-Strauss, spoke with longing/nostalgia for a 'state of nature' prior to the violence of civilisation.

This 'lever', this 'kind of machine' or 'apparatus' – which allowed Derrida to 'formalize and economically decipher, not every text, but that which is dominant in our culture', from which 'everything that would follow it, simply followed it regardless of might happen' – was his idea that the question of writing had the potential to destabilise and possibly overthrow the conceptual bases of many of the human sciences.

As far back as his earliest work on Husserl, Derrida was captivated by the question of writing, which in many ways seemed a great un-problem of philosophy. Problems were proposed, arguments had, tracts published and refuted, aphorisms made, systems erected, ideas generated and logical systems concocted, refined, questioned, embraced and dismissed, without the very strange fact – that this is all being done by writing – presenting itself as problematic or odd.

'However the topic is considered,' writes Derrida, 'the problem of language has never been simply one problem among others.'[5] Where the question of writing has been raised in philosophy, it has always been regarded, from Plato to Saussure, not only as a secondary form of communication after speech, but as a dangerous and malign one, which threatens truth itself. Writing, from Plato onwards, represents a perversion of speech, a contamination of truth. 'The history of truth,' Derrida writes, 'of the truth of truth, has always been ... the debasement of writing, and its repression outside "full" speech.' The nod to Freud – *repression* – is deliberate. The level of resistance to writing in Western metaphysics speaks of anxiety and neurosis, without metaphysics being conscious of it. A vehement denunciation of writing in writing carries a certain irony, and one Derrida is quick to seize upon.

His epigram for the first chapter is taken from Nietzsche: 'Socrates, he who does not write.'[6] This is, of course, more than a simple character note for Plato, it is intrinsic to Socrates' status as a truth seeker. Plato sets out his argument in the dialogue *Phaedrus* (a work which Derrida was to return to in his 1972 essay 'Plato's Pharmacy').[7]

In the dialogue, Socrates has, unusually (and for Derrida symbolically), left the city walls. He encounters the eponymous Phaedrus, who has just heard Lysias give a speech about love – love being the main topic of Plato's dialogue. Socrates tells Phaedrus he is 'sick with passion' for hearing speeches, and so the pair walk into the countryside and sit beneath a tree in order for Phaedrus to repeat the speech. Phaedrus does so, then Socrates gives his own speech on love, gently taking Lysias' oratory apart.

The discussion then turns to the topic of madness (a gift from the gods) and the soul. Then, eventually, to the art of rhetoric, and how to construct a speech. At this point, Socrates asks Phaedrus for an opinion: what feature makes writing good, and what inept? Without waiting for an answer, Socrates waxes periphrastic on the Ancient Egyptian god Theuth who offered King Thamus the gift of writing that, once learned, 'Will make the Egyptians wiser and will improve their memory; I have discovered a potion for memory and for wisdom.'

King Thamus, however, refuses the gift:

> Since you are the father of writing, your affection for it has made you describe its effects as the opposite of what they really are. In fact, it will introduce forgetfulness into the soul of those who learn it: they will not practice using their memory because they will put their trust in writing, which is external and depends on signs that belong to others, instead of trying to remember from the inside, completely on their own. You have not discovered a potion for remembering, but for reminding; you provide your students with the appearance of wisdom, not with its reality.

After this, Socrates goes on to highlight a double bind of writing. Once words are written down, they stay the same, not alive but 'solemnly silent' on the page. But the words can also wander freely from context to context, from reader to reader:

You'd think they were speaking as if they had some understanding, but if you question anything that has been said because you want to learn more, it continues to signify just that very same thing forever. When it has once been written down, every discourse roams about everywhere, reaching indiscriminately those with understanding no less than those who have no business with it, and it doesn't know to whom it should speak and to whom it should not. And when it is faulted and attacked unfairly, it always needs its father's support; alone, it can neither defend itself nor come to its own support.

Without its 'father', the one who speaks, the written word cannot defend itself. Proximity is demanded – the speaker guarantees meaning by his or her presence: his or her author-ity. (Derrida is also alive to the use of the word 'father' in this context, and will revisit it when he extends his criticism of logocentrism to one of phallogocentrism.)

This anxious reaction to the written word was to be a founding act in philosophy. Aristotle is similarly dismissive, regarding writing as defective. He opens his text 'On Interpretation' with the following:

> Spoken words are the symbols of mental experience and written words are the symbols of spoken words. Just as all men have not the same writing, so all men have not the same speech sounds, but the mental experiences, which these directly symbolize, are the same for all.[8]

How he can guarantee the last of these insights is a topic of some debate, but what is key here is the opening sentence: mental experiences are transformed into words, first and foremost. They might then be turned into written words, which exist now, twice removed from the original mental experience. This 'attempts to confine speech to a secondary or instrumental function: translator of a full speech that was once fully present.'[9] And, for Aristotle, as for Husserl, 'it is because the voice, producer of the first symbols, has a relationship of essential and immediate proximity with the mind.'[10] Hearing-oneself-speak, as Derrida asserts, gives the illusion of truth.

Here, also, we find, for instance, the 'voice of conscience', with all its theological implications – 'God's infinite understanding is the other name for logos as self-presence', and

> The logos can be infinite and self-present, it can be produced as auto-affection, only through the voice: an order of the signifier by which the subject takes from itself into itself, does not borrow outside of itself the signifier that it emits and that affects it at the same time. Such is at least the experience – or consciousness – of the voice: of hearing (understanding) oneself-speak.[11]

'And the problem of soul and body,' adds Derrida, 'is no doubt derived from the problem of writing from which it seems – conversely – to borrow its metaphors.'[12]

Phonocentrism, which Derrida diagnosed in *Voice and Phenomena*, then, as translator Gayatri Chakravorty Spivak notes in her preface, 'merges with the historical determination of the meaning of being in general as presence ... the self-presence of the cogito, consciousness, subjectivity ...'[13] This conflation of voice and presence is intimately tied up with the separating of form and matter which takes the form of metaphysics, and the linguistic separation of signifier and signified is of the same order.

Even Saussure argues, 'language and writing are two distinct systems of signs: the second exists for the sole purpose of representing the first'.[14] In fact, Saussure goes further: 'The linguistic object is not defined by the combination of the written word and the spoken word: the spoken form alone constitutes the object.'[15] Writing, in Saussure's schema, need not exist for his model to work.

It is here that Derrida begins his attack, on grounds that are now familiar. First, he declares himself 'baffled as to how [Saussure] can at the same time say of writing that it is the "image" or figuration of language and define language and writing elsewhere as "two distinct systems of signs".'[16] They are either related or they are not. As Derrida notes, the contradiction is revealing – 'By a process exposed by Freud in *The Interpretation of Dreams*, Saussure thus accumulates contradictory arguments to bring about a satisfactory decision: the exclusion of writing.'[17] Derrida also reiterates his argument from the Introduction to *The Origin of Geometry*: writing is the condition of the possibility of the ideal objects in which science trades, and which it passes from generation to generation. Historicity itself is, therefore, 'tied to the possibility of writing'.[18]

In addition, Saussure has already argued that the relationship between the signifier and the signified is arbitrary. Thus, notes Derrida, there can be no 'natural attachment' of any system of signs to any signifieds, and this being so, there is no validity in arguing that the system of signs we ascribe phonetically – speech – is any more natural (true, apt, primary) than any we ascribe graphically, that is as writing. As he notes, the rupture of natural attachment 'puts in question the idea of naturalness, not attachment.'[19]

Again using the tools of psychoanalysis to analyse a mode of thinking, Derrida diagnoses Saussure's vehemence as revealing of a particular crisis. Saussure attempts to protect 'the internal system of language in the purity of its concept against the gravest, most perfidious, most permanent contamination which has not ceased to menace … the contamination of writing, the fact or the threat of it'.[20] Saussure's desire, that which is frustrated by the very operations of difference he himself identified, is the desire for the transcendental signified.

The play of difference forces Saussure into another contradiction. Having argued that 'the spoken form alone constitutes the object', Saussure now needs to protect *langue* from *parole*, the system from its contingent instantiations. Thus he argues:

> It is impossible for sound alone, a material element, to belong to language. It is only a secondary thing, substance to be put to use. All our conventional values have the characteristic of not being confused with the tangible element which supports them … The linguistic signifier … is not [in essence] phonic but incorporeal – constituted not by its material substance but the differences that separate its sound-image from all others.[21]

What is this 'incorporeal signifier'? Well – 'speech thus draws from this stock of writing, noted or not', writes Derrida.[22]

And then Derrida, uniquely in his early work, speaks emphatically in the first person: 'I believe that generalized writing is not just the idea of a system to be invented, a hypothetical characteristic or a future possibility. I think on the contrary that oral language already belongs to this writing.'[23]

It is a breakthrough moment. Derrida was always wary of the use of 'I' (even more so, 'I believe'), acknowledging its constructed and ambiguous state regarding persons, let alone in literature, including philosophy. He is, of course, not unusual in this – philosophy in general utilises a number of rhetorical devices to avoid the first person. It is a subterfuge Nietzsche delighted in exposing and overturning, with his chapter titles in *Ecce Homo*, 'Why I Am So Wise', 'Why I Am Destiny' and 'Why I Write Such Good Books'.

Derrida continues:

> It is not a question of rehabilitating writing in the narrow sense, nor of reversing the order of dependence when it is evident ... I would wish rather to suggest that the alleged derivativeness of writing, however real and massive, was possible only on one condition: that the 'original,' 'natural,' etc. language had never existed, never been intact and untouched by writing, that it had itself always been a writing.[24]

Here he introduces a new term 'arche-writing'. Arche-writing, while carrying within it the implications of an 'origin' or 'source', 'cannot and can never be recognized as the object of a science. It is the very thing which cannot let itself be reduced to the form of presence.'[25] Derrida seeks an original form of language that does not participate in the separation of speech and writing, is unhindered by it. It is already there before we use it. Like différance, it does not (only) exist prior to presence, but it always already is 'there' in the operations of language. This can even be seen in cultures that do not use writing. Notches on a rope, argues Derrida, is a form of language (writing) that does not recognise presence in the sense assigned by Western metaphysical thinking.

The other key term here is 'trace', which in French carries the connotation of a track as well as its 'vestigial' definition. As Saussure's signifiers get their meaning from difference, from what they are not, so the trace of these not-words determines the structure of the sign. Forever absent, they are nonetheless there. Language has a trace-structure. 'The trace is not only the disappearance of origin ... it means that the origin did not even disappear, that it was never constituted except reciprocally by a non-origin, the trace, which thus becomes the origin of the origin.'[26] The congruence of this term with différance is obvious.

Of Grammatology then takes the reader on a tour of writing systems, looking at the phonetic and the ideogrammatic. As expressions of arche-writing, each brings its own idiomatic field of play and possibilities, their own relationship to the interior and the exterior, the spatial, the sensible. The ideogram (the pictogram, the hieroglyph), for instance, by retaining a pictorial relationship to the signified, reminds us that the written is not a transparent field to pass through to get to the thing. The trick of our phonetic language, with its illusion of transparency (given the lack of correspondence between letters and signifieds), is that the words on a page seem to disappear and thus remain unanalysed.

If Saussure, for Derrida, represents a modern example of the metaphysics of presence, then Rousseau represents an exemplary case, not only in his desire to fix presence (be it by extolling the incomparable virtues of speech in the transference of truth, or his nostalgia for a primitivism, for the primordial), but in the multitude of contradictions in his work that reveal the impossibility of his project.

Rousseau had played only a glancing role in Derrida's work to that point, although young Jackie had read him at the age of twelve or thirteen, while also reading Nietzsche. In fact Nietzsche's criticisms of Rousseau upset Jackie, as he worried whether he was allowed to enjoy both.[27] With Proust and Gide, Rousseau was one of the 'writers on the verge of tears' who Jackie always felt drawn to, and whose *Confessions* had a profound effect on him. It was not until his 1965 seminar, with the exorbitant title 'Nature, Culture, Scripture and the Violence of the Letter: From C. Lévi-Strauss to J.-J. Rousseau; Scripture and Civilization', that Derrida considered Rousseau in more detail.

Rousseau argues that humans are fundamentally good in their state of nature, and it is civilisation and culture that corrupt them. Anticipating the Romantic movement, he stresses the importance of feelings and emotions, while waxing elegiac about the natural world, from which we have been cruelly wrenched. It is an ultimately pessimistic view of human progress 'turned towards the lost or impossible presence of absent origin,' and in 'Structure, Sign, and Play …' Derrida contrasted the 'saddened, negative, nostalgic, guilty, Rousseauistic side of the thinking' with its 'other side … the Nietzschean affirmation.'[28]

Rousseau's nature/culture divide is, of course, another of the binary oppositions that deconstruction seeks to investigate and problematise, and his yearning for a state before the fall is, again, the yearning for the transcendental signified, where meaning can be restored. As Rousseau put it in the opening sentence of *Emile*, 'Everything is good as it comes from the hands of the Maker of the world, but degenerates once it gets into the hands of man.'[29] His definition of what this natural state might be is notoriously slippery due, Derrida argued, to this natural state being an expression of yearning rather than a description of an accessible state of affairs.

In *Of Grammatology*, the focus of Derrida's investigation is Rousseau's then forgotten text *Essay on the Origin of Languages*. Unpublished in Rousseau's lifetime, it is a whistle-stop tour of the evolution of human language. In Rousseau's conception, language – like the human race itself – developed in warm southern climes, before journeying northwards in the mouths of men and women, to the colder climates. The ur-language, born of sun, was passionate and musical, but in meeting cold reality it was stripped of this passion and became the more rational form of discourse we use today. As might be expected, Rousseau's view of writing as opposed to speech is particularly savage. In the progression from the passionate musicality of vowels, to consonants, to speech, to writing that Rousseau maps out, each step is a step away from our nature, and one which therefore veils our truth.

Derrida wishes to perform two operations. One, as with Saussure, is to deconstruct Rousseau's privileging of speech over writing. The second is to link this to the nature/culture opposition, which will generate a key term in his thought – that of the supplement. Before doing so, he performs a detour through the work of Lévi-Strauss who, 'like Rousseau, must always conceive of the origin of a new structure on the model of catastrophe'. If metaphysics needs to be defended from the violence of writing, 'what links writing to violence?'[30]

One of the most famous chapters of *Tristes Tropiques* is 'The Writing Lesson'. In it, Lévi-Strauss writes about the Brazilian Nambikwara tribe. They are a population in decline, from 20,000 in 1915 to only 2,000 on his visit in 1938. They are, argues Lévi-Strauss, exemplary in their purity, their 'radical goodness': 'I had been looking for a society reduced to its simplest expression. That of the Nambikwara was so truly simple that all I could find in it was individual human beings.'[31] Writing, that 'strange invention' in Lévi-Strauss's words, is unknown to them.

It is part of his practice of gift-giving to distribute pencils and paper to the non-literate tribes he visits. While writing in his journal, he notices members of the tribe mimicking his behaviour, harmlessly substituting wavy lines for words. But the chief of the tribe grasps its power and convinces the tribe he has mastered the art of writing, using it immediately to increase his prestige, power and authority. The strange invention, rather than being used as a way of storing knowledge, is used as a system of domination. The transition from 'barbarism to civilization' of which writing was generally seen a part, is made, in Levi-Strauss's reading, false. Writing in fact *instigates* barbarism, instigates violence.

It is a neat story – perhaps, and Derrida seems to accord with this view, a little too neat. One objection to Lévi-Strauss's declaration 'And so writing had made its appearance among the Nambikwara!' is, well, no it hasn't. This is not writing, it is the imitation of writing. One does not feel a tremor of fear about the future of AI when one sees someone put a cardboard box on their head and dance like a robot. To blame writing is thus, to use an old-school philosophy phrase, a category error.

Second, and relatedly, the chief simply embraces it as a tool of power, as he might a gun. Nothing in the *character of writing* leads to this, only the behaviours which he perceives flowing from it.

Derrida also notes that the story takes its form from an 'eighteenth century tradition, anecdote, the confession ... calculated for the purposes of philosophical demonstration of the relationships between nature and society'.[32] 'One already suspects,' he writes, '... that the critique of ethnocentrism, a theme so dear to the author of *Tristes Tropiques*, has most often the sole function of constituting the other as model of original and natural goodness, of accusing and humiliating oneself, of exhibiting its being-unacceptable in an anti-ethnocentric mirror'.[33] Lévi-Strauss admits his remorse and, says Derrida, 'it is this remorse that produces anthropology'.[34]

But what Derrida also wishes to contest is the idea that, prior to holding pencils and pushing them on notebooks, the Nambikwara were without writing. In our 'vulgar' use of the term, writing is and only is this system of placing marks on a paper. And we lazily accept that writing 'represents' speech, as though the two systems were linked logically rather than conventionally, which we have no reason to believe. If either vocalisation or graphical representation were integral to language itself, we would not be able to move backwards and forwards between them without changing the language. After all, as he points out, 'no grapheme corresponds to accents of pronunciation ... reciprocally, in pronunciation, no phoneme corresponds to the spacing between words.'[35]

It is, in fact, arche-writing, preceding both writing and speech (and continuing to operate within them), that enables their coming into being. And 'this arche-writing would be at work not only in the form and substance of graphic expression, but also in those of non-graphic expression' – including among the Nambikwara, before Lévi-Strauss handed out his calligraphic trinkets. They are within the field of the trace, as long as we are careful not to imagine this field to be an object with an assignable site.

It is this that 'permits the articulation of speech and writing' as it 'founds the metaphysical opposition between the sensible and the intelligible.' Thus 'if language were not already, in that sense, a writing, no derived "notation" would be possible; and the classical problem of the relationships between speech and writing could not arise.'[36] The moment before the decision, that is always already there at the moment of decision. Or as Derrida puts it, 'The trace is in fact the absolute origin of sense in general. Which amounts to saying once again that there is no absolute origin of sense in general. The trace is the différance which opens appearance and signification.'[37]

A final note: Derrida in fact begins his analysis of *Tristes Tropiques* with an earlier chapter, 'On the Line' in which Lévi-Strauss sees one little girl hit another. The girl who has been hit immediately rushes to him and whispers the name of the offending girl in his ear, breaking a taboo concerning proper names. This taboo, as Derrida notes, already manifests the relevant structural characteristics that he analysed in arche-writing – for instance effacing the connection between a name and its reference, signifier and signified. 'There is writing as soon as the proper name is erased in a system.'[38] Subsequently Lévi-Strauss will use this knowledge to incite quarrels between the children, in order to find out their names. Perhaps Lévi-Strauss's interventions were not so accidental, nor the Nambikwara so pure, as his origin myth required.

From his analysis of Lévi-Strauss, which ends with a more conventional taking apart of his teleological history of language, Derrida returns to Rousseau in the most famous, or perhaps notorious chapter he ever wrote. A little over twenty pages long, '… That Dangerous Supplement …' is Derrida's attempt to link the Rousseau of the *Essay* to the Rousseau of the *Confessions*, his theories on language with his theories on himself.

Derrida picks up on a contradiction running through the *Confessions* as to what constitutes truth. On the one hand, Rousseau argues, 'Languages are made to be spoken, writing serves only as a supplement to speech … Speech represents thought by conventional signs, and writing represents the same with regard to speech. Thus the art of writing is nothing but a mediated representation of thought',[39] and to 'judge genius' from an author's books is like 'painting a man's portrait from his corpse'.[40]

But on the other hand:

> I would love society like others, if I were not so sure of showing myself at a disadvantage, but as completely different from what I am. The part that I have taken of writing and hiding myself is precisely one that suits me. If I were present one would never know what I was worth.[41]

It does not take a huge grounding in Derridean practices to see the contradiction. Only by reading him, Rousseau argues *pace* Rousseau, can we see his true self. A Freudian presented with Rousseau's declared hostility to writing and this passage would have a field day.

Derrida certainly does. In one of his astonishing acts of analysis, Derrida extracts from this a word with little philosophical history – supplement: 'Writing,' argues Rousseau, 'serves only as a supplement to speech'. Note the 'only' – this is speech being privileged over writing in its consummate state. But Derrida wishes to unpack the word *supplement*, to deconstruct it, and search it out in Rousseau's work as a sort of pressure point, a bug in the program.

Derrida analyses supplement from its original French etymology. Supplement can mean either something added on to improve or complete it (the normal English meaning): to supplement one's income, to take a dietary supplement. Or it is something substituted, that which supplants the other. The latter also applies a threat, the supplement replaces the original.

Derrida works through Rousseau's oeuvre seeking out uses of the term, noting that 'the concept of the supplement is a sort of blind spot in Rousseau's text, the not-seen that opens and limits visibility': an invisible and dangerous word which appears at particular moments of stress in Rousseau's texts.[42] He finds it in Rousseau's theory of education, which is a system of substitution of one type of knowledge for another. And in his theory of music. Melody, the ideal, original, musical inspiration is supplemented by harmony (which at a certain level of complexity requires the parts to be written down).

Famously/notoriously, Derrida finds it in Rousseau's series of euphemisms regarding masturbation, one of the preoccupations of *The Confessions*. The phrase 'dangerous supplement' is Rousseau's own, and refers to this act that is 'a condition almost unintelligible and inconceivable [to reason]'. A substitute for sex, it is, Rousseau opines, unnatural, but like the unnatural act of writing, very difficult to give up. It is 'properly seductive' and, according to Rousseau:

> It leads desire away from the good path, makes it err far from natural ways, guides it toward its loss or fall and therefore it is a sort of lapse or scandal. It thus destroys Nature. But the scandal of Reason is that nothing seems more natural than this destruction of Nature. It is myself who exerts myself to separate myself from the force that Nature has entrusted to me.[43]

Derrida has fun with this. When we masturbate, we fantasise about another. And 'it has never been possible to desire that presence "in person" before this play of substitution and this symbolic experience of auto-affection'.[44] You hope, in other words, that they don't walk in – that would ruin the whole point of masturbation. Assuming they don't, 'the presence that is thus delivered to us in the present is a chimera. Auto-affection is pure speculation' such that 'the enjoyment of the thing itself is thus undermined, in its act and in its essence, by frustration …'[45] For Rousseau, no sex he ever has lives up to his masturbatory fantasies; reality is always a falling-short. 'If I had ever in my life tasted the delights of love even once in their plenitude, I do not imagine that my frail existence would have been sufficient for them. I would have been dead in the act.'[46]

At this point Derrida reveals the Freudian kettle logic behind each binary opposition Rousseau establishes, and he writes his most famous/notorious paragraph:

There is nothing outside of the text [there is no outside-text; *il n'y a pas de hors-texte*] ... What we have tried to show by following the guiding line of the 'dangerous supplement', is that in what one calls the real life of these existences 'of flesh and bone', beyond and behind what one believes can be circumscribed as Rousseau's text, there has never been anything but writing; there have never been anything but supplements, substitutive significations which could only come forth in a chain of differential references, the 'real' supervening, and being added only while taking on meaning from a trace and from an invocation of the supplement, etc.[47]

There is nothing outside the text. Derrida does not mean there is nothing outside of writing – that would be *Il n'y a rien en dehors du texte*. He means that everything, like text, can be interpreted multiple ways and is never a pure signifier of the signified, but is always already a chain of supplements. Thus the theme of supplementarity 'describes the chain itself, the being-chain of a textual chain, a structure of substitution, the articulation of desire and language.'[48] Ultimately, the power-relation of the original over the supplement is disturbed when one realises the extent of dependency of the former on the latter. The supplement is not an optional add-on to the original: it is the condition of the original. The 'logic of supplementarity' is Derrida's attempt to tie together all of Rousseau's contradictory declarations to avoid obliterating them. And to set the limits of their scope.

Derrida concludes *Of Grammatology* by bringing this back to the original division of speech and writing. Auto-affection demands the suppression of différance, and this suppression is the origin of what is called presence. We mistake immediacy for presence, and immediacy is a 'myth of consciousness'.[49] It is this presence that philosophy has been chasing for two millennia. 'The great remedy to the miseries of the world,' writes Rousseau, 'is absorption in the present moment.'[50] Husserl would agree.

Near the end of *Of Grammatology*, Derrida returns to Phaedrus. 'The art or technique of writing,' argues Plato, 'is a *pharmakon* (drug or tincture, salutary or maleficent),'[51] and Derrida would immediately follow *Of Grammatology* with the article 'Plato's Pharmacy', printed across two issues of *Tel Quel* in winter and spring of 1968.

The word 'pharmakon' appears throughout *Phaedrus* and, as Derrida had used 'supplement' in Rousseau, so he uses it to deconstruct Plato's text. As with supplement, pharmakon has a 'double, contradictory, undecidable value that always derives from [its] syntax' and it is the interplay of the syntactical connections that is the task of deconstruction to deconstruct.

Like the English word drug, pharmakon is both a remedy and a poison (one takes a drug to cure, one administers a drug to kill). But it has a third meaning, not mentioned in Plato's text, that of 'scapegoat'. Scapegoat is from the ritual of *pharmakós*, human sacrifice. The link is the idea of purification: the ancient Greeks, at a time of crisis (famine, plague, invasion) would sacrifice or exile a human scapegoat to cure their ills. This took place on the first day of Thargelia, the festival of Apollo.

The fact that the dialogue takes place outside the city walls incorporates the idea of sacrifice and exile. What we know, but Socrates does not, is that he himself will be a human sacrifice, executed for corrupting youth, for filling them with the madness of philosophy. Derrida notes that Plato's text, while riffing constantly on *pharmakeia–pharmakon–pharmakeus* does not use the word *pharmakós*; it is absent, but present to those who know Socrates' fate – which includes Plato as he wrote it. It is thus an act of avoidance not to mention it, deliberate or not.

The text is rich with the symbolism of the pharmacy – the pair walk past a pool with 'curative powers', Socrates describes that speech Phaedrus carries beneath his robes as a pharmakon. Asked why he would choose to leave the city, Socrates tells Phaedrus, 'You seem to have discovered a drug for getting me out' (*dokeis moi tis emis exocou to pharmakon heurikenai*).

Pharmakon and its derivatives appear several times in the myth of the origin of writing. Writing is offered as a cure, but rejected as a poison. Derrida, as ever, champions the undecidability of this formulation, and is alive to the possibilities of leaving it undecided, of its ambi-valence. Throughout the dialogue, as Phaedrus carries the written speech beneath his cloak, 'the pharmakon and the grapheme have been beckoning each other from afar' before finally the myth of writing appears, although, as it stands alone, 'in a certain sense, one can see how this section could have been set apart as an appendix, a superadded supplement.'[52]

The word pharmakon is thus 'caught in a chain of significations. The play of that chain seems systematic. But the system here is not simply that of the intention of an author who goes by the name of Plato.'[53] While Plato can declare or clarify the meaning of the word (and all the words he uses) the words 'go on working by themselves. In spite of him? thanks to him? in his text? outside his text? but then where? between his text and the language? for what reader? at what moment?'[54] The privilege of the author in fixing meaning is drastically undermined. The trace is working here too, the unsaid also produces meaning.

The article is a bravura performance, with Derrida working through a number of other ambiguous words in the original text. He ends the piece with Plato closing his pharmacy and retiring 'to get out of the sun', followed by a rhetorical flourish that conjures the night, and has echoes of Lévinas's encounter with the 'there is': 'The night passes. In the morning knocks are heard at the door. They seem to be coming from outside this time ... But maybe it's just a residue, a dream, a bit left over, an echo of the night ... that other theatre, those knocks from without ...'[55]

The essay was collected in the book *Dissemination* with two other texts exploring writing as Derrida analysed it: 'The Double Session', which plays Plato off against Mallarmé's 'Mimique', the poet's essay on mimicry, mimesis and silence in his *Divigations*, which begins 'This is a book just the way I don't like them, scattered and with no architecture'; and 'Dissemination', which analyses three novels of Philippe Sollers, *The Park* (1961), *Event* (1965) and *Nombres* (1968).

Derrida had met Sollers in 1964 after the latter had mentioned the Introduction to *The Origin of Geometry* in the thirteenth issue of *Tel Quel*, the journal he had founded in 1960. Sollers

was already a literary star at that time, having won the Prix
Médicis for *The Park*. *Tel Quel*, meaning 'As Is' quickly became
the premier avant-garde literary magazine in France, perhaps
the world, and attempted to explore and push to the limit the
theoretical revolutions of Marx, Nietzsche, Heidegger, Freud. Its
contributors included Foucault, Umberto Eco, Maurice Blanchot
and Julia Kristeva.

Sollers's *Nombres* (Numbers) was ripe for a Derridean reading.
The novel incorporates quotations, parentheses, dashes, cuts,
figures and Chinese characters in numerically divided sections.
Derrida's analysis continues the radical re-evaluation of writing
started in *Of Grammatology*. Again, Derrida seeks to enact his
theories as much as argue them. 'Dissemination', for Derrida, is
the way that each text disperses itself after inscription, unable to
fix a vantage point from which it demands to be read, whatever
the efforts of the author to police it. Sollers's writing makes this
manifest. The text is 'remarkable in that the reader (here in exemplary fashion) can never choose his own place in it, nor can the
spectator.'[56] The word dissemination, notes Derrida, contains the
'fortuitous resemblance ... of *seme* [the smallest unit of meaning in
language, hence semiotics] and *semen*'.[57] Capturing both semantic
difference and seminal drift, dissemination attacks the idea that
a text can be limited, controlled or owned by any authority, the
author included. All texts have a 'plurality of filiations'. They have
always already begun; they always already continue.

Sollers's response to the text was, while enthusiastic in his
communication with Derrida, otherwise mixed. He was both flat-
tered and scared. Derrida seemed to have appropriated Sollers's
own method, and done it with such dexterity as to have produced
a text which perhaps outdid the original.[58]

The essay also raised tensions with Kristeva. She had arrived in
Paris from Bulgaria in 1964, and her brilliant work immediately
found a place in *Critique* and *Tel Quel*. Her first collection of
essays, 1969's *Séméiôtiké: recherches pour une sémanalyse* (translated into English as *Desire in Language: A Semiotic Approach to
Literature and Art*) ranges across semiotics, literature, the visual
arts and psychoanalysis. Her work would continue to explore

these realms as she teased out the relationship between the semiotic and the symbolic, which she associates with the maternal (the unconscious drives which are manifest in the tone adopted by the writer, the images, the narrative) and the patriarchal symbolic (the rule base aspects of language) which represses the free play of the semiotic.

As Derrida was writing 'Dissemination', Kristeva was working on her own essay inspired by *Nombres*, 'L'engendrement de la Formule', which appeared in *Tel Quel* 37 and 38. In it, she introduces the fused terms, geno-text and pheno-text, between which a text oscillates, the former generating the subject in an infinite chain of signification, the latter fixing (momentarily) meaning and the subject. We can see the proximity of these terms to Derrida's work. In addition, her 1967 'Towards a Semiology of Paragrams' explores in part the way that texts refer to other texts, and how a book, while finite, contains potentially infinite language. Again, the concurrence of her ideas and those of Derrida is striking. There was, therefore, as Sollers later admitted, 'a theoretical competition between Derrida and Kristeva.'[59] Complicating this was the fact that Sollers and Kristeva, unbeknownst to everyone including Derrida, married in August 1967. When Sollers rebuked Derrida for a criticism of Kristeva's work, Derrida didn't know he was taking Sollers's wife to task.

Their 'theoretical' competition became real before long.

Writing and Difference, Speech and Phenomena and *Of Grammatology* – perhaps no philosopher in history has produced such a wealth of texts in a single year. If 1966 had ended with an exhausted Derrida squeezing in a trip to America to speak at a conference in front of formidable thinkers who had basically never heard of him, by the end of 1967 he was the new superstar of French philosophy – a genuine category, with genuine obligations. But already his unique style, his mania for generating neologisms and his odd central premise concerning speech and writing were dividing followers into devotees or antagonists.

The academy could not decide if he was poison or cure. He was immediately regarded as a charlatan by many in the philosophical establishment. The last few years of the 1960s and the start of the '70s were to see a number of battles with other philosophers in France and elsewhere. But if there were a number of intellectual battles to be fought, more immediately there was an actual battle on Derrida's front doorstep – May 1968.

On 2 May 1968, after a series of clashes between students and authorities, the administration of the University of Paris in Nanterre shut down and threatened a number of expulsions. The conflict had begun on 22 March, when 150 students had occupied the council room to discuss the political bureaucracy that was in control of funding the university, and wider questions of class discrimination in France after a decade of de Gaulle. On 3 May, students on the Sorbonne campus met to protest. Six hundred were arrested. On 6 May, 20,000 members of the national student union (UNEF) and teaching unions marched to the Sorbonne to protest the police presence. As they approached, the police charged, and the protestors fell back and began erecting barricades. There were over 400 arrests and over 600 wounded. Not for the first time, nor the last, the streets of Paris had become a battleground between the authorities and the people.

. The year 1968 was one of radical action, not just in France but around the world: the American civil rights and anti–Vietnam War movements, the Prague Spring, the shutdowns of the University of Trento and the Free University of Berlin, student protests in Belgrade, the March of the One Hundred Thousand in Rio de Janeiro and coups d'état in Iraq, Mali and Peru. In France, in the wake of the Algerian War, the atmosphere was particularly explosive, driven by a combination of Third Worldism (Cuba, Vietnam), de Gaulle's patrician rule, and a burgeoning student population which had tripled in the previous decade. The publisher François Maspero brought out new editions of Fanon, Paul Nizan and Sartre, and printed investigations of the use of torture in Algeria.

On 10 May, police attacked a protest on the Left Bank at 2:12 in the morning, injuring and arresting hundreds. Public sympathy turned against the government. On 13 May the major left unions called a one-day strike and workers joined the students in marching through Paris, the biggest demonstration since the Liberation.

Derrida joined the march with the writers of *Tel Quel*. He later remembered with dismay bumping into his old teacher Maurice de Gandillac during the march, who took the opportunity to ask him how he was getting on with his thesis, already twelve years late. Derrida was noncommittal and it would be another twelve before he submitted it.[60]

He had not seen the events of May 1968 coming; in fairness, few did. The revolution over which so much ink had been spilled, not least at the ENS, caught the very intellectuals who had agitated for it on paper and in committees totally by surprise. It was coming at the wrong time, for the wrong reasons, from the wrong people, against the wrong enemy. The slogans of 1968 were too playful, too situationist, too witty (*Je suis Marxiste – tendance Groucho*; *Soyez réalistes, demandez l'impossible*; *Plus je fais l'amour, plus j'ai envie de faire la révolution. Plus je fais la révolution, plus j'ai envie de faire l'amour!*; *Je jouis dans les pavés*). As another put it, *La révolution est incroyable parce que vraie* – the revolution is incredible because it is real.

Althusser, whose books had done much to refresh Marxism in France, was as unprepared for the Real as anyone, and his response was to retire to a sanitorium for the duration (*A quoi sert Althusser? Althusser-à-rien* [What is Althusser for? Althusser's nothing!] was scrawled on a wall in the Latin Quarter). His first response was not until 1969, in a letter valorising the general strike and disparaging the students. That the latter had initiated the rebellion counted for nothing:

> The mass of the students live in a dream based on a misunderstanding. This obviously is an illusion. It confuses chronological order (the barricades came before the 13 May demonstration and therefore before the general strike), the role of 'detonator' or 'the single spark that lights a forest fire' (Lenin), with the historical (non-chronological) role which is determinant in the final analysis. And in May it was the working class, and not the students, who, in the final analysis, played the determining role.[61]

To which the only sane answer is: no, they didn't.

While Derrida participated in the demonstrations, and even organised the first general meeting at the ENS, he again found it difficult to be part of a mass movement. Later, Derrida worked hard at the idea of philosophy and the politics of philosophy being a collegiate activity, but it was indeed something he *had* to work at. As he put it, he was not against May 1968, 'but I have always had trouble vibrating in unison.'[62] His unease was also, as ever, a certain resistance to the moment of decision, and all the falsities one had to endure in making one:

> What really bothered me was not so much the apparent spon-
> taneity, which I do not believe in, but the spontaneist political
> eloquence, the call for transparency, for communication without
> relay or delay ... spontaneism, like workerism, pauperism, struck
> me as something to be wary of. I wouldn't say my conscience is
> clear on the matter and that it's as simple as that. These days
> I would be more cautious about formulating this critique of
> spontaneism.[63]

For Derrida, even caution requires caution.

Derrida's defence of himself is, of course, similar to the defence offered by intellectuals throughout history for a failure to act, and many French intellectuals, Derrida included, were later castigated for this failure, especially in light of the total praxis practised by Sartre. But Derrida's 'caution' received a robust, and quite moving, defence in a beautiful tribute written to him by perhaps the last remaining Maoist intellectual of the era, Alain Badiou.

> In all the questions in which he intervened, Derrida was what I
> call a brave man of peace. He was brave because it takes a lot
> of courage not to enter into the division as it is constituted. And
> he was a man of peace because identifying what excepts itself
> from that opposition is, as a general rule, the road to peace. For
> any true peace is based upon an agreement not about that which
> exists, but about that which non-exists ... This diagonal obsti-
> nacy, this rejection of abrupt metaphysically derived divisions,

is obviously not suited to stormy times when everything comes under the law of decisiveness, here and now. That is what kept Derrida apart from the truth of the red years between 1968 and 1976. Because the truth of those years spoke its name with the words: 'One divides into two.' What we desired, in poetic terms, was the metaphysics of radical conflict, and not the patient deconstruction of oppositions. And Derrida could not agree about that.[64]

પ્

The day before the 13 May general strike, Derrida finished his essay 'The Ends of Man', which he was to deliver in New York in September. It is one of his most important works, and he acknowledges in the introduction that it was written at a time of political turbulence, referencing not only the Paris protests, but the Vietnam peace talks which had just opened and the 4 April assassination of Martin Luther King.

'The Ends of Man' is a close reading of Heidegger. The reception of Heidegger in France – where the majority of his works remained untranslated, *Being and Time* included (only the first forty-four paragraphs in 1962, no full translation until 1985) – still generally depended on Sartre's (mis-)reading of him. Heidegger was therefore regarded as both an existentialist and a humanist in the terms set out by Sartre in his 'Existentialism Is a Humanism'. Humanism still sees the subject as sovereign, and for Sartre that means that humans have both freedom and responsibility. In his famous formulation, existence precedes essence. We are what we do, our choices of what we do define us.

It is a reading Heidegger himself had refuted in his *Letter on Humanism*. 'Existence precedes essence', argues Heidegger, is no more valid than its opposite – 'the reversal of a metaphysical statement remains a metaphysical statement.'[65] And metaphysics is precisely what Heidegger is trying to go beyond with his search for the meaning of Being. Dasein is not a humanist construction in Sartre's terms, nor is he, Heidegger, an existentialist. If Sartre wants to call his own philosophy 'existentialism' that's fine with Heidegger as long as he leaves him out of it. 'The basic tenet of "existentialism" has nothing to do with *Being and Time*,' he wrote, as in that book 'no statement about the relation of *essentia* and *existentia* can yet be expressed, since there it is still a question of preparing something precursory.'[66]

In his paper, Derrida argues that Sartre's 'bad humanism' has led to 'bad readings' of not just Heidegger, but Hegel and Husserl. But his main focus is the way that Heidegger himself is still trapped within a sort of humanism. Derrida picks out the sentence 'This way of being is proper (*eigen*) only to the human being.'[67] *Eigen* is an important word for Heidegger and forms part of *Eigentlicheit*, or authenticity. Dasein should aim for this authenticity, or at least are only true when they dwell in it. But, notes Derrida, to prescribe a proper or authentic way of being, and of relating to being, is to also fall on the side of humans having agency, in just the way Heidegger accuses Sartre of doing. So, as Heidegger regarded Nietzsche's attempt to go beyond metaphysics as failing, so Derrida says the same about Heidegger.

Again, it is worth stressing that Derrida in no way sees himself as 'succeeding' where others have failed; there is after all no way of 'succeeding' in this sense. Criticism of metaphysics can only occur within metaphysics. There is no outside vantage point where one can stand, so 'the enterprise of deconstruction always in a certain way falls prey to its own work'.[68]

Man, Derrida notes, is not an innocuous or self-evident concept. The unity of 'man' remains unexamined. For Derrida, what we call 'man' is in fact a limit, which defines itself by exclusion. As he had argued in *Of Grammatology*, 'Man calls himself man only by drawing limits and excluding his other from the play of supplementarity: the purity of nature, of animality, primitivism, childhood, madness, divinity.'[69] Dasein repeats the unavoidable mistake of all previous metaphysics. In Heidegger's initial definition of Dasein, 'the being whose analysis our task is, is always we ourselves', the 'we' is again that proximate, present voice in our heads we mistake for us.[70]

The tension between humanism and anti-humanism, between Sartre's meaning-creating individual and, for instance, Foucault's declaration of the 'death of man', was, of course, a tension that ran through the May 1968 protests. As Derrida finished 'The Ends of Man', the sound of the protests outside his office door included Sartre on a megaphone. Whatever the faults of his reading of Heidegger, Sartre was making himself useful in the rebellion, addressing huge numbers of students at the Sorbonne on 20 May. Arrested for civil disobedience, he was pardoned by de Gaulle who said, 'You don't arrest Voltaire.'

On the day Sartre spoke, some 11 million French were on strike. The 24th saw the first two deaths, a policeman and a demonstrator. By 28 May, François Mitterrand, then leader of the Federation of the Democratic and Socialist Left, said, 'there is no more state', and declared himself ready to form a government, as did Pierre Mendès France of the Radical Party, the latter in coalition with the Communists.

Then, on 29 May, de Gaulle left the Élysée Palace in a helicopter. No one was sure where he had gone, including the government. The next day half a million protestors marched through Paris chanting *Adieu, de Gaulle!* The general was found to be at the headquarters of the French ministry in Baden-Baden. Forced to dissolve the National Assembly on Prime Minister Georges Pompidou's threat to resign, de Gaulle broadcast that he would not resign himself, but would hold a new election on 23 June, and ordered the workers back to work, threatening a state emergency if they did not.

And then ... it was over. De Gaulle's political genius was always to somehow gauge the mood of the people, or even to change it to suit his own. At the 23 June election, his party won the greatest victory in French parliamentary history, with 353 of 486 seats. Perhaps, in the end, Althusser was, in some way, right: the initial enthusiasm of the students needed the commitment of the workers, and what the workers wanted – better conditions – was very different from what got the students excited. *Travailleurs de tous les pays, amusez-vous!* rung hollow to those on the breadline.

7

Supposing That Truth Is a Woman – What Then?

I too would like to write like a woman. I try ...
                                        – *'Spurs* Roundtable'

Not *just anyone buggers Socrates.*
                                        – *The Post Card*

If that rebellion was fizzling out, another was taking place, and to Derrida's credit it was one he embraced, and embraced critically, working through its implications not only socially, not only philosophically, but for his own work.

At the 1966 Baltimore conference there were fifteen participants and another fourteen colloquists; twenty on the sponsoring and advisory committee; and ten on the student reception committee. Of these, only one, a student committee member, Margaret Meyer, was a woman; the other fifty-eight were men. Baltimore was not unique in this. If the 1960s was the time of second-wave feminism, the academy was particularly resistant to it – or was as resistant as the rest of legislative society.

In France, Simone de Beauvoir's *Second Sex* of 1949 had applied existentialist philosophy to women's oppression – if existence precedes essence, then 'one is not born a woman, but

becomes one'.¹ But the general state of affairs remained oppressive. It was not until 1965 that French women won the right to
work without their husband's consent, while the legalisation of
birth control did not occur until 1967, and even then was delayed
several times in the courts. Derrida's own ENS was an all-male
institution, with women segregated off to the École normale
supérieure de jeunes filles in Sèvres, 10 kilometres south-west of
the centre of Paris. While thirty-five women gained entry between
1927 and 1940 – including Simone Weil and the Franco-Greek
philologist Jacqueline Worms de Romilly – they were officially
banned by a law under Vichy France. It was not until 1985 that
the two campuses were merged.

The events of 1968 inspired the rise of a new radicalism, such
as the 1970 formation of *Mouvement de libération des femmes*,
which advocated for contraception and abortion rights, and
women's autonomy from their husbands. In 1971, de Beauvoir
wrote the text for the 'Manifeste des 343 salopes' [Manifesto
of the 343 Sluts], a petition of that number of women 'who
had the courage to say "I've had an abortion."' The petition
demanded both free access to contraception and free access to
abortion. Alert to male hypocrisy, the satirical weekly *Charlie
Hebdo* asked male politicians, 'Who got the 343 sluts from the
abortion manifesto pregnant?' Eventually, in 1974, abortion
became legal.

If Derrida could laconically use the phrase 'man' in both the
title of 'The Ends of Man' and in its main arguments, it was not a
linguistic or indeed philosophical error he was wont to maintain.
He was one of those men who are lucky enough to find himself
among intelligent opinionated women, or at least lucky enough
to be the sort of person who listens to them – if not without argument. His association with *Tel Quel* and its milieu had introduced
him not only to Julia Kristeva, but also to Catherine Clément,
who had studied at the ENS with both Lévi-Strauss and Lacan
(her interrogation of the latter's thought continuing to inform
her long career), Élisabeth Roudinesco, biographer of both
Freud and Lacan and cultural historian of, among other things
the French Revolution, perversion and Judaism, and Christine

Buci-Glucksmann, whose initial work on Engels and Gramsci led her, via Walter Benjamin, to her groundbreaking study *Baroque Reason*.

And there was Sarah Kofman, the brilliant philosopher who wrote extensively on Freud and Nietzsche, and who also published a book on Derrida. Kofman was the daughter of a rabbi killed at Auschwitz in 1942, when she was eight years old, and she spent the rest of the war in hiding. Her thesis 'Nietzsche and Metaphor' was supervised by Gilles Deleuze, and from 1969 she attended Derrida's seminars at the ENS. Her works, such as *The Enigma of Woman: Woman in Freud's Writings* (1980) and *Le respect des femmes (Kant et Rousseau)* (1982), develop the idea that the feminine functions as a blind spot in philosophical systems, and that male philosophers have repressed their own femininity in producing these systems. Again, her work was to inform Derrida's.

Marguerite Derrida herself, of course, remained a formidable presence, requiring no consent from her husband when she trained to become an analyst at the height of one of Derrida's periodic disputes with Lacan. And then there was Hélène Cixous, with whom Derrida struck up and maintained one of the great intellectual friendships of his life.

Although they did not meet until eight years later, Cixous had in fact attended by chance Derrida's *leçons pour l'agrégation* on 'The Thought of Death' in 1956, having just arrived in Paris. In 1964 Cixous wrote to Derrida, having read his Introduction to *The Origin of Geometry*. As a Joyce scholar – her doctoral dissertation was 'The Exile of James Joyce, or the Art of Displacement', which is longer than *Ulysses* itself – she was fascinated by Derrida's use of this novelist in a philosophical text. Meeting for the first time they were astonished by the extent of their shared reference points. Both were Algerian Jews now in the French university system, and both were eager to shake things up. Like Derrida, Cixous also suffered from 'nostalgeria'.

'A very deep sense of complicity grew up between us,' Cixous wrote, although there were subtle differences in method. 'More than once we say the same words, but we do not live them in the same tone.'² Or as Derrida put it, 'Between her and me, it is as if it were a question of life and death. Death would be on my side and life on hers.'³ They were also both prolific – in 1968 Cixous published her doctoral thesis and her first novel, *Dedans* [*Inside*], which won the Prix Médicis. She was also charged with setting up a radical new university, the University of Paris VIII. Derrida would call her France's greatest living writer.

Always transgressive, always blurring the lines between genres, her essay 'The Laugh of the Medusa' and her collaboration with Catherine Clément, *The Newly Born Woman*, both published in 1975, were among the first works to embrace both the Derridean problematising and destabilising of logocentrism, and his insights into writing and exorbitance. 'By writing her self,' said Cixous, 'woman will return to the body which has been more than confiscated from her, which has been turned into the uncanny stranger on display.'⁴

Cixous coined the term *écriture féminine* for this writing which explored the ways women's sexuality and unconscious shape their imaginary, their language, and their writing. 'Feminine writing' sought to disrupt ordered, logical, phallic language with language which was heterogenous and destructive. Meanwhile Kristeva introduced the concept of the *chora*, a pre-linguistic, pre-Oedipal, unsystematised space for a language process she called semiotic, as opposed to the symbolic order of the patriarchal. *Écriture féminine* became a catch-all for grouping together a number of poststructural feminists, later to include thinkers such as the radical lesbian writer Monique Wittig, who argued that heterosexuality was a political regime, and 'man' and 'woman' political and economic categories, and Chantal Chawaf, whose novels explore the materiality of the female body.

A year before 'The Laugh of the Medusa', the Belgian cultural theorist Luce Irigaray had published *Speculum: De l'autre femme* [Speculum of the Other Woman], which drew directly on Derrida's work in analysing phallogocentrism in Western philosophy from Plato to Freud. Derrida's 'strange notions' she later wrote, had 'shaken the ground of our metaphysical tradition'.⁵ Derrida argued that 'it is no longer possible to go looking for woman, or woman's femininity or female sexuality. At least they cannot be found by any familiar mode of thought or knowledge.'[6] In *Speculum*, Irigaray sought new modes of thought in a critique which identified the 'sexless' notion of the ego which founds philosophy as male, with woman cast in the role of other. Men exist, women are a variation. Women can only become subjects by assimilation, there is no separate subject which instantiates 'woman'. Thus true sexual difference does not exist, as that would require equality in subjectness. The task is, therefore, to reconfigure identity, both male and female.

While many of these writers acknowledged Derrida's influence (as he did theirs), it would be wrong of course to reproduce the phallocentric gesture of awarding him any primacy in feminist philosophy, or to argue that his positions were adopted wholesale. Irigaray herself would come to criticise his deconstruction of the term 'woman' in her 1980 text *Marine Lover of Friedrich Nietzsche*. However, there remains a sense that he played an important role, at least in recognising there was a problem and adapting his writing to incorporate it. As the cultural theorist Avital Ronell put it in her 2010 book of interviews with Anne Dufourmantelle, *Fighting Theory*:

> Derrida cleared spaces that looked like obstacle courses for anyone who did not fit the professorial profile at the time. He practiced, whether consciously or not, a politics of contamination ... Derrida blew into our town-and-gown groves with protofeminist energy, often, and at great cost to the protocols of philosophical gravity, passing as a woman.[7]

Perhaps the strongest commendation for his place as a feminist is, as noted, that the influence went both ways. If the history of the logos was the history of various transcendental signifieds, each designed to keep the instability of the system under some sort of control, then the patriarchy was another example, from sophisticated strategies such as the role of the phallus in Lacan's psychoanalysis, or the blunter instruments of asserting maleness as normative. The man/woman binary opposition was as ripe for deconstruction as any other, and required it just as, if not more, urgently.

Alain Badiou is, once again, particularly perceptive when it comes to Derrida, and goes so far as to ascribe the whole necessity for his philosophy to the rise of feminism. 'Philosophy is the act of reorganising all theoretical and practical experiments by proposing a great new normative division, which inverts an established intellectual order and promotes new values beyond the commonly accepted ones,' he wrote. 'Derrida transformed the classical approach of rigid metaphysical oppositions, largely on account of the growing and unavoidable importance, for our experiences, of the feminine dimension.'[8]

While Derrida continued to publish frequently between 1968 and 1971, in works that would be collected in the books *Margins of Philosophy* (including 'The Ends of Man', 'White Mythology' and 'Tympan', which with its two column layout anticipates 1974's *Glas*) and *Dissemination*, it is a paper written for the 1972 Cerisy conference which marks Derrida's entry into feminist thinking.

Even now *Spurs: Nietzsche's Styles* is a remarkable text – it was even more remarkable then. The history of Western philosophy is not replete with male philosophers intervening from a feminist perspective, outside of, perhaps, vague calls for equality, such as those offered by William Godwin or John Stuart Mill. While Plato in Book V of *The Republic* has Socrates argue the case for women receiving the same education and taking on the same political roles as men, this is part of his scheme whereby spouses and children can be shared in common, sexual intercourse only being permitted at certain festivals, with the spouses drawn by lot, and more than one spouse available over the course of the festival. It sounds a lot like the Summer of Love, and we all know how 'feminist' that turned out to be.

Derrida's intervention in *Spurs* is radical. Ostensibly an essay on style in Nietzsche, Derrida cancels that idea in two sentences. 'The title for this lecture was to have been *the question of style*. However – it is woman who will be my subject'; before adding, 'Still, one might wonder whether that doesn't amount to the same thing.'⁹ It is reasonable to say that no one before Derrida had, in fact, wondered that.

What does Derrida mean by 'the question of style'? Style has tended to be seen as a secondary question for philosophy, if that. As philosophy has attempted to make itself transparent in order to get to truth, so style has been regarded simply in terms of how close it gets to this achievement. Displaying 'clarity' is one of the highest epithets a philosophical work can achieve. This is not to say that complex edifices can't be built – what Hegel, for instance, had to say was obviously complicated, so he is forgiven by followers for a deal of abstruse terminology, as Heidegger is for his neologisms. But the goal still remains to make the explanation as clear as it can be, whether discussing apodictic arguments, the negation of the negation, or the-Being-present-at-hand-together-of-things-that-occur. If there is a simpler way to say it, it should be said more simply.

Here we have another binary opposition, matter/style, as though the matter of a philosophical text somehow lay behind its style, which in this sense 'gets in the way'. It is like the stupidity of the question 'What does this poem mean?' as though behind the text of the poem is a clear and definable meaning. For Derrida, who had argued among other things that there is nothing 'behind [outside] a text', and argued that all language is metaphorical such that there is no coherent way to separate the language of philosophy from any other, this is obviously anathema. Separation is neither possible, nor makes sense.

Nietzsche knowingly *performed* his style as his philosophy. Disjointed, ecstatic, boastful, aphoristic, exuberant, hyperbolic, it argued for the overthrowing of the grand narratives of Western metaphysics by not indulging in grand narratives. Like Derrida's own work, it is argument through enaction. And Nietzsche, in Derrida's reading, does not just have one style, he has a multitude that he deploys when necessary. What we must not do, for Derrida, is reduce these styles, attempt to make of them a coherence that can only be an imposition.

Derrida's argument here is with Heidegger who, in order to situate Nietzsche as the last metaphysician and himself as the first to go beyond metaphysics, flattens Nietzsche under the rubric of *Will to Power*. The author of *The Revaluation of All Values* is presented by Heidegger as arguing for exactly the sort of universal prime mover he was attempting to complicate, the value he was attempting to re-evaluate. Like Roussel's analysis of Proust, Heidegger allows for a 'grand style' in Nietzsche, proclaiming the blind force that is will, and disregards anything that does not meet the criteria.

Derrida has fun disrupting this totalising strategy by examining a sentence which appears in Nietzsche's unpublished manuscripts, quotation marks and all – 'I have forgotten my umbrella.' Mimicking a traditional philosopher, Derrida interrogates the meaning of this pronouncement – where does it fit into Nietzsche's corpus? Is it 'true Nietzsche', or should it be disregarded, treated as supplementary? On what criteria? 'Could Nietzsche have disposed of some more or less secret code, which, for him or for some unknown accomplice of his, would have made sense of this statement?'[10] And with perhaps just a touch of self-satire he asks, 'What if Nietzsche himself meant to say nothing, or [at] least not much of anything, or anything whatever? Then again, what if Nietzsche was only pretending to say something? In fact, it is even possible that it is not Nietzsche's sentence ...'[11] The umbrella, notes Derrida, is also a Freudian symbol for male genitalia, in, according to the *Introductory Lectures on Psychoanalysis*, the pre-Oedipal phase. But it is also a bisexual symbol, embracing the maternal in the sense that it protects us from both the hot and the cold. Finally, gleefully, with tongue firmly in cheek, Derrida settles on 'Everyone knows what "I have forgotten my umbrella" means. I have ... an umbrella. It is mine. But I forgot it.'[12]

That these games undercut philosophy's pomposity is part of the point. And philosophical pomposity, Derrida argues, is and has always been masculine. In his work, Nietzsche, as he plays with the idea of the philosophy's favourite transcendental signified, Truth, opens the possibility of a different metaphor, that of the feminine. *Beyond Good and Evil* starts:

Supposing that Truth is a woman – what then? Is there not ground for suspecting that all philosophers, in so far as they have been dogmatists, have failed to understand women – that the terrible seriousness and clumsy importunity with which they have usually paid their addresses to Truth, have been unskilled and unseemly methods for winning a woman? Certainly she has never allowed herself to be won; and at present every kind of dogma stands with sad and discouraged mien.[13]

Here, as Derrida notes, 'All the emblems, all the shafts and allurements that Nietzsche found in woman, her seductive distance, her captivating inaccessibility, the ever-veiled promise of her provocative transcendence … they all belong properly to a history of truth by the history of an error.'[14]

Derrida is not attempting to make a feminist of Nietzsche. The anti-female spiels come thick and fast throughout Nietzsche's work (although arguments can be made that it is the male-constructed female whom he attacks). But here, and in analyses of Nietzsche's frequent use of metaphors of castration, pregnancy, birth and so on, Derrida sees the same disruptive potential which informs *écriture féminine*. (Irigaray's *Marine Lover* takes up Nietzsche in similar ways, 'not a book on Nietzsche but with Nietzsche, who is for me a partner in a love relationship'.[15])

Derrida notes that Nietzsche makes three aporetic propositions joining 'truth' to 'woman'. The traditional philosopher is linked to the 'castrated woman', whom he reviled; the 'masked artist' to the 'castrating woman', whom he dreaded; and the 'free thinker' to the 'affirming woman', whom he loved. 'Woman' is a plurality gathered into a matrix of interrelations, which don't form a unified system but multiple aporias and paradoxes.

Throughout, *Spurs* plays with metaphors of cutting and castration. Style begets *stylus*, which begets *stiletto* and so on; and Nietzsche's intervention into Western metaphysics is given as a cutting gesture, right back at the umbilicus of philosophy:

Once this inaugural moment has given way to the second age, here where the becoming-female of the idea is the presence or

presentation of truth, Plato can no more say 'I am truth.' For
here the philosopher is no longer the truth. Severed from himself,
he has been severed from truth.[16]

Heidegger, notes Derrida, ignores the question of women in
Nietzsche. Even a sentence by Nietzsche such as 'Our aesthetics
heretofore has been a woman's aesthetics, inasmuch as only the
recipients of art have formulated their experiences of "what is
beautiful"' is simply regarded by Heidegger as a call for better
artists.[17] Heidegger's style remains a masculine style, whereas
Nietzsche's parenthetical remarks, quotation marks and dashes
should no longer be viewed as purely semantic devices but as
deliberate deviations from the expected normal and continuous
flow of the text, and they constitute in their 'gay science' a play
of possible meanings.

Which is to say, as Derrida does in closing:

> There is no 'totality to Nietzsche's text' not even a fragmentary
> or aphoristic one. There is evidence here to expose one, roofless
> and unprotected by a lightning rod, as he is, to the thunder and
> lightning of an enormous clap of laughter.[18]

One must not forget one's umbrella.

Closer to home, the tensions in Derrida's relationship with
Sollers and Kristeva blew up. Sollers had sent Derrida his new
novel *Lois*, which took his experimental textual strategies to
their limit, including incorporating *Finnegans Wake*. Derrida's
response was lukewarm at best. In addition, Derrida agreed to be
interviewed for the communist journal *La Nouvelle Critique*, an
ideological and personal enemy of *Tel Quel*. Sollers and Kristeva
then stood Derrida and Marguerite up for dinner as punishment,
and the break was complete. It was a banal end to a mutually
fruitful relationship.

On the domestic front, he and Marguerite had moved to the
anonymous Paris suburb of Ris-Orangis where he was to live
for the rest of his life. On the top floor at Ris-Orangis, Derrida's

ever-expanding office overflowed with books, along with, it would seem, every piece of paper, every document, every old computer and typewriter he had touched. His personal library, now housed at Princeton, ran to almost 14,000 books, a large number of them bearing, as Derrida put it in an interview, 'traces of the violence of pencil strokes, exclamation points, arrows, and underlining.' He nicknamed this unheated office his 'Sublime', both for its elevated position and for its being 'subliminal, under heaven, the workshop and departure lounge for my sublimation.'[19]

The notion of the archive was to play a large part in his later work, and again, his philosophical concerns seem to have more than a passing resemblance to his personal concerns. It was in this library, surrounded by what he called his witnesses and promises for the future, that Derrida would start writing at 6 a.m., after his first cup of coffee, and work indefinitely, missing meals and failing to change out of his pyjamas. Precise and punctual in his social life, when writing he was an obsessive. 'I can't help it,' he told a friend, 'it's my way of fighting against death.'[20]

Marguerite was going through her own personal transformation. In 1974 she was admitted to the Société Psychanalytique de Paris to train as a psychoanalyst (her supervisor having been warned that accepting Mme Derrida would open the door to her dangerous husband).[21] Convinced that her Jacques was the greatest philosopher of their generation, she took over management of their daily life while carving out her own successful career (there were, it seems, limits to Derrida's questioning of phallocentrism). As well as her work as an analyst, Marguerite continued to work as a translator, including the works of Melanie Klein (for instance *Psychanalyse d'enfants*, Klein's revolutionary text on the psychoanalysis of children) and Vladimir Propp's *Morphologie du conte*, which analysed the structural elements of Russian folktales.

Just as psychoanalysis worried about Jacques Derrida, Jacques Derrida worried about psychoanalysis. His relationship with it was always restive, combative and therefore – this being Derrida – productive. His early essay 'Freud and the Scene of Writing' had established Freud and psychoanalysis as being simultaneously accomplices and antagonists to the methods of deconstruction. The psyche is not, in psychoanalysis, a given, from which meaning radiates. Rather it is a series of speculative negotiations with the outside world, a world which it resists or incorporates (or both). Like language, it has a trace-structure not a presence-structure.[22] Meaning is always contingent, restless, up for grabs. Freud's model of the workings of the psyche in *The Interpretation of Dreams*, where it refers by metaphor and metonymy, applies, Derrida argued, to our non-dream life too, our non-oneirological selves. That Freud sought to tie meaning to a point of origin, a childhood trauma for instance, was how psychoanalysis remained trapped by the metaphysics of presence.

Derrida's own growing engagement with psychoanalysis informed 1970–71's ENS seminar series 'Psychoanalysis in the Text', but his range of topics remained catholic; he also lectured that year on the proto-Surrealist poet Lautréamont and on the no doubt terrifying to students 'Theory of Philosophical Discourse: Part One, The Metaphor'.

The next year he lectured on 'The Hegel Family', and it was from this seminar that he took the themes for what was his first fully realised manuscript that was through-written as a text, rather than a collection of essays, or made up of them. But this was no conventional book, let alone a conventional book of philosophy.

Glas, published in 1974, enacted in both text and layout the theories that Derrida had been worrying into print for the previous decade. As we have seen, for Derrida, books create a false (falsified in fact) coherence; they impose on writing a form that has only conventional justification. Finite in material construction, they are infinite in the construction of meaning. Enacting this, *Glas* has no recognisable beginning or end, starting and ending mid-sentence, and appears in two columns (mostly), in different type sizes: on the left an essay on Hegel, in particular *Principles of the Philosophy of Right*, and on the right a paean of sorts to Jean Genet. There are no footnotes. No bibliography. It contains, if we are to believe Derrida, 'not one pun'.[23] Occasionally a third column joins the other two: 'side notes' commenting on Hegel (mostly) to the far left, or, on the right, commenting on

Genet (mostly) or quoting from him ('I fuck the Mother of God in the ass!'). There are no keys to help the reader understand, and the relationship between the two columns is mysterious.

In *The Principles of the Philosophy of Right*, Hegel had argued that the bourgeois family was an embodiment of Absolute Knowledge, where the domain of reason is the prerogative of the father (even in Hegel, psychoanalysis lurks surreptitiously). By pairing his analysis of Hegel with his analysis of the subversive, distinctly un-heteronormative Genet, whose writings celebrate all that is not family, all that is not bourgeois, Derrida disarranges Hegel's schema. The juxtaposition means that Hegel, the great thinker of the triad – thesis, antithesis, synthesis – is denied his third term. Thesis and antithesis, now and forever, to infinity.

The form had in fact been in part suggested to Derrida by an article Genet had written, titled 'What Remains of a Rembrandt Torn into Four Equal Pieces and Flushed Down the Toilet', in which the text is divided into blocks of four per page, like four paintings. Susan Handelman notes a similarity to the layout of the Talmud, while Gayatri Chakravorty Spivak, first translator into English of Derrida's *Of Grammatology* and aware of his critique of phallocentrism, interprets the columns as female legs, and the side notes as phallic penetration. 'As the father's phallus works in the mother's hymen, between two legs, so Glas works at origins, between two columns, between Hegel and Genet.'[24]

Derrida had met Genet in 1965 at the apartment of Paule Thévenin, the publisher of Artaud's *Complete Works*. Genet had become a sort of second Artaud to her – she typed up his texts, and even did his washing.[25] Much to everyone's astonishment, including perhaps their own, Derrida and Genet hit it off immediately, falling straight into intense conversation. Genet was usually extremely wary of intellectuals. His initial resistance had been made worse by the overwhelming experience of being the subject of Sartre's 1952 text, *Saint Genet: Actor and Martyr*. Sartre's analysis of Genet's psychology and morality had left him unable to think, unable to act. Also, in 1964 his long-term partner Abdallah had killed himself, and in his grief Genet had stopped writing and burned what he could of his previous work. Thévenin was hoping that the brilliant young Derrida might do for Genet what his essay 'La Parole soufflée' had done for Artaud, reclaiming the holy madness, safely pathologised into a neatly labelled illness of which writing was mere symptom, as holy madness again.

Immediately a friendship was forged between Derrida and Genet, despite each admitting to being intimidated by the other. During May 1968 the pair walked the streets of Paris all night, talking. In 1972, having published nothing for years, Genet wrote a letter for the review *Les Lettres françaises*, which was dedicating an issue to Derrida. He quotes the opening lines of 'Plato's Pharmacy', comparing them to the opening of Proust's *À l'ombre des jeunes filles en fleurs*. 'The usual coarse dynamism that leads a sentence to the next seems in Derrida to have been replaced by a very subtle magnetism, found not in words, but beneath them, almost under the page.'[26]

Flowers were to be one of the central motifs of the right-hand column of *Glas* – *genêt* means broomflower in French, and the author of *Our Lady of the Flowers* was alive to its symbolism. The first hundred or so lines of *Glas*'s Genet column riff on this, combined with 'Jean', which carries the name of his mother, a prostitute who gave him up for adoption, as an author gives up a text. Genet also alludes to a horse, as the name Hegel carries in it 'eagle'.

And as is so often the case with Derrida's texts, Joyce lurks somewhere in the interstices: Glas means knell, as in death-knell, and Derrida himself referred to the book as a kind of wake. It was Joyce of course who was Derrida's exemplar of the equivocal, disturbing the univocality of philosophy. Here Derrida ups the ante, the two columns, talking to each other or not, representing philosophy and literature.

For Derrida, Hegel too is intrinsic to the form. Hegel represents 'The end of the book and the beginning of writing', the name of the first chapter in *Of Grammatology*. Everything Hegel writes, except his eschatological work, argues Derrida, can be read as 'a meditation on writing ... he has reintroduced the essential necessity of the written trace into a philosophical discourse.'[27] The endpoint of his eschatology includes the resolution of writing: once the realm of Absolute Knowledge is achieved, there will be no metaphors (nothing to compare to something else, there is not something else) and thus no writing. The great book will close.

Unsurprisingly, reaction to *Glas* was varied, from being proclaimations it was a masterpiece to a witty review in the *New York Times* by John Sturrock, who said, despite its cleverness, it 'asks too much of one's patience and intelligence; our defence against a text declaring itself to be unreadable may be to call its author's bluff and simply leave it unread'. Sturrock points out that the book 'mocks ... the notion that translation achieves a semantic identity from one language to another'.[28] The word 'mocks' might be replaced with 'refutes' and we would be close to Derrida's own position.

Of his own friends, it was Althusser, perhaps surprisingly, who was most enthusiastic.

> You've written something extraordinary ... You've got in ahead ... but we'll catch up, only to find you've moved on ... Please forgive me for these ridiculous words, but it 'says' completely new things, that go past Hegel and Genet; it's a philosophical text without precedent which is a poem of a kind I've never come across before.[29]

Genet himself said a few supportive words, then the pair never spoke of it again. Meanwhile Thévenin, feeling her Genet had been stolen, said a few not so supportive words, and didn't speak to Derrida again for years.

Another person not speaking to Derrida was Jacques Lacan. In the summer of 1974 Derrida was invited to write an essay for the review *Poetique*, which based its issue around his work. He decided to rework a lecture he had given in 1971, and, as was his wont, ended up producing a text far longer than he meant to. The essay, 'The Purveyor of Truth', was a response to Lacan's 1956 'Seminar on the Purloined Letter'. The latter was not only Lacan's best-known work, but was the psychoanalyst's calling card to such an extent that he had insisted was first in the otherwise chronological *Écrits* (perhaps to keep it more secure if the book fell apart).

Lacan's seminar was based on the Edgar Allan Poe story 'The Purloined Letter', which turns on the idea of 'hiding in plain sight' – the missing letter, which one would expect to be concealed, is placed out in the open, and thus remains hidden. Lacan turns the story into an exploration of signifying chains, the characters mirroring each other, failing to mirror each other, and revolving around a master signifier, the letter, which is empty – no one, the reader included, ever knows the contents.

Derrida's attack is complex, but the main problem he wants to expose is what he terms phallogocentrism. In Lacan's psychoanalysis, entry into the Symbolic Order, the universal structure which encompasses all human activity, is made possible by the child's acceptance of the Name-of-the-Father, the laws and restrictions that govern desire and communication. The phallus here is the transcendental signifier of desire, either to have or to be. Men are positioned as men insofar as they wish to have the phallus. Women, on the other hand, wish to be the phallus. Lacan thus joins the phallic to the linguistic ('logos is conjoined to the advent of desire') – falling into the trap of both phallocentrism and logocentrism.[30] Derrida, perhaps taking his lead in this case from writers such as Irigaray, again intervenes on the side of that which disrupts. 'Dissemination', he writes, 'mutilates the unity of the signifier, that is, of the phallus.'[31]

Lacan did not take kindly to Derrida's intervention, and the latter's crime was exacerbated by his writing a foreword to *The Wolf Man's Magic Word* by Nicolas Abraham and Maria Torok. Their book re-examined Freud's famous case of Sergei Pankejeff, the 'Wolf Man', whose childhood dream included the image of a tree full of white wolves. Freud used this 'primal scene' as one of his exemplary cases, confirming his hypotheses about the unconscious, infant sexuality and the Oedipus complex – proof, as it were, that his product worked. Abraham and Torok analysed the case differently, focusing on Freud's doubts and evasions, and proposing the idea of a *crypt*, an intrapsychic vault within the ego that protects secrets from the return of the repressed, a sort of false unconscious, producing, if it produces anything, false memories.

The idea, with its accompanying cryptonym, a secret or code word, fascinated Derrida, and his foreword, 'Fors', introduces a number of themes that haunted the rest of his work: death, ghosts, mourning, memory and the secret. These themes led Derrida to the notion of hauntology, the near homonym of ontology – except that while the latter is a taxonomy of things which exist, the former is a taxonomy of those which do not. The ghosts of the Wolf Man, in Abraham and Torok's reading, are attendant in discourse, language, the order of knowledge.[32]

In a sense, the hauntological was always attendant with Derrida. The trace, différance, arche-writing are, to pun badly, nothing if not not-existent. All words carry with them that which they are not; this was, after all, Saussure's original insight. So it is that life carries with it things that are *not*: the ghosts of the dead, of possible futures not realised, pasts that could have been. Every decision is a renunciation, and the path renounced still in some sense exists, commenting on the choice taken.

Derrida is not indulging in mysticism, although he is more than happy to draw on mystic language. To take a solid example, there are, as we know, more people living on earth now than ever before, but there are also more dead. Thus the world we are thrown into by our birth carries these dead with it. Also, we are thrown into history; the laws of our country, for instance, were originally codified by people long dead. In fact, most things we engage with are inventions of dead people, and films and television, music and radio, philosophies and cultural practices bring the dead to us without their cessation being an issue. Sometimes we encounter the dead up close, as Derrida did with his brother, dead before his own birth, for whom Jackie felt himself a substitute, a supplement. 'One must stop believing that the dead are just the departed and that the departed do nothing. One must stop pretending to know what is meant by "to die" and especially by "dying". One has, then, to talk about spectrality.'[33] Philosophy has busied itself, in the main, with existents; ontology is a sort of mathematics of objects, while simultaneously generating incorporeal transcendental signifieds – Truth, Ideas, Forms. And it has done so while ignoring the ghosts that are absolutely proximal, leaving them to religion and poetry.

Derrida's fascination with Freud at this point is of a piece. Freud is the great writer of secrets and ghosts – what is the unconscious if not a repository of them, what is neurosis if not a haunting by secrets and ghosts that will not stay buried? At the same time, the number of ghosts in Derrida's own life was increasing; Abraham himself died before the book was published, another ghostly presence.

The Wolf Man's Magic Word was popular with Lacanians, which infuriated Lacan himself. He saw it, essentially, as a land grab and responded with all guns blazing. What 'surprised him most' was 'someone I didn't know … I think he's in analysis to tell the truth… a certain Jacques Derrida' who has written 'an absolutely fervent, enthusiastic preface in which I can perceive a throbbing which is linked – I don't know which of the two analysts he is dealing with – what is certain that he couples them … I don't think this book, or this preface is in very good taste.'[34]

It was a breach that never really healed, with Lacan's death in 1981 forestalling any rapprochement. But ten years later Derrida was to deliver a paper titled 'For the Love of Lacan', which explored, in generous terms, Lacan's influence on his own work. At Baltimore, Derrida noted, Lacan had wondered what people would say about him after his death, a ghostly future, and here was Derrida doing the talking, about a man who was now a ghost.

What will I not have said today! But if I had said that we loved each other very much, Lacan and I, and thus we promised each other very much, and that this was for me a good thing in this life, would I have been in the truth? Stephen Melville said that the promise always risked being also a threat. That's true. But I would always prefer to prefer the promise.[35]

Still, the rumour put about by Lacan that Derrida was in analysis, while at times amusing Derrida, at times frustrated him too. The rumour would get a mention in his next major work, his most personal yet, and one which involved the telling of a secret.

This secret was, compared to the elevated ones he was discussing in his philosophical works, banal. In 1972 Derrida had started an affair with twenty-seven-year-old Sylviane Agacinski, who had attended his seminars in 1970 with her then boyfriend, the writer Jean-Noël Vuarnet. The affair started shortly before the Nietzsche conference at Cerisy, and the opening of *Spurs* quotes a letter by Nietzsche which surely had a coded meaning for Derrida and his lover: 'At last my little envelope is ready for you, at last you hear from me again, after it must have seemed I had sunk into a dead silence ...'[36]

Agacinski was to be one of the strong, intellectual women to whom Derrida was drawn – her first book in 1977 was *Aparte: Conceptions and Deaths of Søren Kierkegaard*, and she would go on to publish several volumes on such topics as the question of the other, modernity, Ibsen and Strindberg and the politics of architecture.

But it was in the field of sexual difference that she made her name, with books such as *Metaphysics of the Sexes* (2005), *Women Between Sex and Gender* (2012) and, perhaps her most controversial work, *Gender Policy, Gender and Parity* (1998), in which she argues that differences between the genders were to be acknowledged and 'parity' sought, rather than 'equality', which was a meaningless concept within the context.

This was not simply a theoretical position. By 1998 she was directly involved in politics – in 1983 she met future prime minister Lionel Jospin at a party, and they married in 1994. In 1999, she was one of the originators of the Parité amendment that forced political parties to present 50 per cent female candidates or lose a corresponding share of their campaign funding. During Jospin's presidential bid, his wife's secret relationship with Derrida became front-page news, to the latter's dismay.

How secret Derrida's relationship with Agacinski was at the time is a mystery. They avoided being seen together, but it seems many of their colleagues were aware, and Derrida's sons were later to say they had some knowledge of it, implying Marguerite herself knew too. In fact, Marguerite was to intervene decisively in 1986. In 1978 Agacinski had aborted a child; in 1984 she chose to see another pregnancy with Derrida to term. Their son, Daniel Agacinski, was born on 18 June 1984. By then the affair was over, but Marguerite persuaded her husband to acknowledge the child as his. Derrida saw Daniel only once, accidentally bumping into him at an airport in 1994, a young boy with his aunt Sophie whom Derrida recognised.[37]

Back in 1980 the relationship was in the midst of the frantic stage which characterises any affair. How much sympathy one musters for Derrida's predicament is a personal choice, but it did yield one of his most fascinating works. *The Post Card: From Socrates to Freud and Beyond*, as the name suggests, is written in the form of postcards, or *envois*, sent by a man to his lover. The postcard form fascinated Derrida; here was a (secret) correspondence hiding in plain sight.

The idea had come to him in an episode recounted in the book. On visiting Oxford in 1977, his friends Jonathan Culler and Cynthia Chase gave him a postcard, depicting Socrates seated at a desk, taking dictation from Plato, who stands behind him. This reversal of the historical relationship between the two, and all its disruptive metaphysical implications, became an obsession for Derrida (the 'Derrida' of *The Post Card* anyway, although here more than ever the distinction may be paper thin), and became cleaved to the obsessive nature of the affair he was having with his 'Mistress of the equivocal'.[38] These *envois* (sendings) create a psychosexual web or matrix, in which the familiar themes of Derrida jostle with the newly minted.

> The card immediately seemed to me, how to put it, obscene ...
> For the moment, myself, I tell you that I see Plato getting an
> erection in Socrates' back and see the insane hubris of his prick,
> an interminable, disproportionate erection ... slowly sliding, still

warm, under Socrates' right leg ... Imagine the day, when we will be able to send sperm by post card. [... and finally, Plato] wants to emit ... to sow the entire earth, to send the same fertile card to everyone.[39]

The book does seem painfully autobiographical. Spivak had noted the autobiographical elements in *Glas*, all the derivatives of Derrida's name 'scattered [disseminated?] all over the pages', so that 'I can read *Glas* as a fiction of Derrida's proper name turning into a thing ... crypting the signature so that it becomes impossible to spell it out'.[40] But here there is both scattering and bringing together. He retells the story of his mother playing cards during his birth; of his expulsion from school: 'Is it not for this reason that I have for ever ensconced myself in it in order to provoke them to it and to give them the most urgent wish, always at the limit, to expel me again?';[41] his melancholy over his own philosophical position – 'it is so sad, to be right I mean';[42] his guilt – 'Literature has always appeared unacceptable to me, a scandal, the moral fault par excellence, and like a postcard seeking to pass itself off as something else';[43] and his ambiguous relationship to his writings – 'I have published a lot, but there is someone in me, I can't quite identify him, who still hopes never to have done it.'[44] He also gently mocks the analytical philosophers of the English tradition: 'I adore these theorizations, often Oxonian moreover, their extraordinary and necessary subtlety, as much as their imperturbable ingenuity, psychoanalytically speaking: they will always be confident in the law of quotation marks.'[45]

He also offers what may be read as the pithiest statements he would ever make about his philosophical aims – 'I want to reread the entire *corpus platonicum* and to settle into it as if into a very refined brothel, with confessionals and peepholes everywhere, mysteries without the slightest vulgarity' – and his philosophical method: 'like a little boy in his playpen, with his construction toys. That I spend the clearest part of my time taking them to pieces and throwing them overboard changes nothing essential in the matter.'[46]

His depression at the time was deep, and while it is in the nature of notebooks to be more morbid than their author, his during this period seem to reflect a state of real crisis – unable to write (a first), consumed with guilt about the affair and exhausted by the quiddities of maintaining it. It was a time of furtive meetings and letters. This – as so many personal things were destined to do – found expression in his work, in particular the postal effect, this failure of language to arrive at its proper destination (and the failure of a text to inhabit a singular meaning). Derrida coined the neologism *destinerrance* for this effect, and presented it as a structural aspect of, in particular, psychoanalysis.

Thus the second half of the book contains three articles on Freud and Lacan – the first of which, 'Speculations of Freud', is an extended commentary on *Beyond the Pleasure Principle* and takes Freud's encounter with 'The Mystic Writing Pad' as an encounter with hauntology. Punning on secular imagery, Derrida here links the Freudian psyche to Plato's conception of the *khôra*, from the dialogue of Timaeus, in which the myth of the creation of the world is given. Reminiscent of Derrida's trace and, of course, Kristeva's *chora*, *khôra* is the space 'logically' prior to the division of the sensible and the intelligible that inaugurates the world (and metaphysics). It is both prior to and critiques spatiotemporality. This territory outside the city proper, *khôra*

> 'means': place occupied by someone, country, inhabited place, marked place, rank, post, assigned position, territory, or region. And in fact, khôra will always already be occupied, invested, even as a general place, and even when it is distinguished from everything that takes place in it. Whence the difficulty – we shall come to it – of treating it as an empty or geometric space.[47]

The Post Card was published in the winter of 1980, causing unease among his friends and family, but receiving generally enthusiastic reviews, albeit fewer than he was used to. The reaction of Sylviane Agacinski, or indeed Marguerite Derrida, is not known.

The air of melancholy deepened in March with the accidental death of Roland Barthes. Barthes had championed Derrida from the beginning and perhaps of all the 'structuralists' of the time was both the first to absorb Derrida's theoretical challenge. He was the one whose thought changed most under its influence. But it was another death soon after which was to have the most dramatic effect.

At 7 a.m. on Sunday the 16th of November 1980, the doctor at the École normale supérieure, Pierre Etienne, was awakened by a knock on the door. Outside was Louis Althusser, 'extremely agitated'. 'Pierre, come and see, I think I've killed Hélène.' Althusser and his wife lived on the campus, and Dr Etienne went, in his dressing gown, straight to their bedroom, as Althusser kept repeating, 'I've killed Hélène, what comes next?' Hélène was at the foot of the bed, dead.

Dr Etienne made two calls, one to the police, and one to the Sainte-Anne hospital, a sanitorium, to have Althusser committed. Althusser had, in fact, recently been in the clinic for a number of months, only to return to the ENS a few days before. The ambulance arrived ten minutes before the police.

In his memoir, *The Future Lasts a Long Time*, written five years later and only published in 1992, two years after his death, Althusser opens with his 'precise memory of those events, engraved on my mind through all the suffering.' He recalls Hélène resting on the bed, and that he was 'massaging her neck ... I had learnt the technique as a prisoner-of-war.' But 'I was massaging the front of her neck ... the muscles in my forearms began to feel very tired.' Hélène, he noticed, was just staring at the ceiling. Suddenly he was 'terror-struck ... I had seen dead bodies, of course, but never in my life looked into the face of someone who had been strangled.'[48]

He had killed Hélène. For many, what came next was a scandal. Rather than being taken to a police station, Althusser was taken to the hospital and placed in an isolation ward. The police initially found no evidence of strangulation; it was the post-mortem a few days later which revealed her broken windpipe. The day after the murder an examining magistrate visited Althusser to charge him with 'voluntary homicide'. Althusser, however, was in a state of 'total mental collapse' and the hospital did not allow the magistrate to see him. Three psychiatrists were then appointed by the state, and judged him unfit to stand trial. Two months later the magistrate declared that there would be no prosecution – Althusser was declared 'non-lieu' (no grounds to prosecute), under Article 64 of the French Penal Code, based on the assessment of the psychiatrist that he had committed the murder 'in the course of an iatrogenic hallucinatory episode complicated by melancholic depression',where 'iatrogenic' means a hallucination brought on by his treatment, or his medication.[49]

There was uproar both at the time of the murder and at the time of the judgment. The right-wing press was particularly virulent, going to town on the reputation of this Marxist philosopher and eminent member of the Communist Party. 'How dare the paragons of virtue who protest against inequalities and class justice attempt to organise this inequality for their own benefit?' asked Le Quotidien de Paris, which in its editorial turned its guns on Althusser's colleagues, neatly conflating their specific reactions with a general suspicion of their obscure writing:

> So many precautions, Messieurs, so many reticences, so many pious lies, so many pens dipped repeatedly in the inkwell until they no longer come out again, so many friendships, to the point of complicity, so many silences or half-silences, some stemming from self-censorship, others, in all probability, from political or social censorship.[50]

The polemics continued when Article 64 was invoked, despite the Procureur de la République, the French Attorney General, pointing out that the procedure was unexceptional.

Derrida was hit hard – Althusser had been a huge part of his life, and they had exchanged the role of father figure between them more than once. Utterly different philosophers, with utterly contrasting philosophies, they had nonetheless never quarrelled, in life or in print. It was often the work of those closest to him that Derrida felt compelled to deconstruct, but not Althusser's.

There was, no doubt, an element of protectiveness in this. Althusser was always a fragile figure, his long bouts in the sanitorium rounded by disturbing episodes and an inability to work. Overall, his output was small – even the great books of the mid-sixties were short, essayistic. Douglas Johnson, in the introduction to the English version of *The Future Lasts a Long Time*, recalls visiting his office and seeing the same papers strewn on the floor from year to year, going yellow. Derrida, in failing to engage with his work, was in some sense doing him a service.

Derrida's despair was heightened when the press made him the chief representative of the cohort of intellectuals who they alleged had formed a barrier around Althusser. 'Crushed by despair, Jacques Derrida, loyalest of the loyal, refused to make any comment.'[51] He had indeed taken charge of many of the legal and administrative tasks, visiting Althusser often and even taking him back to Ris-Orangis on the occasions that he was allowed out. He also arranged for Althusser to be transferred to another clinic when Sainte-Anne's proved inadequate for his needs. As was often the case with Derrida, the scrupulousness of friendship trumped other considerations.

The rights and wrongs of the affair are difficult to untangle. Any retelling of the facts leading up to the event, of the powerful psychosexual, even Oedipal, relationship between the Althussers, risks making the victim culpable and the perpetrator guiltless, a risk which *The Future Lasts a Long Time* does not avoid. As Richard Seymour puts it, 'It is a shame that, in the discussion of the murder, [Hélène] Rytman hardly ever appears as a woman with qualities'.[52]

Hélène Althusser, née Rytman, had fought in the Resistance as a communist militant. She too suffered from manic depression, although was apparently more robust than her husband. His dependence on her was absolute; he had, before meeting her, been almost phobic about women. Althusser's mother had named him after the dead lover whose brother she married in the Mediterranean tradition, and she treated her son like a husband.

He claimed never to have masturbated until he was twenty-seven, that is, not until after his five years as a POW. Hélène had broken through all of that, but at the cost of having to take on, as we might say, baggage:

> She loved me as a mother loves a child ... and at the same time like a good father in that she introduced me ... to the real world, that vast arena I had never been able to enter ... Through her desire for me she also initiated me ... into my role as a man, into my masculinity. She loved me as a woman loves a man![53]

In addition, Althusser's philosophy, perched on the precipice of the self, was, like Derrida's (and as Derrida claimed, like all philosophies), a deeply personal expression. He fed it, and it fed him. A philosophy like Althusser's, where all our subjectivity is the creation of malign powers, and there is no way out of the trap of ideology, is a strong liquor, and Althusser's defences were paper thin.

None of this leads to murder, but all of this complicates it. While there is only one victim here, Althusser claimed he felt cheated that he was never charged. He was never, therefore, able to take responsibility for his actions. In a sense he died the night Hélène did, and was left a ghost. After his release in 1983 he lived by himself in the north of Paris, sending the occasional letter to the press, writing his memoirs. Occasionally he walked the streets yelling at passersby, 'Je suis le grand Althusser!' He died in hospital in 1990.

While the actions of Derrida and other colleagues such as Étienne Balibar and Régis Debray have been questioned, these were not questions, rightly or wrongly, they felt they had to ask themselves. They came to the aid of a friend, and at no time, it would seem, attempted to intercede in the legal proceedings. Nowadays, they might have been more explicit about their sympathy for the victim, but their acts were those of friendship, a quality Derrida was to hold in greater esteem than just about any other, and which he would soon make the subject of one of his books, and one of the key terms in his work on ethics, to which he turned in the 1990s. That he was now famous added to the pressure, but it was not his central concern. It did mean, however, that everything he did, and every pronouncement, was under the microscope like never before.

8

Here Comes Everybody

There is no one, single deconstruction. Were there only one, were it homogeneous, it would not be inherently either conservative or revolutionary, or determinable within the code of such oppositions. That is precisely what gets on everyone's nerves.

– Limited Inc

The world is going very badly.

– Specters of Marx

'I'm in love with a Jacques Derrida/Read a page and know what I need to/Take apart my baby's heart.' While Scritti Politti's Green Gartside was never afraid to trade in lyrical obscurities, the eponymous hero of the song 'Jacques Derrida' would have been familiar to most listeners in 1982. It is hard to exaggerate how present the magus of non-presence was in the popular culture of the 1980s and '90s. As the field of 'cultural studies' spread throughout the world, so did the name of Derrida, who seemed to bring all the disparate disciplines together, not only to have an opinion on them but to find new ways of seeing them. The obscure philosophy assistant of 1965 had become an international superstar. France has generally had a celebrity philosopher, embraced by the world, regenerating like Doctor Who. Sartre had died in April 1980, and this new iteration, with his pipe, his shock of white hair and his open-necked shirt, seemed a hip new one invented especially for Generation X.

An easy misreading of Derrida (or a non-reading more likely) by both those 'for' and 'against' was to take his disavowal of transcendental signifiers for the sort of ironic detachment that Gen X traded in. If, as Jean Francois Lyotard had put it, postmodernism was a suspicion of grand narratives, where one 'waged war on totalities', this fit perfectly with the temper of the times, and Derrida was taken to represent postmodernism.[1] And why not? This was a man who paused what he called the 'theatrical genre of the interview'[2] to point out the artificiality of the construct, and who answered perfectly straightforward questions with:

> I should not have to reply right away to such fully elaborated and serious questions – and by improvising no less. Our agreement for this exchange is that I should try to improvise a response even when I am not sure that I can do so adequately. Well, I am sure that in a few sentences I will not be able to meet the demands of a question whose elaborations and presuppositions are of such a vast scope. Nevertheless, I'll take my chances with an answer.[3]

For a generation whose relationship with media was in the first stages of dissociation, this was heady stuff.

There is nothing, of course, wrong with any of this – philosophy in popular culture, even high popular culture, is different from philosophy in the academy. To wish for anything different is a fallacy. For this generation, seeing Madonna dry her armpits with the hand-dryer in a bathroom sent as potent a feminist message as reams of theory, and may have empowered more women.

Derrida himself – like Madonna – had feminist cred, as well as postcolonial cred, and deservedly so. The enthusiasm with which his theories were embraced by French feminists, whether they agreed with them wholeheartedly or not, was shared around the world. He also had media cred. He had avoided being photographed until the 1970s, but suddenly his image was everywhere; T-shirts appeared emblazoned with cartoon Derridas and slogans such as 'There is nothing outside the text', 'I always dream of a pen that would be a syringe', 'There is no simple answer to such a question' and 'I have nothing to say about love'. The difficulty of reading him was negotiated by not doing so – slogans would do.

Music was composed about him, plays were written, he was asked to help design buildings and *Glas* was turned into a series of paintings by the Italian painter Valerio Adami. Woody Allen made a film called *Deconstructing Harry*. Derrida was present even when he was not: anything postmodern, or at least ironically hip, was ascribed to his influence. It is hard not to smile, but feel some sympathy – empathy even – for the Australian television interviewer who asked him about *Seinfeld*: 'Jerry Seinfeld made this sitcom, about a group of people living together. Everything is about irony, and parody, and what you do with your kitchen cupboard is imbued with as much feeling or thought as whether someone believes in God if you like. Do you see anything in that?' To which a clearly baffled Derrida answers, 'Deconstruction the way I understand it doesn't produce a sitcom and if the people who watch it think that deconstruction is this, the only advice I have to give them is stop watching the sitcom, do your homework and read.'[4]

In 1973 David Allison had produced the first major translation into English of Derrida, *Speech and Phenomena*, followed by the essay 'Différance', with which it was paired. *Writing and Difference* appeared in 1978, translated by Johns Hopkins student and future psychoanalyst Alan Bass, its jagged black-and-yellow cover, diagonal chapter headings and marginal epigraphs immediately becoming familiar on university campuses across the English-speaking world. Bass had worked intensely on the project for years at the New York Public Library, checking each reference meticulously. 'When there was a quotation from Leibniz's *Monadology*, I read the whole work.'[5]

Derrida's relationship with his English translators was often an intense one. Some, like Geoffrey Bennington and Peggy Kamuf, became as much collaborators as translators. His works were often translated by novices who had become devotees of deconstruction, and yet the quality of the translations is extraordinary, particularly given the difficulty of the source material, with its conscious use of puns, wordplay and neologisms.

Perhaps the most miraculous translation is *Of Grammatology* by Gayatri Chakravorty Spivak, for whom neither French nor English was a first language. Indian born, and only twenty-five at the time, Spivak was an assistant professor at the University of Iowa and, although Paul de Man had advised on her dissertation about W. B. Yeats, she had no idea who Derrida was when she ordered his book. 'I was trying to keep myself intellectually clued in. So I would order books from the catalogue which looked unusual enough that I should read, so that's how I ordered the book.' She found the work extraordinary:

> This was before the internet, so nobody was telling me any-thing about Derrida. My teacher had not met Derrida when I left Cornell, so I truly didn't know who he was. So I thought, 'Well, I'm a smart young foreign woman, and here's an unknown author. Nobody's going to give me a contract for a book on him, so why don't I try to translate him?' And I had heard at a cock-tail party that the University of Massachusetts Press was doing translations, so I wrote them a very innocent query letter in late 1967 or early 1968. They told me later that they found my query letter so brave and sweet that they thought they should give me a chance. [Laughs.] It's really ridiculous, but there it was.[6]

She had also asked to write a 'monograph-length' introduc-tion, which remains a classic account and perhaps more read than the book itself. The pair did not meet until 1971 – she had seen no photographs and didn't realise they were in the same room together. 'When he came up to me and said, in French, "*Je m'appelle Jacques Derrida*," I almost died.'[7]

Derrida's influence inside the academy grew exponentially. Aside from philosophy and literature, areas as diverse as cinema studies, gender studies and postcolonialism and, outside the humanities, politics and law, were all explicitly impacted by his methods. Derrida had, on a number of occasions, drawn attention to the parasitical nature of deconstruction. It is not something imposed from outside, rather it exists within a text, working away both to produce and complicate meaning. It is also parasitical in its adaptability to new hosts, and in the 1980s it moved through academic disciplines, challenging their founding notions and calling into question their grand statements.

In the UK, the growing interdisciplinary field of Cultural Studies received new impetus from deconstruction. A product of 1950s British Marxism, its exploration of how cultural practices, high and low, generated social phenomena, from class to gender to ideology to ethnicity, was ripe for the sort of radical examination which Derrida enabled.

Founded in Birmingham in 1964 by Richard Hoggart, author of *The Uses of Literacy*, the Centre for Contemporary Cultural Studies (CCCS) had, under the directorship of Stuart Hall, received new inspiration in attempting to grapple with the question of why huge portions of the population were switching allegiance from the left to Margaret Thatcher, whose policies were instrumental in causing the very decline that had left them devastated. With Althusser's theories on base and superstructure already incorporated, the Birmingham School, through its own and wider efforts, made questions of race, gender and sexual orientation central to their studies. Rather than being made up of immutable categories, they contained constructs – which could therefore be deconstructed.

Hall's 1981 essay 'Notes on Deconstructing "The Popular"' is representative of the trend in the way it analyses what we might define as 'popular culture' ('those forms and activities which have their roots in the social and material conditions of particular classes ... embodied in popular traditions and practices'): in its complicating of the binary opposition of 'high' culture and 'low', alternative and popular ('We tend to think of cultural forms as whole and coherent ... [but] this year's radical symbol or slogan will be neutralized into next year's fashion'); and in its analysis of the sort of semiotic shifts Derrida identified as being intrinsic to all language and communication ('Not only is there no intrinsic guarantee within the cultural sign or form itself, there is no guarantee that, because at one time it was linked with a pertinent struggle, it will always be a living expression of a class').[8]

The essay is also representative in that the word deconstruction

itself had begun to shift in meaning, loosened from the strict philosophical technique first proposed by Derrida, into something
more broad and labile. The 'deconstruction of popular culture'
in Hall's fashioning is more a 'taking apart' than an analysis of
any metaphysics of presence. The tools of deconstruction were
becoming blunter, but effective in ways that Derrida could not
have predicted.

The English novelist Candida Clark captures a sense of his
star power in an article about seeing him at Cambridge in 1992.

It certainly struck me that way, that day in autumn, or spring –
or was it a particularly cool summer? – when Derrida came to
talk to whoever cared to hear him in Cambridge. Many stayed
away; many turned up simply to bask in the thrill of the forbidden. That kind of hullabaloo was a definite ruck in the texture
of Cambridge life, and his visit had the aura of celebrity about
it, too. Non-philosophers came, and were made nervous by the
excitement: had they done the wrong degree? Did this kind of
thing happen all the time over in the philosophy faculty? ...
Derrida, in making his case for evidence-as-witness, was soft-
spoken, his gestures economical, and he was not a tall man,
though his hair was, it's true, startling, a vivid mop of light – the
kind of whiteness that often comes overnight, after a profound
emotional shock. His argument seemed ethereal: not just hard to
catch hold of, but liable to go anywhere, pass through walls. Its
ghostliness was an aspect of its modernity: it might have been
an offshoot of cybernetics; it was entirely relevant, and to the
entire business of thinking, too, in whatever faculty – and it was
this, I suppose, that certain quarters found alarming. There was
just that whiff of mortality about it: if they followed this line of
argument, where might it lead? It was emotional.[9]

The apotheosis, although far from the denouement, was perhaps
the 1983 film *Ghost Dance*. Derrida plays himself – can one say
badly? – in a film dominated by two women, played by Leonie
Mellinger and Pascale Ogier, wandering around London and
Paris, theorising earnestly about ghosts and cinema, and their

philosophical ideas. Twice we encounter our hero, once in a café (he asks Pascale about her ideas; she replies, 'The idea behind my idea is I have no idea' – he looks on sympathetically), and once in his office where he speaks portentously to them about the topic of the film, baffling as it is. At one point he is interrupted by the telephone and stops being 'Jacques Derrida' to be Jacques Derrida. *Très* pomo.

For all its nonsense, the film did have a lasting effect on Derrida. In 1984, a year after the film was released, Pascale Ogier died of a drug-related heart attack. Derrida recalled that, after his own improvised section, the script had him ask her if she believed in ghosts, as she had asked him at the start of the scene. It took thirty takes – thirty times of him asking, and each time she replied, 'Yes, now I do, yes.' Watching the film a few years later in Texas, seeing the 'dead woman's face on screen', he said he had the 'unnerving experience of the return of her spectre, the spectre of her spectre, coming back to say ... Yes, believe me, I believe in ghosts.'[10] That, says Derrida, 'is why the experience of seeing a film is so rich. It lets one see new spectres appear while remembering (and then projecting in turn onto the screen) the ghosts haunting films already seen.'[11]

It was odd interventions into popular culture like this that, while adding to Derrida's cachet outside the academy, was increasingly raising hackles inside it. Derrida seemed to be at the head of an army of French theorists, gleefully relativising their way through all the shibboleths of philosophy; deconstruction, it turns out, *was* destruction, after all. That its theories were being reduced to slogans fuelled this reaction; that the texts from which they were garnered seemed impenetrable saved his critics the bother of reading them.

Meanwhile, much of the seventies and early eighties was taken up for Derrida in generating work, establishing his ENS position, and deputising where necessary for Althusser. On top of his teaching work he became an active and ongoing advocate for the Groupe de recherches sur l'enseignement philosophique (GREPH) (Sarah Kofman was also a member), which mobilised in opposition to the Giscard government's plans to 'rational-ise' the teaching of philosophy. GREPH championed continued teaching of philosophy at secondary school, which Giscard's reforms threatened, and Derrida wrote a number of polemics in support, many of which were later to appear as the collection *Who's Afraid of Philosophy?: Right to Philosophy 1*. In them we see the germ of later deconstructive texts about academies, archives and institutions. To those who would later demonise Derrida as an anti-philosopher, these texts stand as a monument to his devotion to the discipline and to rigour in its teaching. As he later noted, 'So you see, at the same time I am a very conserva-tive person. I love institutions.'[12]

The movement had been given greater impetus by the arrival of a group of self-styled 'New Philosophers' who emerged in 1976. Led by Bernard-Henri Lévy, who came to be known as BHL, and including in their number names such as André Glucksmann and Alain Finkielkraut, the *nouveaux philosophes* were united by their split from Marxism, having been influenced by Solz-henitsyn's *Gulag Archipelago*, which documented the horrors of the Soviet Union. Although they denied being right-wing, each of them would move that way across the political spectrum at various speeds. To Derrida, as to many others, they were united by their superficiality, representing a marketing concept as much as a philosophy. This was philosophy dumbed down to a series of media events and fake scandals.

When Derrida was part of a 1979 meeting of the Estates General to protest the change in philosophy teaching, the New Philosophers invaded the hall, asking, for instance, why the protest was about school reform, and not the Gulag. Derrida responded, 'Stop talking rubbish.'[13] BHL later claimed to have been expelled from the meeting after a scuffle but, as with so many of the New Philosophers' pronouncements, self-promotion seems to have trumped reality.

While the New Philosophers sought the attention of the French press, Derrida was getting it. In 1973 *Le Monde* featured a double-page spread on 'Jacques Derrida, the Deconstructor', noting the influence his work was already having outside of France, and the growing wave of Derrideanism. Derrida appeared as a cartoon, having forbidden any public photographs to appear, believing that they, particularly the headshot with books behind, or the upper body in the act of writing, fetishised the author. He also admitted to a narcissistic horror of seeing his own face, and the death effect it implied.[14] For a philosopher who later theorised and enacted philosophy as biography, let alone one who enjoyed worldwide fame, it was a position that could not be sustained. The Estates General meeting marked the first time his photograph appeared in a newspaper; subsequently his image proliferated around the world.

He also became involved in the first of what were to become a theme of his later career – international battles with other philosophers, particularly those from the analytic tradition. In many ways his dispute with John Searle, the American philosopher of language was not only the first such contretemps, it set out the terms on which later battles would be fought.

In 1969, Searle, then forty-seven, published his first major work, *Speech Acts*. It built on the work of his teacher, John L. Austin, whose 1962 text *How to Do Things with Words* had introduced the concept of 'performatives' – words and phrases which 'do' things, rather than simply denote or describe things. Austin was arguing against the model of language which had reached its (logical) conclusion with the logical positivists, that the only meaningful statements are those that describe a state of affairs which can be either verified or proved false, such as 'The cat is on the mat.'

While these are a part of language, they are not the whole of it, as there are statements that are neither true nor false, but are still meaningful. These 'performatives' carry out an action – 'I declare you man and wife', 'I name this ship Queen Victoria', 'I bet you £100 my horse will win.' Promising, naming, betting, agreeing, swearing, declaring, ordering, predicting, warning, insisting, declaring or refusing are all meaningful speech acts, but neither true nor false.

Having identified these 'illocutionary' acts, Austin then analyses in what way they are valid, which is to say, in what cases do they fail? For instance, declaring a couple man and wife is not, for Austin, a valid illocutionary act if, for instance, I am not legally authorised to do so, or I am but the circumstances are not right (a priest cannot just go up to two people and legally declare it), if I don't speak English and thus don't know what I am saying, if one of them is already married or if the sentence is in a poem, play or novel.

Austin calls these invalid performative acts 'infelicities' and explores a number of strategies regarding how they may be identified and/or avoided. Ultimately he is forced to propose a sort of ideal situation, where the context of the utterance is correct and unambiguous (not on a stage then), and the intention of the speaker is in earnest (not a joke, or in a poem). Speech acts which fail to meet these criteria are, for Austin, 'parasitic'.[15]

Searle takes up this claim, arguing that it is the intention of the speaker which separates the normal from the parasitic. He then offers rules for performing 'normal speech acts', their necessary and sufficient conditions. That this requires an idealisation of the situation, and therefore the concept is something he admits to – in his analysis of 'promising' he notes, 'I am ignoring marginal, fringe, and partially defective promises.'[16] This is anathema to Derrida's view on language, and in his 1972 text 'Signature Event Context' he carries out an extensive analysis of both Austin's and Searle's positions.

For Derrida, Austin's initial insight is powerful and correct, a move away from language as logic towards language as rhetoric. However, the argument that the context of a performative can be successfully demarcated (be 'exhaustively determinable'), and, more importantly, that the intention of the utterance can ever be transparent (to the speaker, let alone anyone else) is, for Derrida, a false construction, relying on notions such as a centred (knowing) self, a (fully) comprehensible set of speech structures, and the idea that an uttered sentence has a particular meaning which permanently inheres, and is available to all hearers (and readers).[17]

Austin and Searle are forced to declare all sentences which do not meet this criteria 'parasitic', which basically rules out all literature, as well as every lie, misunderstanding or joke, and to assert, *pace* for instance psychoanalysis, that I as a speaker have complete and incontrovertible access to my intentions, which I can then transfer wholesale to another human being, who will potentially understand them completely. In fact, Derrida argues, Austin and Searle are forced to go further than this. They exclude *all writing* from normal discourse. Writing, by its very nature, both breaks with its context and, as evidenced by the endless attacks on it from Socrates to Rousseau and beyond, moves away from the agent who gave it utterance.

In 'Signature Event Context' Derrida introduces what will become a key term in his thinking – iterability. It is a structural necessity of writing that it can function without the writer being present – you can read this book without, thankfully perhaps for both of us, me being there with you, as nice as we both may be. Someone else may read this book long after I am dead. The meaningfulness or otherwise of the text is not contingent on my presence, or even my continuing existence. It is the structural necessity of writing that it is repeatable in different contexts, today, tomorrow, in a hundred years' time. 'A writing that was not structurally legible – iterable – beyond the death of the addressee would not be writing.'[18]

And for Derrida it is writing that, in fact, grounds speech, by enabling the transfer of words and therefore concepts. All language is iterable, any linguistic expression must be capable of being repeated, which introduces the possibility, or even the inevitability, of a deviation from its 'intended meaning' (supposing for the moment one could be assigned). This does not render utterances invalid or unmeaningful, as they all have significance within whatever contexts they find themselves. 'Infelicities' in fact constitute the very structure of language, as every statement can escape its context. A corruption that is always possible cannot be an extrinsic or accidental property of something – the clue is in the word 'always'. The difference between the normal and the parasitic cannot be maintained.

Thus,

the theoretician of speech acts will have to get used to the idea that, knowingly or not, willingly or not, both his treatment of things and the things themselves are marked in advance by the possibility of fiction, either as the iterability of acts or as the system of conventionality.[19]

Derrida also raises the issue of 'citationality'. All communication can be taken from its context by being quoted – again this is a structural necessity of language, 'the possibility of extraction and citational grafting belongs to the structure of every mark, spoken or written.'[20] For Derrida, Austin's (and Searle's) claims for 'normal speech acts' cannot incorporate this.

'Signature Event Context' was translated into English in 1977, in the first issue of the journal *Glyph*, and Searle's response the same year was swift and vicious. His paper 'Reiterating the Differences: A Reply to Derrida' begins in a mode of contempt from which it seldom attempts to rouse itself:

> It would be a mistake, I think, to regard Derrida's discussion of Austin as a confrontation between two prominent philosophical traditions. This is not so much because Derrida has failed to discuss the central theses in Austin's theory of language, but rather because he has misstated Austin's position at several crucial points, as I shall attempt to show, and thus the confrontation never quite takes place.[21]

Searle then accuses Derrida of having misunderstood and misrepresented Austin's (and, by implication, his own) work. He begins by focusing on Derrida's argument which sees iterability as fundamental to writing. Searle's first move is an odd one – he argues that writing is not unique in this, it is the same for speech. This is, of course, exactly what Derrida argued: that the speech/writing distinction is unsustainable.

Furthermore, argues Searle, what Derrida calls iterability is in fact, simply, permanence. The fact that my words can be read after my death shows only that they are permanent. *This* is what, for Searle, distinguishes writing from speech. Derrida would not, and does not, argue with this – yes, written words have a permanence. However, this is not a *necessary* aspect of writing, whereas iterability, the possibility of my absence, and the possibility of my communicating with an absent receiver (you), is.

Here Searle again makes an odd manoeuvre. Yes, 'writing makes it possible to communicate with an absent receiver, but it is not necessary for the receiver to be absent.' He then gives two examples of writing occurring in the presence of a receiver – me making a shopping list for myself, or me passing a note to a companion 'during a concert or lecture' (one notes the world in which Searle's missives reside).[22]

As Derrida points out, the putative presence of the receiver does not alter the fact that writing assumes the possibility of their absence. I would not bother, for instance, writing a shopping list if the 'I' that writes it was the same as the 'I' that opens it in the shopping aisle with my total list of gustatory needs and desires as present and complete as they were as I sat at the kitchen table. I wrote the list to an absent future self. And if I write a note to be passed to my neighbour between movements at a concert, the meaning of the note is not obliterated if they have gone to the loo. In fact, I can leave it on the chair and it will still be meaningful when they get back.

Regarding intentionality, Searle argues that when we read the words such as 'On the twentieth of September 1793 I set out on a journey from London to Oxford' we can say with total confidence, 'The author intended to make a statement to the effect that on the twentieth of September 1793, he set out on a journey from London to Oxford,' even if the author is dead.[23]

This sentence is, of course, ripe for deconstruction. In this novel, who is speaking? The author? The character? What assumptions are contained in the sentence? Searle immediately assumes it is a 'he' (the author, the character). Why does Searle assume that? What are his assumptions as related to the context in which he reads it, in which he repeats it, and how he relates it to his own cultural history? To take another example, why 'London to Oxford'? What does that tell us about the putative author, the possible character or, if the sentence has been made up by Searle to give as an example, his own cultural positioning, or that of the assumed reader? London to Oxford carries with it a whole different set of cultural assumptions than, say, 'Hull to Dagenham'. And, invoking 'citationality', could not this sentence be used in a cut-up poem, by a spy to show another spy he is the contact, or in an essay against Derrida as an example of the 'obvious' transparency of intention?

Finally, Searle argues that Austin's distinction between normal and parasitic discourse in analysing speech acts is not, as Derrida argues 'a matter of great moment', rather it is 'a matter of research strategy.' Austin strategically decides he had better not start his analysis 'with promises made by actors on stage' but with normal, everyday utterances.[24] Again, the objections to this are not hard to imagine – Derrida himself did not argue one should start with the theatrical or literary fiction either, but one cannot exclude such speech acts. They are, after all, a fairly standard part of discourse.

If Searle's article carries an air of condescension, Derrida's equally swift reply – it came out in the next issue of *Glyph*, again in 1977 – is one of unprecedented savagery, and makes for uncomfortable reading, even for his defenders. Derrida himself would later read it 'with a certain uneasiness', calling it 'not devoid of aggressivity'.[25]

Titled 'Limited Inc a b c ...', Derrida plays on the fact that Searle's article carries the signature 'Copyright © 1977 by John R. Searle.' Why, if Searle is saying things that are 'obviously true' would he be worried about copyright, which prevents the theft of ideas? Is this a business transaction? Is Searle a limited company? Or in French a *société à responsabilité limitée* – that is, an SARL, which Derrida snarkily calls Searle throughout.

In addition to the rebuttals above, Derrida sees in Searle's paper an attempt by the latter to replace the dead father Austin, a case of parricide even, evidenced by Searle's 'forgetting to mention' Derrida's own closeness to Austin's thought, as stated in 'Signature Event Context'.

Having thus introduced the Oedipal, Derrida riffs on his Freudian theme, pointing out that the axiomatics of speech act theory in both Austin and Searle must, insofar as they argue that all intentions must be conscious, exclude therefore the unconscious, must in fact treat the unconscious 'as the great Parasite of every ideal model of a speech act'.[26]

Bringing all of these threads together, Derrida focuses his attention on a sentence in Searle's paper, namely, 'There are two obstacles to understanding this rather obvious point, one implicit in Derrida, the other explicit.' Leaving aside the point under discussion where Searle says this (we shall; Derrida, like a dog with a bone, does not), the essay here appears to be arguing that there is a meaning *behind* Derrida's utterances, an *implicit* one. Something unconscious? Are, Derrida asks, 'Derrida's intentions' not transparent here?

Searle did not respond directly to the paper, and when, in 1988, Derrida published *Limited Inc*, collecting both 'Signature Event Context' and 'Limited Inc a b c ...' together, he refused permission for 'Reiterating the Differences' to be included. He did, however, fire one last salvo, the 1983 *New York Review of Books* article 'The World Turned Upside Down'.[27]

The essay is *echt* anti-deconstruction and inaugurates many of the tropes that would become part of a veritable cottage industry. Derrida and his followers are accused of obscurantism, obfuscation, banality, philosophical sloppiness, superficiality, breathtaking implausibility and a wilful ignorance of concepts basic to analytical philosophy. So obscure is Derrida, writes Searle, that he cannot even be misread, as this would imply that there is a clear argument that can be extracted.

Five years later, *Limited Inc* concludes with one final paper, 'Afterword: Toward An Ethic of Discussion'. In it, Derrida reflects for a final time on both the dispute and its tone. Yes, the tone of his response to Searle had been unconventional, 'I multiply statements, discursive gestures, forms of writing.'[28] But in doing so, Derrida was providing instances of speech acts which in themselves invalidate Searle's concept of 'normal'. In proposing that in serious and literal language 'sentences are precisely the realizations of the intentions' one is not, as Searle thinks, making a philosophically neutral statement. Rather 'it is tantamount to stating, in a normative or prescriptive manner, that toward which language ought to tend.'[29] Derrida would continue to deconstruct this philosophical manoeuvre throughout his work.

If the intervention of Derrida's theories, or approximations of them, into all areas of the academy was proving controversial, it was his embrace by literature departments which was seen as most threatening by those who saw his work as poisonous. As we have seen, a central plank of the Western metaphysical tradition was that literature and philosophy are different things. Plato had as a first order of business expelled the poets from his Republic – 'the poet is an imitator, and therefore, like all other imitators, he is thrice removed from the king and from the truth.'[30] Moreover, they corrupt the youth and their verse 'feeds and waters the passions instead of drying them up; she lets them rule, although they ought to be controlled, if mankind are ever to increase in happiness and virtue.'[31] In a well-ordered state, usefulness is the chief virtue, and Plato is good enough to suggest that if any poet wants to argue – in prose – that 'there is a use in poetry as well as a delight' then he might give them a listen.[32]

Derrida, of course, wishes to deconstruct the binary opposition philosophy/literature, and a great deal of his work, from the Introduction to *The Origin of Geometry*, to *Glas*, to *The Post Card*, attempts to do just that. That all language is metaphorical – there is no direct correspondence between it and the world, words aren't exact labels, sentence structure does not, *pace* early Wittgenstein, represent the structure of reality – means that philosophy is a series of metaphors as much as literature is.

He tackled the question of metaphor in philosophical discourse directly in his 1971 paper 'White Mythologies'. Taking language in its entirety, metaphor cannot be a singular entity, there can be only the plural 'metaphors':

> The word is written only in the plural. If there were only one possible metaphor, the dream at the heart of philosophy, if one could reduce their play to the circle of a family or group of metaphors,

that is, to one 'central', 'fundamental', 'principal' metaphor, there would be no more true metaphor but only, through the one true metaphor, the assured legibility of the proper.[33]

This singular metaphor would of course again be a transcendental signified, it would be Hegel's Absolute Knowledge.

The plurality of metaphor gives rise to texts, including philosophy. Each philosopher has their set of metaphors – the 'metaphorics proper to Descartes [for instance] – the ivy and the tree, the path, the house, the city, the machine, the foundation, the chain; the wax and the pen, dress and nudity, the ship, the clock, seeds and the magnet, the book, the stick ...'[34] We then take the metaphor for the concept. For the thing itself.

Metaphysics, built out of such metaphors, is 'the white mythology which reassembles and reflects the culture of the West: the white man takes his own mythology, Indo-European mythology, his own logos, that is, the mythos of his idiom, for the universal form that he still must wish to call Reason.'[35] As Christopher Norris puts it, Derrida, 'unpicks the elements of metaphor and other figurative devices at work in the texts of philosophy ... acting as a constant reminder of the ways in which language deflects or complicates the philosopher's project.'[36]

Literature, of course, trades in metaphors – hence the old joke, 'Okay poets, we get it, things are like other things', or in Derridean language, signifieds are like other signifieds. But literature does so knowingly, part of the art is to inhabit the artifice. No Leopold Bloom actually exists, circumambulates Dublin or meets Stephen Dedalus. There is no wine dark sea or swift footed Achilles. Whether there was a Trojan War or not does not affect the *Iliad* qua *Iliad*.

Derrida, obviously, did not see literature as having a secondary relationship to truth or reality. He wrote, 'My most constant interest, coming even before my philosophical interest I should say, if this is possible, has been directed towards literature, towards that writing which is called literary.'[37] He was always drawn to complex works. Unlike, say, Wittgenstein, who would spend his weekends watching B-movie Westerns, Derrida indulged in little 'down time' when it came to reading and writing. As he himself said, he rarely read for pleasure, except in the sense that his pleasure was to dig deep into the greatest of literature and seek to deconstruct it. 'Literature', he said in one interview, 'is the most interesting thing in the world, maybe more interesting than the world.'[38]

There was Joyce, obviously, and Proust, and later Shakespeare, whose work he would use in one of his more spectacular and brilliant interventions, *Specters of Marx*. Poetry was of particular importance, from his first 'lit crit' paper on Edmond Jabès, to Mallarmé (*Dissemination*), Francis Ponge (*Signsponge*) and particularly Paul Celan.

Derrida's 1992 paper on Celan, 'Che cos'è la poesia' – 'What [thing] is poetry', is a small masterpiece. The answer to 'what is poetry' is, argues Derrida, 'poetry', but how do we get there? He riffs on the idea of dictation – writing which puts 'knowledge' to one side. 'I am a dictation, pronounces poetry, learn me by heart, copy me down, guard and keep me, look out for me, look at me, dictated dictation [*dictée*], right before your eyes: soundtrack, wake, trail of light, photograph of the feast in mourning.'[39]

Celan holds a special place in Derrida's thinking. He was born Paul Antschel into a German-speaking Jewish family in Romania in 1920 and studied medicine in France (as a Jew he could not study in Romania or Vienna). Returning to Cernăuți in Romania to study literature, he was driven, like the rest of the Jewish population, into a ghetto, where he translated Shakespeare's Sonnets and began writing poetry before being forced into labour, which included burning Russian books. His parents were deported to a labour camp, his father dying of typhus, his mother subsequently shot for being too exhausted to work – facts he learned when he himself was deported to a camp.

Perhaps his most famous poem, 'Todesfuge' – 'Death Fugue' – was written in 1947, but it was not until the 1950s that he began to gain prominence. In 1955 he moved back to France, becoming a French citizen, and shortly after, became a lecturer in German at the ENS. Celan was as self-effacing, if one might use that loaded word casually for the moment, in his life as in his poetry. Derrida was embarrassed to admit that he had often crossed paths with Celan at staff meetings without knowing who he was, despite being consumed by his poetry.

The affinities between Celan and Derrida are obvious – their Jewishness, their ambiguous identities, their adoption of a language that is not their own (Celan insisted on writing in German, the language of his oppressors), even a sense of survivor's guilt, although Derrida would never claim any sort of parity. Both, like many Jewish intellectuals of their era, lived in a world where the Holocaust was a fact which could not be elided.

But it was perhaps at the level of language – not separable from any of these things of course – that their paths met most fruitfully. Celan's use of ellipsis, condensation and allusion (each central to Derrida's argument in 'Che cos'è la poesia') enact an indirect use of speech, fusing his own 'natural' style with the problem of writing the horrors of the Holocaust (among other things, although not too many other things). In a sense, all of Celan's work was an answer to Theodor Adorno's statement, 'To write poetry after Auschwitz is barbaric' – the answer being that not to write poetry would be more so. As he said in his speech on accepting a prize in Bremen in 1958,

> Only one thing remained reachable, close and secure amid all losses: language. Yes, language. In spite of everything, it remained secure against loss. But it had to go through its own lack of answers, through terrifying silence, through the thousand darknesses of murderous speech. It went through. It gave me no words for what was happening, but went through it. Went through and could resurface, 'enriched' by it all.[40]

Derrida wrote about Celan often – 'Poetics and Politics of Listening', 'The Truth That Wounds', 'Language is Never Owned', all later collected in *Sovereignties in Question: The Poetics of Paul Celan*. 'Shibboleth for Paul Celan' is one of his greatest essays. Drawing on 'shibboleth' as that which marks out a particular group of people, he generalises from it, noting that 'every insignificant, arbitrary mark becomes discriminative, decisive, and divisive'.[41] The essay's other concern is the experience of 'the date'. A date – signing with a time and a place – is a 'singularity, solitude, the secrecy of the encounter.'[42] It cannot be repeated, and so the enigma of the date (the 'today, on this date') 'seems to resist every philosophical question and mode of questioning, every objectification, every theoretico-hermeneutic thematiza-tion.'[43] Central is the idea of 'the encounter', which is what a poem is:

> Encounter – in the word encounter two values meet without which there would be no date: 'encounter' as it suggests the random occurrence meeting, the coincidence or conjuncture which comes to seal one or more than one event once, at a given hour, on a given day, in a given month, in a given region; and 'encounter' as it suggests an encounter with the other, the ineluc-table singularity out of which and destined for which the poem speaks. In its otherness and its solitude (which is also that of the poem, 'alone', 'solitary'), it may inhabit the conjunction of one and the same date. This is what happens.[44]

This idea of singularity would prove vital to Derrida in trying to understand and write about a date which would take on awful significance a few years later – September 11, 2001.

Derrida's theories of literature were taken up with some alac-rity by departments of literature. To deconstruct a literary object was regarded by some theorists as being as valid a work of art as the original object itself, so criticism should not be shy of adopting literary techniques and tropes in creating its critique. Philippe Sollers's discomfiture at Dissemination, the sense that the critic was in some sense stealing his soul through mimesis, is the first example of what would become an increasingly common complaint against deconstruction. Those who can, do; those who can't become critics, thinking they do.

At the forefront were the so-called Yale School thinkers, of whom Paul de Man was perhaps the most brilliant theorist. Derrida had met de Man at the Baltimore conference, the then forty-six-year-old an attendee but not a speaker, although he was active in the discussions. Derrida's paper affected him greatly, and he soon responded with the essay 'The Rhetoric of Blindness', which analysed Derrida's discussion of Rousseau in *Of Grammatology*, not always to Derrida's advantage. Despite this, the friendship between de Man and Derrida was immediate, deep and enduring ('the space for friendship is shrinking strangely, dangerously [in me], as the other grows broader, increasing the number of its networks, its machines and its traps', Derrida wrote to him in 1976), and de Man was instrumental in obtaining for Derrida a visiting professorship at Yale.[45] In person, de Man was known as possessing 'warmth, generosity and loyalty to colleagues and friends,' in contrast to 'that self-abnegating spirit that marked both his writing and his conduct of personal relationships.'[46]

He was born Paul Deman in Belgium in 1919, and had emigrated to the United States in 1948, studying comparative literature at Harvard from 1952. The encounter with Derrida was life-changing, and his work shifted dramatically as he applied deconstructive 'techniques' to Romanticism; Rousseau, Nietzsche, Rilke and Proust; Blanchot, Yeats and Holderlin.

Of all the thinkers influenced by Derrida, it was de Man perhaps who not only stayed closest to deconstruction's original insights, but who displayed an intellectual rigour on a par with Derrida's own. He argued, in the words of Barbara Johnson, that 'philosophy is defined by its refusal to recognize itself as literature; literature is defined as the rhetorical self-transgression of philosophy.'[47] Both fields, argued de Man, are constituted of the interplay of the Platonic trivium of logic, grammar and rhetoric (themselves unstable concepts, defined against each other, but which must be preserved while acknowledging their contingency and the uncertainty of their priority), and it is the task of the critic to analyse each, and to look at the interstices where the demarcation between them fails.[48]

Philosophy attempts, in particular, to expunge itself of rhetoric – the 'false', the 'fictive'. And yet even the most 'rigorous' philosophical text can be exposed for its reliance on metaphors, symbols and allegories. Meanwhile, literature 'is fiction not because it somehow refuses to acknowledge "reality", but because it is not a priori certain that language functions according to principles which are those of the phenomenal world ... it is not a priori certain that literature is a reliable source of information about anything but its own language.'[49] Unlike, say, the Romantics, who privileged the symbolic – where word and world coincide, ideally for eternity – de Man insofar as he argued any hierarchy of styles, privileged allegory, as this was fiction glorying in its figurative nature, acknowledging its language game.

There is no such thing as unrhetorical language, whatever the discipline. Rhetoric is indeed the enabling condition of all articulate thought, as language of 'pure information' is impossible. All language fails in that it cannot possibly have a successful referential relationship with the world. Meaning remains, can only be, ambiguous, and it is that ambiguity which poetry speaks of, the 'fundamental one that prevails between the world of the spirit and the world of sentient substance. The spirit cannot coincide with its object and this separation is infinitely sorrowful.'[50]

Like Derrida, de Man's work resists all totalising strategies, exploring rather the particular and the fragmentary. His essay on Percy Bysshe Shelley's final unfinished work *The Triumph of Life* is exemplary here, noting that not only is the poem a fragment that uses fragmentary tropes and images (statues and architecture) but that the coincidence of Shelley's violent death while writing the poem (the fragmentation of his life and body) cannot fail to inform our reading of the poem, and is in fact paradigmatic of one of the conditions of literature. All literature (and everything else) is but a fragment as all life is cut short by death, and a writer's oeuvre is always already partial no matter how much they write.[51]

Some saw de Man's contention that there is no relationship between literature and the world as enabling a quietism which renders all political action pointless. For critics, de Man's work was a sanctioning of the ahistorical, of relativism, and 'a fundamental hostility toward the political, a stacking of the cards against actions political felicity.'[52] Everything just became a language game, with texts endlessly chattering to each other. It was a criticism to which Derrida was not immune, and which would force him to think deeply about deconstruction's relationship to both the world and the social forces at play.

The Yale School flourished in the 1980s, and de Man was joined by such thinkers as Geoffrey Hartman, who wrote on Wordsworth, and the notion of testimony based on his video archiving of the Holocaust; J. Hillis Miller, who explored such ideas as 'The Critic as Host', and asked 'when a text contains a citation from another text, is it like a parasite in the main text or is it the main text that surrounds and strangles the citation?';[53] and, more briefly in terms of his embrace of deconstruction, the prolific Harold Bloom, whose breakthrough work *The Anxiety of Influence* in 1973 looked at the ways in which a new poet struggles to escape from the influence of those who came before, breaking the texts into what he described as six 'revisionary ratios', with the forbidding appellations of *clinamen*, *tessera*, *kenosis*, *daemonization*, *askesis*, and (of course!) *apophrades*.[54]

Hillis Miller's definition of deconstruction as the 'searching for the thread in the text in question which will unravel it all, or the loose stone which will pull down the whole building' captures what made other critics furious about the process.[55] Seen as wilfully destructive, their endless 'playful' readings seemed to offer the possibility that any reading was not only legitimate, but as legitimate as any other reading. A 1986 article by Colin Campbell in the *New York Times*, headlined 'The Tyranny of the Yale Critics' summed up the objections in lurid terms. The 'Elizabethan Pavilion' of Yale, where the occasional 'dewy-eyed deer or tame peacock would walk past' now has a 'dense jungle' around it, caused by poststructuralism, 'a term that lumps together various French and other thinkers who write as though they want to overthrow oppressive philosophic structures by subverting language.' The whole ruse was invented by Jacques Derrida, 'still the movement's leading theoretician and King Babar.' Derrida, whose *Glas* features 'two parallel columns of quotations: one from Hegel, one from the literate French criminal Genet,' dominates the Yale School and is spreading through other universities 'like kudzu'.

What, asks Campbell, is deconstruction?

> To 'deconstruct' a text is pretty much what it sounds like – to
> pick the thing carefully apart, exposing what deconstructors see
> as the central fact and tragic little secret of Western philosophy –
> namely, the circular tendency of language to refer to itself...[and]
> the 'meaning' of a piece of writing – it doesn't matter whether it's
> a poem or a novel or a philosophic treatise – is indeterminate ...
> Derrida, in a typically bold and outrageous way, has gone so far
> as to say that writing is more basic than speaking, that speaking
> is only a form of writing.[56]

And so on.

The following year Allan Bloom (no relation to Harold) had
a surprise bestseller with *The Closing of the American Mind:
How Higher Education Has Failed Democracy and Impoverished
the Souls of Today's Students*. While not exclusively targeting
deconstruction, Bloom saw it as part of the moral relativism
that had taken over American universities, with students react-
ing by instinct, rather than with cool, rational thinking. Such
thinking has also led to the decline of the Great Books. Students
had lost their taste for reading, or only read theory, and so had
lost their critical faculties. Deconstructionism, as he calls it,
shares the premise of Freudian criticism, Marxist criticism, New
Criticism (!) and structuralism that 'what Plato and Dante had to
say about reality was unimportant'(!!).[57] It is the 'last predictable
stage in the suppression of reason and the denial of the possibility
of truth.'[58]

Bloom's book was a hit, but 'deconstructionism' and its like
received support from an unlikely quarter – Noam Chomsky,
no great friend of continental philosophy, described the book as
'mind-bogglingly stupid'.[59]

In all of these criticisms there is, of course, some truth – as
Derrida knew better than anyone, a letter doesn't not necessarily
(or cannot possibly) arrive at its proper destination, and a theory
cannot generate perfect adherents. There was undoubtedly a lot
of rubbish generated in the name of deconstruction by literature departments throughout the world; that said, there was, no
doubt, a lot of *Scheisse* generated by epigones of Hegel who tried

to crowbar his theories into their own analyses or who built entire careers out of misunderstanding him, no doubt to the detriment of his standing. As noted in the 1980s film *A Fish Called Wanda*, apes do read philosophy, they just don't understand it.

While these battles played out in both philosophical journals and the popular press, they also had an effect closer to home, at the ENS. In 1981, shortly before his son Pierre passed his exam for the Normale Sup at his first attempt (thus outdoing his father), a sustained campaign was launched against Derrida. Again the terms are familiar: he was accused of producing work that was 'pure literature' with nothing to do with philosophy and indulging in 'cunning verbal acrobatics deprived of any seriousness'. In truth, Derrida felt less and less affinity with the ENS – the Althusser affair had seemed like the end of the era. He moved to the École des hautes études en sciences sociales (EHESS) where he would teach for the next fifteen years as director of studies. That the university focused on interdisciplinary studies and the social sciences is apt, as Derrida's work was about to turn outwards.

9

Before the Law

God separated himself from himself in order to let us speak, in order to astonish and to interrogate us. He did so not by speaking but by keeping still, by letting silence interrupt his voice and his signs, by letting the Tables be broken.
— 'Edmond Jabès and the Question of the Book'

A future that would not be monstrous would not be a future; it would already be a predictable, calculable, and programmable tomorrow. All experience open to the future is prepared or prepares itself to welcome the monstrous arrivant.
— 'Passages: From Traumatism to Promise'

From the *New York Times*, 1 January 1982:

Jacques Derrida, a French philosopher, was arrested Monday in Prague for alleged drug smuggling, official sources said today

The French Government demanded that Czechoslovakia release him immediately.

The demand was made to Ambassador Jan Pudlak when he was called to the Foreign Ministry this afternoon, the sources said. Mr. Derrida, fifty-one years old, a noted specialist on the French language whose wife is of Czechoslovak origin, was taking part in an unofficial seminar on philosophy organized by the dissident Charter 77 human rights group in Prague, ministry sources said. They expressed astonishment at the allegations of drug trafficking, which they described as totally out of character.

Derrida had gone to Prague as a guest of the Jan Hus Educational Foundation, named for the Czech hero who was burned at the stake in 1415 for heresy. Set up by a group of British philosophers from Oxford, it aimed to bring philosophy from outside Czechoslovakia to dissident intellectuals suffering under the oppressive Communist regime. There had been an aggressive attack on these dissidents after Charter 77, a petition calling for basic human rights, with signatories including the then playwright and future president Václav Havel and the philosopher Jan Patočka, a former student of Husserl and Heidegger. In March 1977, at sixty-nine, Patočka had died after ten hours of police interrogation. Derrida wrote about him in his 1995 collection *The Gift of Death*.

As well as supplying books, the foundation also organised seminars with overseas philosophers, known as *bytové semináře*, residential seminars, as they were held in the home of one of the dissidents. Other lecturers over the course of the few years of its operation included Roger Scruton, Anthony Kenny, Thomas Nagel and Jürgen Habermas, but Derrida was the biggest name. When a French chapter was set up, Derrida took up the post of vice-president – Marguerite was born in Prague and had Czech heritage on her mother's side, so the Derridas had a special interest. It was organised for him to go to Prague on 26 December 1981, less than two weeks after a state of siege was declared in Poland by the Soviet government, raising tensions.

Coincidentally, Derrida was at the time working on his paper 'Before the Law', based on the Kafka story of the same name. It is his first work in an area that was to fascinate him and inform his philosophy from then on: the law. In Kafka's story a man goes to an open door behind which is the Law. He asks the gatekeeper for entry. 'It is possible,' says the gatekeeper, 'but not now.' The man considers simply going through the door, but the gatekeeper tells him that each door leads to another door, each with a more powerful gatekeeper. The man decides to wait, and waits until the end of his life. Before he dies, he asks, 'Everyone strives after the law, so how is it in these many years no one except me has requested entry?' To which the gatekeeper replies, 'Here no one else can gain entry, since this entrance was assigned only to you. I'm going now to close it.'

Derrida's paper spins out the implications of the story as exemplifying 'the law of literature'. The law is always deferred – and Kafka's story presents the ultimate deferral – a deferral until death. Derrida notes that the gatekeeper also stands before the law, and also has no access. In addition, 'before' also means 'prior to'. And prior to the law, prior to the decision, the making of the law, there is différance. While his focus is mostly literature, the wider legal implications are present, and will form the basis of his investigations into justice.

Kafka's parable, and his own paper, took on a significance he did not expect during his trip to Prague. At Orly airport, as he prepared for departure, Derrida felt as though he was being followed but dismissed his fears as being too like a spy novel, the product of an overactive imagination. But at Prague the surveillance became obvious. A man followed him onto the Metro causing Derrida, he later wrote, to summon up his 'knowledge of novels and psychology, I tried to remember all the techniques of the genre' – which turned out to mean waiting until the doors were about to close and jumping out.[1] Later that day he visited Kafka's grave in the New Jewish Cemetery, then gave his seminar on Descartes and language (to which one of the students responded, 'How is that supposed to help?'). Still being followed, he returned to his hotel. Terrified, he decided not to give the second seminar he was scheduled to deliver, but just to wait and catch his 30 December plane home.

As he checked his bags a 'huge guy' stepped forward and led him into a little room. He imagined they were looking for manuscripts. But in the lining of his bag they found four small bags filled with a brown powder. The room filled with customs officials and police, and Derrida was arrested for 'producing, trafficking and transferring drugs'.

Derrida was interrogated for seven hours and then taken to Ruzyně Remand Prison where he was placed in a small dark cell. At 5 a.m. a Romani Hungarian was also locked in, and the pair played noughts and crosses to attempt to assuage Derrida's distress. The next morning he was photographed, clothed and then naked, then dressed in prison uniform and taken to a cell with five other inmates who explained he would probably get two years minimum.

It was not until the next day that Marguerite, who had waited at the airport growing increasingly agitated, found out about the arrest from her aunt who lived in Czechoslovakia. The news became public soon after, Foucault took to the airwaves, and the Czechoslovakian ambassador was summoned by President Mitterrand at 4 p.m. It soon became clear that, while the ambassador had no idea who Derrida was, the authorities were well aware, and were testing the French reaction. Derrida was released and taken to the French Embassy. They put him on a train which arrived at Gare de l'Est on 2 January at 7:30 a.m., where he was swamped by journalists. For a man who had for so long avoided having his photograph taken, it was another humiliation.

The experience was one of the most traumatic of Derrida's adult life, perhaps *the* most traumatic, and brought back memories of his expulsion from school. 'Whether they expelled me from school, or threw me into prison, I always thought the other must have a good reason to accuse me.'[2] Questions about the law, so present in his early life, dominated much of his thinking for the last twenty years of it.

'I shall speak of ghost [revenant], of flame and of ashes. And of what, for Heidegger, avoiding means.'

In October 1987, the Chilean historian Victor Farías published *Heidegger and Nazism*. It chronicled the relationship between Heidegger and the National Socialists. While the book contained little that was new and was written in a sensationalist style (Derrida wrote that the work was 'sometimes so rough one wonders if the investigator [has read] Heidegger for more than an hour'), it caused a sensation, and Derrida again found himself on the front pages, by an accident of timing as much as anything else.

Farías's book was published, coincidentally, at the same time as Derrida's own 'Of Spirit: Heidegger and the Question'. While Derrida's work had been delivered back in March, it was immediately seen as responding to Farías's and the new controversies the book stirred up, and has been ever since. With its subtle, nuanced, dense, allusive, digressive – Derridean – style, it was found, in an atmosphere of polemics, wanting. Farías himself wrote a polemic, '13 Facts for Jacques Derrida', and responded to Derrida's assertion that his book offered nothing new with 'If Derrida knew all that, why didn't he tell us?'[3]

Heidegger's association with Nazism had often been treated as a dirty secret, to be put to one side, after a brief consideration of the usual questions about separating the art from the artist. In the case of Heidegger, one would like to say 'the facts are straightforward', and some of them are. But many are not, a point crucial to Derrida. 'Why', he asks, 'does this hideous archive seem so unbearable and fascinating? Precisely because no one has ever been able to reduce the whole work of Heidegger's thought to that of some Nazi ideologue.'[4]

The facts not being straightforward was not only crucial to Derrida and others who 'defended' Heidegger. It was crucial to Heidegger too. If Derrida's 'style of philosophising' included obfuscation as a structural necessity, to draw attention to the undecidability of certain notions, or to foreground their complexity – 'I think you'll find it's not quite as simple as that' – Heidegger's style is similarly designed to flummox those seeking clear declarative sentences.

For many the problem was not simply Heidegger's participation in Nazism. While it revealed his ambition, his lack of loyalty (particularly towards Husserl, whose funeral, in a final insult, he failed to attend, citing illness) and his venality, many people are ambitious, disloyal and venal and are fortunate enough not to live in a time where that leads to a brown shirt. A Heidegger thrown into different historical moment may have come up with *Being and Time* while living a perfectly blameless public life, albeit without being great company.

What made people most uncomfortable was his evasiveness after. He never expressed any regret or apologised. This was exemplified by an interview he gave *Der Spiegel* in 1966, on the agreement it would not be published until his death. It appeared in 1976, under the title 'Only a God Can Save Us'. In it, Heidegger gives a masterclass in dissembling; he says he had no alternative but to join the Nazi party, and that after The Night of the Long Knives, the extrajudicial purge Hitler ordered in 1934, he changed his mind and distanced himself. All of which may or may not have been true, although the subsequent release of the 'Black Notebooks' with their anti-Semitic 'jottings', complicates this. But whatever the balance between mendacity, collusion and double dealing, at no point does Heidegger directly express remorse. The interview, in fact, has the feel of a small man caught in a crime, trying to blame others. As Jürgen Habermas put it, 'He detaches his actions and statements altogether from himself as an empirical person and attributes them to a fate for which one cannot be held responsible'.[5]

'Of Spirit' turns, as implied, on the word 'spirit' (*Geist*) in Heidegger's work. In *Being and Time* Heidegger explicitly argues against its use – he warns (*avertit*) it must be avoided (*vermeiden*). It is a metaphysical trap into which we have fallen, like 'consciousness' and 'soul'. This exclusion is a vital move in setting the terms of Heidegger's enquiry, as the concept of *Geist* (with its polysemic semantic field including ghost, spirit, mind and intellect) had blown through German philosophy (in particular) since Hegel.

And yet, shortly afterwards, in his 1933 speech accepting the rectorship of Freiburg, titled 'The Self-Assertion of the German University', he uses the word freely, and moreover begins to give it a capital initial, which he had not done previously. What, asks Derrida are we to say of this 'sudden inflammation and inflation of *Geist*?' and its accompanying word 'spiritual' (*geistig*), which Heidegger, this most careful and precise of thinkers, bandies about throughout.[6]

And what is 'spirit' in this incarnation? 'At the center of the "Address" for the first time to my knowledge ... Heidegger offers a definition of spirit. It is certainly presented in the form of a definition: S is P. And without any possible doubt, Heidegger takes it up for himself.'[7] Heidegger says:

> 'Spirit' is neither empty sagacity nor the gratuitous game of joking ... but spirit is the being-resolved to the essence of Being. And the spiritual world (*geistige Welt*) of a people is not the superstructure of a culture, and no more is it an arsenal of bits of knowledge and usable values, but the deepest power of conservation of its forces of earth and blood, as the most intimate power of emotion. Only a spiritual world (*Eine geistige Welt allein*) guarantees the people its grandeur.[8]

This is, as Derrida points out, an 'exaltation', a 'raising aloft'. Note that 'spirit' still appears in quotation marks, and Derrida toys with the idea that this is a strategy of irony; perhaps this is a game of joking, and not a gratuitous one. But later, in Derrida's particularly memorable phrase, these quotation marks around spirit are lifted off in a '*coup de théâtre*, the raising of the curtain'.[9] Later again, after the war, Heidegger will denounce spiritual decadence, *sans* quotation marks.

As well as lifting the quotation marks, Heidegger performs another operation, the erasure of an erasure – the crossing out of the word spirit is reversed, the repressed returns. Placing words and concepts under erasure (*sous rature*) in philosophy was Heidegger's own conception. He first used the technique in *The Fundamental Concept of Metaphysics*, where he crosses out the word 'being'. As Spivak neatly puts it, 'Since the word is inaccurate, it is crossed out. Since it is necessary, it remains legible.'[10] Derrida popularised *sous rature*, this identifying of the inaccurate and necessary; it is a kind of *present trace*, and it enacts the impossibility of speaking of the death of metaphysics without using metaphysical terms. Thus ~~metaphysics~~.

Derrida draws out disagreeable parallels between the metaphysical tradition, Nazi racism and Heidegger's thought, the last of which becoming, in his reading, entangled in both the others between 1934 and 1945. From here, however, Heidegger's relationship to spirit takes another turn. The erasure and quotation marks return as Heidegger explores language, poetry in particular. Language precedes the question of Being, and language requires the call of the Other. Thus ethics precedes ontology. We return to ethics as first philosophy, and to Lévinas, not mentioned in the work, but present, hidden. Secret.

Derrida's essay is deep and nuanced, and it is no apologia. But it does work within the ambit of a 'question', not a definitive statement. And questions, as Derrida notes in the essay, 'are not things, like water, stone, shoes, clothes, or books.'[11] But coming after the publication of *Heidegger and Nazism*, stones and their casting were more to people's taste. Heidegger's later works are also about questions, his book *The Question Concerning Technology* for instance, and it did not go unnoticed that in warning of the dangers of mechanised killing machines of the future, Heidegger uses Bolshevism as an example of dehumanisation through technical means, and never mentions a perhaps more grievous, certainly more proximal example of industrial slaughter, which had taken the lives of six million Jews.

Ten months after his interview in *Der Spiegel*, one of Nazism's survivors, Paul Celan, visited Heidegger at his home at Todtnauberg. The poet was on a leave of absence from Saint-Anne hospital (where Althusser would be interned thirteen years later). They were admirers of each other's work. They went for a walk together. What was discussed on their walk is not known – some have speculated they discussed their shared interest in botany. But what was not discussed was the obvious, and what was not forthcoming was an apology. Celan wrote a poem memorialising their meeting, named after the house, with its meaning of Death Mountain. The poem is dated 1 August, a week after this singular encounter. On 20 April 1970, Hitler's birthday, Celan drowned himself in the Seine.

It was not the last time Derrida was accused of evasiveness in the 1980s, and the next time was much more personally harrowing.

In 1983 he had been deeply saddened by the death of Paul de Man. Suffering from cancer, de Man had talked to Derrida most days on the phone. On hearing of his death, Derrida cancelled all his other plans and went to the States, subsequently delivering a eulogy, 'In Memorium: Of the Soul', at a ceremony at Yale in memory of his friend. They had, he recalled, met at the breakfast table in Baltimore in 1966, surprised to find they were both working on an obscure text of Rousseau's, *An Essay on the Origin of Language*. 'From then on,' noted Derrida, 'nothing has ever come between us, not even a hint of a disagreement.'

In 1986 Derrida published *Memoires: For Paul de Man*, which was to have been a book about deconstruction in America, but on the death of his friend became a meditation on friendship and memory, the deconstruction of pastness and of the future. 'Underlying and beyond the most rigorous, critical, and relentless irony ... Paul de Man was a thinker of affirmation. By that I mean – and this will not become clear immediately, or perhaps ever – that he existed in memory of an affirmation and of a vow: yes yes.'[12]

But in August 1987 a past that Derrida had not imagined entered the now. A Belgian student, Ortwin de Graef, working on a thesis on de Man visited the Flemish Archive to see if he could read de Man's earliest work. He found some articles which had been published in 1942 in the newspaper *Het Vlaamsche Land* (The Flemish Land). He also obtained 170 articles de Man had written for *Le Soir vole*. The articles showed that the young de Man was a fascist. He wrote for Nazi newspapers – *Le Soir volé* was the most significant of them and often ran anti-Semitic articles on its front page. Having taken over the newspaper in 1940, the Nazis staffed it with collaborationists; one could not have worked there without being regarded as one.

De Man started writing for *Le Soir volé* in December 1940, at the age of twenty-one, eventually contributing a weekly column, 'Our Literary Chronicle', which associated Jews with degeneracy and assured readers that 'the New Order had come to Europe'. The title of one of de Man's articles was 'The Jews in Contemporary Literature' which concluded that 'our civilization ... [b]y keeping, in spite of Semitic interference in all aspects of European life, an intact originality and character ... has shown that its basic character is healthy'. Remarkably, the articles had always been freely available, published as they were in his own name. Like Poe's purloined letter, they were hiding in plain sight.

In July 1987 de Graef attended a literary conference in Louvain, which included Gayatri Spivak and Samuel Weber, like Spivak an ex-student of de Man's. He passed the articles on to them, they passed them on to Derrida. He was, as can be imagined, severely shaken. A few weeks later he sought advice at a conference at the University of Alabama, and handed out copies to former students and colleagues of de Man, who were as shocked and upset as he was. Debates broke out about how quickly they should be published. Derrida argued that they should be published as soon as possible as 'one did not have to have second sight to foresee the whole spectre of relations to come.'[13] He was convinced to delay. It was a mistake – on 1 December, the *New York Times* printed on its front page 'Yale Scholar's Articles Found in Pro-Nazi Paper'. While the article contained many inaccuracies, it didn't matter. The affair was out there.

Worse was to follow. Some scholars hoped that the articles were a youthful folly, a serious one, but one which could then be separated from the rest of his work, both in terms of their history (he had, after all, left the paper in 1942) and ideologically. But it soon became clear he had not left of his own accord, rather he had overreached. His dream of being a powerful editor led him to show his ambition a little too obviously, accusing a colleague of mismanagement in order to replace him, for which he was sacked. Being regarded as morally repugnant by a pro-Nazi paper is quite an achievement.

De Man then worked at a publisher, also pro-Nazi, and attempted to establish an art journal promoting Nazi ideologies. Avoiding jail at the end of the war – he was too small a fish – he opened what might now be called a shell company to publish books which, with two small exceptions, never emerged. He forged receipts, cooked the books, took money from fake contracts and paid himself a salary. When the business collapsed, he fled to South America and was sentenced in absentia to five years in prison if he ever returned to Belgium. Arriving in New York, he blagged his way into Harvard with an imaginary master's thesis, 'The Bergsonian Conception of Time in the Contemporary Novel', and an 'unfinished' doctoral dissertation, 'Introduction to a Phenomenology of Aesthetic Consciousness'. Having left his wife in South America he then bigamously married Patricia Kelley, who was unaware of his other marriage for ten years. Then he got into Cornell, and then he got into Yale. And that was that. Although in 1954 a letter was sent to Harvard accusing him of collaborating, his defence – that he had written the articles under duress and 'stopped doing so when Nazi thought-control did no longer allow freedom of statement' – was accepted.

The astonishing thing about the whole story – well one of the astonishing things – is, as Louis Menand put it in the *New Yorker*, 'the sheer magnitude of the risks he took'.

> If you were an émigré trying to hide a criminal past, would you default on your rent pretty much everywhere you lived? Would you claim to hold fictitious academic degrees, and doctor transcripts that could easily be checked? Would you talk your way out of a jam by pretending that you were the son of your uncle? For that matter would you become the leader of a high-profile and controversial school of literary criticism? You would not.[14]

The uncle Menard refers to is Henri de Man, who had been a father figure of sorts to his nephew. This de Man had written a text famous in Belgium, *Beyond Marxism*, but then made the not unique journey from socialism to National Socialism, rising to the rank of de facto prime minister of Belgium under Nazi rule. 'For the working classes and for socialism, this collapse of a decrepit world, far from being a disaster, is a deliverance,' he wrote.[15] Convicted in absentia of treason after the war – he had fled to Switzerland – he died in a car accident in 1953. It was almost certainly suicide.

In the light of these revelations, Paul de Man's arguments for the ahistorical and the apolitical became more sinister, and it is tempting to see in all of de Man's works a sort of autobiography told through renunciation. Scholars combed his work for evidence linking the man who wrote Nazi propaganda with the man who wrote *Allegories of Reading*, and it is hard not to feel a shiver when reading quotes such as 'indecision between fictional discourse and empirical event makes it possible to excuse the bleakest of crimes,' in the chillingly named essay 'Excuses (Confessions)'.[16]

It is not known in what order Derrida became aware of each revelation – it is unlikely he knew all of it, perhaps he knew none of it, when he sat down to write his defence of de Man, 'Like the Sound of the Sea Deep Within a Shell: Paul de Man's War', only a month after the *New York Times* front page. But it is a depressing read, and as annoying as its title. While Derrida is open about his shock and dismay, and acknowledges the anti-Semitism of 'Jews and Contemporary Literature', it is an actual *defence*, in a way that *Of Spirit* is not. It is hard to swallow such paragraphs as:

> Paul de Man's war is finally, in a third sense, the one that this man must have lived and endured in himself. He was this war. And for almost a half century, this ordeal was a war because it could not remain a merely private torment. It has to have marked his public gestures, his teaching and writing. It remains a secret, a hive of secrets, but no one can seriously imagine, today, that in the course of such a history, this man would not have been torn apart by the tragedies, ruptures, dissociations, 'disjunctions' ... How did he live this unliveable discord between worlds, histories, memories, discourses, languages? Do we have the means to testify to this? Who has the right to judge it, to condemn or to absolve?[17]

To which one might answer, the law courts from which he fled and the victims of his propaganda.

When he wrote it, Derrida was probably unaware of the sheer scope of de Man's sociopathy. But of course it is not just de Man he is defending; he is defending himself. Critics were quick to use the Paul de Man affair as a stick not only to beat de Man but

Derrida and deconstruction, that malign corrupter of philosophy and literature departments.

In response Derrida asked:

> What does deconstruction (in the singular) have to do with what was written in 1940–42 by a very young man in a Belgian news-paper. Is it not ridiculous and dishonest to extend to a 'theory', that has itself been simplified and homogenized, as well as to all those who are interested in it and develop it, the trial one would like to conduct of a man for texts written in Belgian newspapers forty-five years ago and that moreover, once again, one has not really read?[18]

Yes and no. Of course a simple dismissal of deconstruction because one of its main theorists was morally corrupt is an injustice, but so is dismissing moral corruption because it is done by a main theorist of deconstruction. Derrida had after all once said we should not condemn Nietzsche just because the National Socialists had taken him up, but we should try and understand why they did.[19]

The rest of Derrida's response displayed precisely the sort of relativism and moral slipperiness of which deconstruction often stood accused. The facts of the de Man case were plain and the only ethical response was denunciation, not what was at best hair splitting, at worst a defence which amounted to little more than 'we liked him, so we forgive him', however technical the language it was couched in. Derrida was certainly in an invidious position, but that was the fault of Paul de Man, not the critics. As Geoffrey Hartman put it, 'Rereading the later work we will always be troubled by the fact that de Man did not explicitly address his past. I regret his silence, which shifts a moral burden to us: are we now obliged to speak for him, to invent thoughts he might have provided?'[20]

The central refrain of Derrida's paper, that de Man had radically broken with his past, is, well, untrue. Simply, he was not caught. As with Althusser, the case was never brought. Derrida's decade, in which he became the most famous philosopher on

Earth, had seen him having to defend friends who were never tried for the crimes they committed, bookmarking his own incarceration for a crime of which he was innocent.

The end of the decade also saw what has been called the 'ethical turn' in Derrida's work. A turning outwards towards the social and the political, and a new concern with law, and friendship, the gift, and hospitality – terms which form a sort of mobius strip in his thinking: possible-impossible aporias, Derrida called them. He would strenuously argue that these concerns were not in fact new, but grew logically from his earlier thinking.

That said, that this dimension of his thinking need not have occurred to him is a very strong possibility, and it is hard to ignore the effect that the ethical quandaries, and the accusations made against him for failing to respond 'correctly', had had on him. The previous decade, while bringing extraordinary fame, had also seen him suffer a series of bruising encounters, personally and philosophically. If Derrida's argument is that one's philosophy is not separable from one's life and that any work has a specificity of time and place, he was to enact this fully in the years between 1989 and 1994.

Certainly, he knew from the off that his ideas were different, but they were also painstakingly gained and argued. One could disagree with them, but one had to acknowledge how meticulous his arguments were. They were also, Derrida must have felt, reasonably arcane. Yes, he was aware that they had implications for more than the small corner of philosophy he was beavering away at, but the idea that these implications would not only be recognised (with amity or without) but would spread through philosophy into so many diverse fields, establishing disciplines and departments throughout the world, was simply unthinkable.

Derrida's reaction to the level of fame he enjoyed was ambivalent in all the right ways. But the hostility he began to receive surprised him. Academic disputes, in books, tracts and inside the walls of the academy, are of course grist to the intellectual mill, in a world of competing visions and competing egos. It is, as Derrida noted, not inexplicable to find a desire for power in the sort of person who might do philosophy.

> The philosopher is someone whose desire and ambition are absolutely mad; the desire for power of the greatest politicians is absolutely minuscule and juvenile compared to the desire of the philosopher who, in a philosophical work, manifests both a design on mastery and a renunciation of mastery on a scale and to a degree that I find infinitely more powerful than can be found elsewhere ... He wants to situate himself in a place where everything done and said can be thought, theorized, and finally mastered by him. It is the place of absolute mastery, the project of absolute knowledge.[21]

The impossibility of this absolute knowledge changes nothing, in fact it makes any small gain require more defending. This goes with the territory. But the sometimes visceral level of the attacks from outside were very difficult for him. While he seldom hit back with the force he displayed in the de Man defence, he felt he had to re-argue constantly that *deconstruction* wasn't *destruction* (he would have used that word if it was). It retained what it analysed.

He was aware that he brought some of this animus on himself. In a 2004 interview he noted that when he thought something needed to be said, 'No force in the world can stop me.' But sometimes

> just as I was drifting off to sleep, half-asleep, there was someone inside me, more lucid and vigilant than the other, who kept saying, 'But you're completely crazy, you shouldn't be doing this, you shouldn't be writing this ...' and then when I opened my eyes and settle down to work, I do it. I disobey that council of prudence.[22]

Of all the accusations, what seemed to sting most of all was the notion that his thinking was relativist, anything goes, and thus nihilistic. 'Deconstruction', he had reiterated in *Memoires: For*

Paul de Man, 'is anything but a nihilism or a scepticism. Why can one still read this claim despite so many texts that, *explicitly, thematically and for more than twenty years* have been demonstrating the opposite?'[23] Nihilism is an ontological claim that there is no truth. Deconstruction has no opinion on this. Nor does it on, say, pink elephants. What it does say is that we cannot know whether there is truth or not, which is an epistemological claim. So any assertion that there is truth is unprovable, and therefore whatever truth is offered should be analysed for the reasons why it is being offered.

This question of truth opened the question of ethics. In the works of the early 1990s – 'The Force of Law: "The Mystical Foundation of Authority"', 'Given Time: Counterfeit Money', 'The Politics of Friendship' and 'Spectres of Marx' – Derrida explored new ethical territory. If we are to be in a world where we cannot know truth, how are we to *be*? Or, perhaps better descriptive rather than prescriptive, how is it that we are like this? What rules and laws guide us? How? And why?

Derrida's first explicit writing on the idea of Law was, as we have seen, 'Before the Law' on Kafka. But it is his 1989 paper 'The Force of Law: The Mystical Foundation of Authority' that represents his most significant intervention. This is in fact two papers, joined together, the first part from October 1989 and the second from April 1990. While the second part, an exploration of Walter Benjamin's text 'Critique of Violence', is a fascinating piece of work, which Derrida handed out at the conference, it is the first part which was to have the greater influence, both on the legal profession itself and on Derrida's own subsequent thought.

'The Force of Law: "The Mystical Foundation of Authority"' takes its subtitle from Michel de Montaigne – 'Custom creates the whole of equity, for the simple reason that it is accepted. It is the mystical foundation of its authority.' The paper was given at a conference called 'Deconstruction and the Possibility of Justice' and Derrida homes in immediately on the word 'and' in the conference title, noting that 'and' is 'the conjunction that brings together words that do not belong in the same category.'[24] By doing so it not only joins them, but assumes that they are distinct: they need an 'and' to bring them together. This title voices a suspicion.

> Does deconstruction ensure, permit, authorize the possibility of justice? Does it make justice possible, or a discourse of consequence on justice and on conditions of possibility? Do the 'deconstructionists' have anything to say about justice, anything to do with it? Why basically, do they speak of it so little. Does it interest them, finally? Is it not, as some suspect, because deconstruction does not itself permit any just action, any valid discourse on justice but rather constitutes a threat to law, and ruins the condition of the possibility of justice?[25]

The paper has the feel of a court case, and one can almost see Derrida pacing before the jury as defence counsel for his own theories, which are being tried on a charge of political and social irrelevance. The tone is discursive, often conversational, occasionally confrontational. The jury is appealed to, the mood shifts between belligerence and emollience. Gripping his robe, he asks why, m'lud,

> does deconstruction have the reputation, justified or not, of treating things obliquely, indirectly, in indirect style, with so many 'quotation marks', and while always asking whether things arrive at the indicated address? Is this reputation deserved? And, deserved or not, how does one explain it?[26]

His paper, he notes, will speak of the *force* of law. Why force? Because, argues Derrida, enforceability 'is not an exterior or secondary possibility that may or may not be added as a supplement to the law. It is the force implied in the very concept of justice as law.'[27] This is Derrida's first mention of 'justice'. It is a word that is notably absent in his work before its invocation here, but Derrida will dispute this absence, it is simply that the theme has not been foregrounded. It is always there, perhaps under erasure.

The question then becomes, Derrida continues, what is the difference between force that is just and force that is unjust? It is hard not to imagine that this is the Derrida of Prague speaking, as he has his photograph taken, his spirit for that moment stolen. This is Derrida's moment of 'unjustice', falling outside of the law, while being held within it.

At this point Derrida makes a startling declaration, but one which will inform the rest of his work. He argues that

> the most radical programs of a deconstruction that would like, in order to be consistent with itself, not to remain enclosed in purely speculative, theoretical, academic discourses but rather to aspire to something more consequential, to change things and to intervene in an efficient and responsible (though always, of course, in a mediated way), not only in the profession but in what one calls the city, the polis, and more generally the world.[28]

This is a mission statement. Deconstruction must and will engage with 'the world', the social, and thus the ethical. This is of course precisely what it has been accused of not doing. In Derrida's argument, of course, deconstruction always already was engaged in this way. But, needs must, it will now do so overtly.

What then is this 'mystical foundation' of authority? Prior to the law, notes Derrida, there is no law. It is the founding of the law – insofar as it is accepted, as Montaigne reminds us – which instigates the law. It is a performative which both inaugurates and justifies the law, and establishes also what is unlawful. We are again in the moment of decision, of violence.

He takes a practical example: the signing of the American Declaration of Independence. It is written before it is signed, so those who sign it in fact have no right to do so, they are not yet representative of the people. The signing is the performative act, which gives them the right to sign. It is a request for consent which could possibly not be given; that it is given is an act of assent.

And if law is founded from nothing, that means it is constructed and so can be deconstructed. It is, in fact, argues Derrida, the deconstructible structure of law that ensures the very possibility of deconstruction. This is, after all, what deconstruction does. It seeks laws of law, of literature, of philosophy, and looks at how they were constructed, where the gaps and contradictions are, what is left out, what the hidden assumptions are, and then what all of this means. Here Derrida makes another breathtaking move. This being so, then 'Justice in itself, if such a thing exists, outside or beyond law, is not deconstructible. No more than deconstruction itself, if such a thing exists. Deconstruction is justice.'[29]

Deconstruction is justice. Hidden – perhaps in plain sight – within the system of law, the law of law, the law of literature, the law of philosophy, is justice. Perhaps surprised by his own audacity, Derrida says here for perhaps the only time in his whole oeuvre, 'I am not sure this is altogether clear. I hope without, being sure of it, that it will become a little clearer in a moment.'[30]

Justice is, he argues, an experience of the impossible. In practical terms, no punishment can fit a crime, there is no possible exact eye for an eye – the scales of justice can never balance. To kill one who has killed achieves no parity, unless the dead one comes back to do it in exactly the same way, with exactly the same consequences (there can never be exactly the same consequences). 'Law is not justice. Law is the element of calculation, and it is just that there be law, but justice is incalculable.'[31]

Deconstruction, in its demand for infinite justice 'would not all correspond (though certain people have an interest in spreading this confusion) to a quasi-nihilistic abdication before the ethico-politico-juridical question of justice.'[32] Again, aware of the high-wire act he is performing, Derrida assures the jury that 'I know I will not fail to surprise or shock not only the determined adversaries of said deconstruction … but also the very people who pass for or take themselves to be its partisans or practitioners.' But it needs to be emphasised, 'Deconstruction is mad about and from justice, mad about and from this desire for justice.'[33]

Deconstruction foregrounds undecidability, but we must not forget:

> The undecidable is not merely the oscillation between two significations or two contradictory and very determinate rules, each

equally imperative ... A decision that would not go through the test and ordeal of the undecidable would not be a free decision; it would only be the programmable application or the continuous unfolding of a calculable process.[34]

If a judge brings down a judgment based on the law, as he or she must, that is simply a case of following a rule, not a unique, singular event predicated in its totality by the specific crime. Therefore it is not justice.

Summing up – while we want justice, here and now, it cannot arrive. Justice is always justice 'to come', *à venir*, a phrase which would be key to later Derrida. Our legal system is predicated on its arrival, but it cannot arrive, as Jewish law is predicated on the arrival of the Messiah who cannot arrive. Like our own death cannot arrive. Like democracy which cannot arrive.

The case rests.

It is an audacious intervention on Derrida's part at a moment of considerable political tumult. In the time between his giving the two halves of the paper, the Berlin Wall fell and Nelson Mandela was released from prison, and from 17 November to 19 December 1989, the Velvet Revolution in Czechoslovakia consigned Derrida's own judicial tormentors to defeat, and those he had discussed philosophy with into places in the government. These were seismic changes. Derrida's turn to ethics and the law thus works within this same matrix of what would be perceived as a moment of liberalism and democracy. On a philosophical level, Derrida's relationship to these shifts was, unsurprisingly, ambivalent, and some of his theoretical work of the time anticipated how complicated the events actually were. But on what we might call a practical level, he displayed at this time some of his most committed activism, guided by either the temper of the times, a personal whim, or his private concerns about the increasingly carnivalesque reception of his work.

Whatever his reasons, apartheid in South Africa in particular became an issue he involved himself with directly, on the ground from 1983 as part of the guiding council of the Foundation against Apartheid, and in his writing – from his 1985 essay 'Racism's Last Word' ('Apartheid – may that remain the name from now on, the unique appellation for the ultimate racism in the world, the last of many. May it thus remain, but may a day come when it will only be for the memory of man') to his speech at the University of Western Cape on 'Forgiving the Unforgivable'.[35] Nelson Mandela was, in some senses, the inspiration for 'The Force of Law', as Derrida began exploring some of the ideas he later included when he wrote 'The Laws of Reflection: Nelson Mandela, in Admiration' for a 1986 book about Mandela, which included contributions from Cixous, Susan Sontag, Samuel Beckett and Nadine Gordimer. Derrida's piece analysed both Mandela's writings and the statements he made in his own defence during his 1962 trial, teasing out the implications of a 'man of law' who must break it in a search for justice. He would later visit Mandela's jail cell on Robben Island and, in 1998, meet Mandela himself.

Mandela had in fact visited Algeria in 1961 to participate in the ANC's joint exercises with the FLN. It was the first country he visited after his release from prison in 1990. It is hard not to think that in Mandela Derrida saw the sort of figure who might have achieved rapprochement between the Algeria of now and the Algeria he had lost.

Derrida's 'turn' was simultaneously political, ethical and juridical (and indeed theological), and the congregation of these terms is no coincidence. In thinking one, one must think the others. In asserting this he was, he argued, again going back to the roots of our thinking, to the rules of engagement established by Plato and Aristotle.

It was indeed to Aristotle he turned in an extraordinary set of seminars in 1988–89, later collected as *The Politics of Friendship*: in particular a 'saying' of Aristotle's, the odd and unnerving *O philoi, oudeis philos* – 'O my friends, there is no friend.' Derrida's text is a series of meditations on this strange sentence, and sees him at his most abundant in terms of references – he ranges far and wide, not to establish what Aristotle means, but freely to interpret all manner of possible connotations. Each week of the seminar, notes Derrida, 'voices, tones, modes and strategies were tried on, to see if its interpretation could then be sparked, or if the scenography could be set in motion around itself.'[36] The still centre of this speculation is the entanglement of politics and friendship.

For Derrida, as we have seen, friendship was, in his personal life, a fundamental ethic. In contemporary political philosophy it had become a marginal concept if that, despite the word 'fraternity' having such prominence in the founding of the French state, and therefore the founding of a certain type of democracy – the type we are closer to now than we were before the French Revolution. This is not, of course, true democracy because, and Derrida is explicit here, democracy, like justice, is always 'to come', à venir. It is an ideal beyond material possibility – not only due to inadequacy or mendacity on the part of the legal system or political parties, but also because the idea of democracy carries an unresolvable contradiction. On the one hand, it assumes to respect the singularity of each individual in what is a heterogenous polity, and thus their freedom. On the other, democracy means equality for everyone. And equality is a numerical concept – one 'I' is equal to another 'I' as citizens. Singularity is effaced in an achieved democracy of equality. Equality is effaced in achieved democracy of singularity. Liberté and égalité have a relationship of tension, not amity.

Democracy is thus always deferred, and there is a necessary restlessness at the heart of it, and lazy proclamations of democracy having been achieved by current nation-states or their practices must be radically questioned and dislodged. But democracy to come calls for engagement and intervention, and an openness to the coming of the event. This doesn't mean a future democracy 'correcting or improving the actual conditions of our so-called democracies,' it means democracy is 'a promise'. The notion of improvement is inscribed in the concept, and seeking equality, justice, respect for the singularity of the other and equity is an injunction. Participation in 'democracy' demands our participation in this struggle.

In addition, notes Derrida, the concept of democracy has

always, without our necessarily being aware of it, been associated with the canonical concept of friendship as set out by Plato and Aristotle, whose political writings always include explorations of the theme. Thus brotherhood, roots, soil. Derrida is alive to the destructive capabilities of each of these terms, and to their phallocentrism – words such as 'fraternity' and 'filial' depend on an androcentric conception of the human. There is 'inequality and repression' in the concept of friendship as we inherit it, and 'for the sake of democracy' so friendship must be deconstructed, an endless task.

Friendship is a type of recognition, both of the friend and ourselves. Unlike familial relationships (but not excluding them), friendship is voluntary. It also implies obligation, although this varies both between friendships and within them. It also contains the possibility of a wound – one can lose a friend through death or disagreement. One can also, in one of the text's most moving sections, entrust a friend with one's secrets, without judgement. It is, for all of these reasons, a relationship of responsibility, and one to which we might aspire for politics to aspire to.

Aristotle's version of what he calls complete friendship, and thus that to which we are all heirs, is based on the notion of 'good will' and the 'virtuous'. It is virtuous that I love my friend, and friendship is something that radiates from the self. 'Loving' is privileged over 'being loved'. For Derrida, this misses the reciprocity of friendship. It also overlooks the 'otherness' of the other, where friendship is in fact a radical ethical act of the self in relation to the other. One cannot have friendship, inhere in it, without this openness to the other. A human relationship which only enacts itself through negotiation is not friendship.

In a surprising move, the text then turns to the work of the German political theorist Carl Schmitt, at that time virtually forgotten. Born Catholic in 1888, Schmitt was what one might call an 'unreconstructed Nazi' – he was known as 'the crown jurist of the Third Reich' – a radical anti-Semite who served as editor-in-chief for a number of National Socialist newspapers and who, after the war, refused all attempts at de-Nazification, which barred him from academic posts. Derrida pulls no punches this time in his assessment, and is also forensic on any sloppiness or lacunas in his thinking. Nonetheless, for Derrida, Schmitt's thinking is of interest in framing a certain mode of the political and of political thinking.

While born Catholic, Schmitt fell out with the religion while retaining a structural fidelity to theological thinking – one of his earliest works is titled *Political Theology*. In it, Schmitt argues that all modern theories of the state 'are secularized theological concepts'. Also, all states have within them a dictatorial element in that they allow states of emergency – exceptional circumstances in which the leader can step outside the rule of law. 'Sovereign is he who decides on the exception.'[37] It has the flavour for Schmitt of a religious miracle.

Schmitt's most thoroughgoing work of political analysis is *The Concept of the Political*. For Schmitt, 'the political' is an existential state of being shared by all (Western) humans. Contemporary politics is a system of compromises, and therefore lacks decisiveness, and all decisions are weakened by their temporary, contingent nature. This is the fault, argues Schmitt, of liberal democracy. We are in danger of losing the political – or, by failing to enable it, of driving it down, internalising it, making it into resentment.

So how can one define the political? 'Let us assume', writes Schmitt, 'that in the realm of morality the final distinctions are between good and evil, in aesthetics beautiful and ugly, in economics profitable and unprofitable. The question then is whether there is also a special distinction which can serve as a simple criterion of the political and of what it consists?'[38]

Notoriously, Schmitt argues that the final distinction defining the political is between 'friend' and 'enemy'. One defines one's own political beliefs – ultimately, what one would die for – by recognising, or even creating, an enemy. The political enemy need not be morally evil or aesthetically ugly; they need not appear as an economic competitor, and it may even be advantageous to engage with them in business transactions. But they are, nevertheless, the other, the stranger; and it is sufficient for their nature that they are, in an especially intense way, existentially something different and alien, so that in the extreme case conflicts with them are possible.

Derrida proceeds to deconstruct this friend/enemy, amity/enmity distinction. To invoke the distinction is to partake in a haunting, as each carries within it the phantom of the other. All decisions are made in the name of the other, 'of the absolute other in me the other as the absolute that decides on me in me.'[39]

The political world we inhabit is full of invisible enemies; the principal enemy is unidentified. While this obviously invokes the gap in belligerence newly minted by the fall of the Soviet Union, it always applies as our enemies are chosen for us, and is always a revelation of our own anxieties, and that of the polis.

> The invention of the enemy is where the urgency and the anguish are; this invention is what would have to be brought off, in sum, to repoliticise, to put an end to depoliticisation. Where the principal enemy, the 'structuring' enemy, seems nowhere to be found, where it ceases to be identifiable and thus reliable – that is, where the same phobia projects a mobile multiplicity of potential, interchangeable, metonymic enemies, in secret alliance with one another: conjuration.[40]

This conjuration of an enemy is the way a nation-state asserts its rights, the way it unifies its citizenry. Those who resist this conjuration are expelled from citizenship, by methods benign or malignant, such as being called un-[insert name of country here], or by literal expulsion (including being imprisoned and thus outside of citizens' rights). Or they are excluded from ever attaining citizenship, in the case of immigrants who are part of the otherness chosen as enemy ('refugee' might be conjured as an enemy regardless of nationhood, or because of it).

Against this, Derrida calls for a new cosmopolitanism (which itself has a tradition, from the Greeks, to the Stoics, to St Paul and his call for citizens of the world) grounded on what he calls the 'groundless' experience of friendship. In everyday life, notes Derrida, we see that the classical concept of democracy, the way it inhabits all the rhetoric of politicians and parliament, is shaken, that we need something else. Concepts such as immigration, border and citizenship are under a terrible seismic displacement and need to be rethought.

But when will we be ready, he asks at the end of *The Politics of Friendship*, 'for an experience of freedom and equality that is capable of respectfully experiencing that friendship, which would at last be just, just beyond the law, and measured up against its measurelessness? O my democratic friends ...'[41]

10

Of ~~God~~

Let's suppose I have a secret proper name that has nothing to do with my public proper name or with what one may know about me...

— *Octobiographies*

Circumcision, that's all I've ever talked about, consider the discourse on the limit, margins, marks, marches, etc., the closure, the ring (alliance and gift), the sacrifice, the writing of the body, the pharmakos excluded or cut off, the cutting/sewing of Glas, the blow and the sewing back up...

— 'Circumfession'

In a 2004 dialogue with Hélène Cixous, subsequently published as 'From Word to Life', Derrida, uncharacteristically, tells a joke. There are three people isolated on an island, a French citizen, a German citizen, and a Jew. The only other creatures on the island are elephants. Bored, one of them says, 'Let's do something, the three of us. Why don't we write about the elephants? We could compare the styles and the national idioms.' A week later the French citizen comes back with a short, bright, very superficial but very brilliant essay on the sexual drive of the elephants. Three months later the German comes back with a large scientific book, with an endless title, on the ecology and taxonomy of the elephants. The two of them then ask the Jew, where is your book? The Jew says, sorry, but for something this serious I need more time. Every year they ask him where it is. Finally, ten years later he arrives with his book – Elephants and the Jewish Question.

Derrida always resisted being cast as a 'Jewish philosopher', but without ever renouncing his fascination with Jewish thought or downplaying its influence on his own. While noting that he 'rightly passes for an atheist', he also asserted that 'the constancy of God in my life is called by other names.'[1] To impose a purely Jewish reading on Derrida – Derrida and the Jewish Question – is, of course, to do a fundamental violence to the scope of his thinking, but from his earliest works onwards he is open to the claims of Jewish thought in ways that are profoundly and radically vital to his ideas. As he noted in 'Violence and Metaphysics', there is a sense in which Greek philosophical thought narrows its concerns in a way that Jewish philosophical thought resists – or at least, if it too had narrow concerns, these served to disrupt mainstream Western philosophy. 'Jewgreek is Greekjew' appears more often in Derrida's work than any other quotation. In an early essay, he quotes from Edmond Jabès's *Book of Questions*, about the 'difficulty of being a Jew, which coincides with the difficulty of writing: for Judaism and writing are but the same waiting, the same hope, the same depletion'.[2]

His interest in ethics intersected with a new, or at least newly overt, interest in the religious, in particular the Abrahamic religions. His 2002 collection *Acts of Religion* brings together a number of his essays on the topic. This interest was not a form of conversion, rather a recognition of a multitude of shared concerns between religious narrative and his own way of doing philosophy – from the secret, to the idea of testimony, to spirits, to mourning and to memory. It was a shared affinity. As Harold Bloom noted in his *Kabbalah and Criticism*, 'Kabbalah is a theory of writing, but this is a theory that denies the absolute distinction between writing and inspired speech ... Kabbalah speaks of a writing before writing (Derrida's trace), but also of speech before speech.'[3]

In the ethical thinking we can still sense the (ghostly) presence of Lévinas, and Derrida's ethics form a conversation with those of his great friend. Speaking at his funeral upon his death in 1995, Derrida gave a moving eulogy and noted that for Lévinas,

> Yes, ethics before and beyond ontology, the State, or politics, but also ethics beyond ethics. One day, on the rue Michel-Ange, during one of those conversations whose memory I hold so dear, one of those conversations illuminated by the radiance of his thought, the goodness of his smile, the gracious humor of his ellipses, he said to me: 'You know, one often speaks of ethics to describe what I do, but what really interests me in the end is not ethics, not ethics alone, but the holy, the holiness of the holy.'⁴

If 'the holiness of the holy' did not flow through Derrida, or the works of Derrida, with quite the same constancy as it did through Lévinas, it was a question which remained open.

Looking further back, we can find a fascinating contiguity between Derrida and the twelfth-century philosopher Rabbi Moshe ben Maimon, known as Maimonides, whose *Guide for the Perplexed* (1190 BCE), especially in terms of language, wishes to argue that there can be no contradiction between the Word of God, as found in the holy texts, and the findings of the human mind.

In his introduction, Maimonides states that what we find 'perplexing' about biblical language, compared to the language of logic, is that scripture deals in words that are polysemic, where the meaning is not ostensive. Their meaning is equivocal (more than one meaning); derivative (they contain supplemental meanings derived from other, different, words); or what he terms amphibolus (understood as containing sometimes one, sometimes many meanings, depending on, for instance, the context). Here, of course, we find more than an echo of Derrida – the sensitivity to equivocality as a condition of language, supplementarity of meaning, meaning's generation by différance, and the importance of context – *il n'y a pas de hors-texte*.

Maimonides also argues against anthropomorphising God. He cannot be given human attributes. Where the Bible does so – for instance, the 'hand of God' – it must be read metaphorically. As John of Damascus put it in the eighth century, 'God is infinite and incomprehensible and all that is comprehensible about Him is His infinity and incomprehensibility.'[5]

This is an example of apophatic, or negative, theology. God is described by what 'He' is not. Any transcendental signified, God included, cannot be captured in concepts. This anticipates a new and fruitful interpretation of Derrida's work which finds its apotheosis in John D. Caputo's 1997 text, *The Prayers and Tears of Jacques Derrida*, and in other works of the clumsily named 'postmodern theology'.[6] As noted, justice, democracy, the Messiah, God, are always already *à venir*, to come. We exist in the *espace vital* – to use a term from Lévinas, the space in which we can survive – of their coming, and their actual coming would be so fundamental a change, such an 'abrupt invasion', that the space they enter ceases to be.[7] To say what justice is, we point to its failures; to see what God is, we point to the things which are not God.

Caputo subtitles his work, quoting Derrida, 'Religion without Religion'. But he warns, this theology is not 'only' or 'simply' negative – rather, as he puts it in a later interview:

> In its most condensed formulation, deconstruction is affirmation, a 'yes, yes, come' to the future and also to the past, since the authentic past is also ahead of us. It leads to, it is led by, a 'yes' to the transforming surprise, to the promise of what is to come in whatever we have inherited – in politics, art, science, law, reason and so on. The bottom line is 'yes, come.'[8]

For Maimonides this is the 'World to Come' (*Olam Ha-Ba*) and, in common with the tradition of Halakha, the collective body of Jewish laws, it is impossible for living human beings to know what the World to Come is like. However, we must prepare for it, by carrying out our devotions, our prayers, in this life, in anticipation. This is an ethical position, and it was here that Derrida established his problematic: How are we to live, in anticipation of that which does not arrive?

Here the work of another Jewish philosopher, Hermann Cohen, was to exert considerable influence on Derrida, particularly in his 1991 study 'Interpretations at War: Kant, the Jew, the German'. The son of a rabbi, Cohen was born in Coswig, Anhalt, in 1842, and studied the history of Judaism, philosophy, philology, physiology and linguistics. He is seen as the main founder of neo-Kantianism, which dominated German thought from the 1870s to the First World War. Cohen contends that Judaism has a special status among religions as the original monotheistic religion, as only monotheistic religions can be religions of reason and can thus be universalised in a way polytheistic religions are not. Cohen's question is: How can God and human beings – who are infinitely different from each other – have any sort of relationship with each other? For Cohen, particularly in 1915's *Concept of Religion in the System of Philosophy* and 1919's monumental *Religion of Reason Out of the Sources of Judaism*, this relationship is one of 'correlation'.

Kant's fundamental moral insight, notes Cohen, is the categorical imperative, the first dictum of which is 'Act only according to that maxim by which you can at the same time will that it should become a universal law',[9] while the second, 'Act in such a way that you treat humanity, whether in your own person or in the person of another, always at the same time as an end and never simply as a means',[10] is crucial in this context. The Other – 'Thou' in Cohen's formulation – is recognised in that we can see their particular moral failings, and how they suffer due to them. One such 'thou', a morally responsible individual existing in the world, is oneself. We recognise our moral selves by recognising our moral failings. We acknowledge them through prayers and confession, and thus seek moral improvement. It is this striving for moral improvement which establishes the correlation between ourselves and God. But this striving can never reach its goal, it can never become 'congruent' with the ideal, God. Reconciliation is an infinite, unachievable, task. And yet pray and confess we must.

For Derrida the notion of *task* is vital. It is precisely the disruptive possibility of 'task', with its temporal structure (it is a 'doing' word), that Husserl sought to eliminate in his frozen moment of transcendental apprehension, the living present. Husserlian truth strives for presence as humanity strives for God, but it cannot be attained.

Derrida seeks to deconstruct 'ontotheology'. The term, first used by Kant, does what it says on the tin, combining the ontological with the theological. For Heidegger, again, this was, indeed, what metaphysics is, and thus contributes to the forgetting of Being. The mystery of faith is reduced to an investigation into the order of beings. For Derrida, again, Heidegger remains trapped in the very type of thinking he seeks to overcome, as only différance 'encompasses and irrevocably surpasses onto-theology or philosophy'.[11]

The bridge here is language and, as we have seen, Derrida also identified language with its own necessarily temporal constitution, as one of the fundamental threats that Husserl, and much of the Western philosophical tradition, tries to neutralise, and which Derrida's project seeks to de-neutralise, to keep in the world as it does, in fact, exist, in all its messy, non-transcendental immanence. How are we to reconcile the language of God with the language of humans?

Derrida turns to Walter Benjamin, in particular his 1923 text 'The Task of the Translator' – note, again, the word 'task'. For Benjamin, translation cannot be the simple transmission of meaning from one language to another. The translating language has to be transformed and adapted to 'match' the original. Translation is thus generative – it does not replace the original, but *supplements* it and, more than that, forms a work in itself and performs change in the host language. The translation, thus, 'instead of resembling the meaning of the original, must lovingly and in detail incorporate the original's mode of signification, thus making both the original and the translation recognizable as fragments of a greater language'.[12] This greater, or 'pure' language, argues Benjamin, 'resides' in all languages, and is revealed as residing precisely by their translation, without which no 'pure language' would be hypothesised, in part because the absence of translations would assume the existence of only one language. As Benjamin puts it, 'To redeem in his own tongue that pure language exiled in the foreign tongue, to liberate by transposing this pure language captive in the work, such is the task of the translator.'[13]

But this 'pure' language, residing in all languages, hypothesised by translation, a language where all meaning would be transparent for all humans, is, again, a transcendental concept, and like God, like justice, like democracy, like the Messiah, is always *à venir*.

If it is the unattainable telos, it is also the irretrievable origin ('the concept of origin remains indispensable', writes Benjamin), and here Derrida turns to the story of the Tower of Babel in 'Des Tours de Babel' (1991). In destroying the Tower, and punishing humans by forcing them to speak different languages to each other, God eliminates forever this singular language, a pure, untranslated language with its immediate access to meaning. This forces humanity into a double bind. Claims to universality must be given up, and all speech requires translation. While translation for Benjamin is, in its generative power 'holy growth' (*heiliges Wachstum*) towards a 'kingdom which is at once "promised and denied where the languages will be reconciled and fulfilled"', the kingdom can never be reached.[14] In Derrida's words, 'Translation promises a kingdom to the reconciliation of languages. This promise, a properly symbolic event adjoining, coupling, marrying two languages like two parts of a greater whole, appeals to a language of the truth.'[15]

We are on the one hand forced to translate, as there is more than one language, and on the other prohibited from doing so, as no absolute faithfulness between languages can be achieved. 'There is something untouchable, and in this sense the reconciliation is only promised.'[16] But while translation 'promises a kingdom' that can never be attained, it is the act of promising which is important. To 'promise' is to orientate a discourse (a way of being, a life) towards something 'to come' (*à venir*) to which I am then drawn, enticed. The 'task of the translator' – note that it is the *task of the translator*, not the task of 'translation'; this is an ethical duty and thus human – is to draw me into the text with the promise of fidelity, of revelation. That this is a 'task' draws us into a whole economy. As Derrida notes:

> The recurrence of the word 'task' is remarkable enough in any case, for all the significations that it weaves into a network, and there is again the same evaluative interpretation: duty, debt, tax, levy, toll, inheritance and estate tax, noble obligation, but labor midway to creation, infinite task, essential incompletion, as if the presumed creator of the original were not also indebted, taxed, obligated by another text, and a priori translating.[17]

Translation is thus, as a responsibility, a debt that can never be discharged. 'The translator is indebted, he appears to himself as translator in a situation of debt; and his task is to render, to render that which must have been given.'[18] Here Derrida introduces the idea of the debt, and also the gift, which he will go on to explore in greater detail.

Translation is also an act of hospitality, a word which became increasingly prominent in his later works. What is hospitality? Derrida differentiated conditional hospitality (the *laws* of hospitality), where the rules are at least partially set by the host, and unconditional hospitality (the *law* of hospitality), which is, again, an unachievable limit, as it requires the host to accept the guest without any constraints (behaviour, time), obligations, and, if truly unconditional, to not know the guest, to be surprised by their arrival, and for both guest and host to forget the hospitality after the event. All other forms imply some sort of indebtedness. Obviously this (impossible) unconditional is proposed in order to analyse the conditional, as (impossible) justice is proposed to analyse the law.

The translator cannot make their hospitality absolute post-Babel – a perfect translation would render the meaning exactly. In addition, two texts require a third, a reference outside themselves to guarantee their fidelity to each other, and this third can only be God, whose name in the Jewish tradition, notes Derrida, cannot be pronounced. He appears *sous rature*. He is ~~God~~. All we say of Him is inaccurate and necessary.

The Bible itself enacts the mystery; it demands to be translated – to spread the word of God, to spread the word God – but it contains within an injunction preventing exactly that. God's 'text is the most sacred, the most poetic, the most originary, since it creates a name and gives it to itself, but it is left no less destitute in its force and even in its very richness; it pleads for a translator.'[19] God Himself, Derrida writes, 'weeps over his name'.[20] Present at origin, present at telos, God meanwhile waits, as Judaism and writing wait.

As prayer is to God, so philosophy is to truth.

When the Berlin Wall fell on 9 November 1989, a narrative of Western triumphalism rushed into the space it had occupied. This was, so the story went, a victory for Western liberalism against the malign forces of communism. Poland had already elected a non-communist prime minster and Hungary was preparing for a multi-party election. A week after the fall of the Wall, Czechoslovakia began its Velvet Revolution, with Bulgaria and Romania following soon after. On 26 December 1991 the Soviet Union was dissolved, the Soviet flag having been lowered at 7:32 p.m. on the night before.

By now Derrida was combining his teaching at the EHESS with teaching at the University of California, Irvine, having followed J. Hillis Miller there from Yale after the death of de Man. He did keep a visiting professorship at Yale, as he did at Johns Hopkins and New York University. The States at the time seemed to him more open to French Theory. '*L'Amerique, mais c'est la deconstruction,*' he once joked. 'America is deconstruction.'[21]

America was also now globally ascendant. Famously, Francis Fukuyama declared, in a bestselling book, that this was *The End of History*. Fukuyama argued that Western liberal democracy is the final form of government – no other form can supersede it – and humanity had reached an end point of ideological evolution. It will achieve a universal hegemony, without rupture, without disruption.

On 22–24 April 1993, the University of California held a conference titled 'Whither Marxism? Global Crises in International Perspective', which sought to address the question of whether the fall of communism meant the end of Marxism and Marxist theory. Though the euphoric epistles to Western liberal democracy were crude, did they have a point? Could any of Marxism be saved from what was regarded, whatever the reservations, as its testing ground? Derrida's plenary address was delivered over two nights on the 22nd and 23rd of April, under the title 'Specters of Marx: The State of the Debt, the Work of Mourning, and the New International' and later became a book of the same name.

It is impossible to displace *Of Grammatology* as Derrida's most astonishing work, but *Specters of Marx* runs it close, given the historical context and Derrida's long-term resistance to a Marxist political position (or any political position, some might have argued, certainly before his outpouring of juridico-ethical works of the late 1980s and '90s). To intervene on the question of Marxism at precisely this point in history was shocking. Few heads were seen above the parapet offering any sort of defence of a system whose internal flaws – contradictions even – seemed to have brought it down, and whose victims were celebrating its demise. It was only just over ten years since Derrida himself had been a victim, jailed for attempting to bring Western ideas into a communist country, while the brief reign of the New Philosophers seemed to have made the conflation of Marx and the Gulag indisputable in intellectual circles.

Specters of Marx is, as one might expect, no simple paean to Marxism – unable to produce such a document in 1968, Derrida had no reason or temptation to produce one now. What he is writing, he notes, 'will not please anyone. But who ever said that someone ever had to speak, think, or write in order to please someone else?'[22] Rather he wishes to complicate what he sees as two particular dangers this singular moment inaugurates.

The first is that which has been noted – the fall of communism being misread as the triumph of Western liberalism, and as giving license to its uncontested dominion. As well as triumphalism, he sees a certain set of neuroses in the heralding of the new dawn, noting that

> this neo-liberal rhetoric, both jubilant and worried, manic and bereaved, often obscene in its euphoria, obliges us, then, to interrogate an event-ness inscribed in the gap between the moment in which the ineluctable of a certain end was heralded and the actual collapse of those totalitarian States or societies that gave themselves the figure of Marxism.[23]

Derrida takes Fukuyama and those who speak through him to task. While attempting 'not to be unfair' to *The End of History*, he notes that with books of this sort 'their very incoherence and sometimes their distressing primitivity play the role of symptomatic signal which one must account for as well as possible.'[24]

Fukuyama's drew on a Hegelian framework, via Alexandre Kojève's famous 1933 lectures on *The Phenomenology of Spirit*. Hegelian progress, Kojève argues, posits moving towards a global order without classes or other types of distinction, conferring universal recognition on all individuals, who in turn recognise each other. Human needs will not, as Marx argued, be eliminated by the end of capitalism, but by capitalism itself that, in Kojève's version, will overcome its own contradictions, unleash its full productive power and create wealth more than sufficient for human freedom. The capitalist West will thus achieve dominance through economic rather than military means. Absolute Knowledge, Hegel's dream of complete self-consciousness and self-possession of spirit, will replace ideology. And, like the utopia Marx desired, this post-historical world will leave absolute space for 'art, love, play, and so forth; in short, everything that makes Man happy.'[25] Fukuyama proclaimed we were now approaching that end-game. While it may still take centuries, and still go through reversals, the model for human emancipation has been found.

While one thread of human existence might, at a pinch, be conducive to Fukuyama's thesis, it took a lot of nerve, Derrida argued in reply, to avow this as anything but a local phenomenon, and to fail to hold Western liberal democracy accountable for those conditions in the world that were at odds with its sunny positivism.

> For it must be cried out, at a time when some have the audacity to neo-evangelize in the name of the ideal of a liberal democracy that has finally realized itself as the ideal of human history: never have violence, inequality, exclusion, famine, and thus economic oppression affected as many human beings in the history of the earth and of humanity. Instead of singing the advent of the ideal of liberal democracy and of the capitalist market in the euphoria of the end of history, instead of celebrating the 'end of ideologies' and the end of the great emancipatory discourses, let us never neglect this obvious macroscopic fact, made up of innumerable singular sites of suffering: no degree of progress allows one to ignore that never before, in absolute figures, have so many men, women and children been subjugated, starved or exterminated on the earth.[26]

These conditions were not outside the remit of capitalism, they were not exceptions to it, and they certainly were not its antithesis. They were as much part of the structure of capitalism as Fukuyama's bullish diagnosis.

Derrida is also prepared to give a history lesson, noting that the sort of eschatological thinking in which Fukuyama is indulging is nothing new, not even when it comes to proclaiming the end of Marxism. He pulls no punches: the 'end of communist Marxism' did not 'await the recent collapse of the USSR'.

> Many young people today (of the type 'readers-consumers of Fukuyama' or of the type 'Fukuyama' himself) probably no longer sufficiently realize it: the eschatological themes of the 'end of history', of the 'end of Marxism', of the 'end of philosophy', of the 'ends of man', of the 'last man' and so forth were, in the 50s, that is, forty years ago, our daily bread.[27]

The question being asked now of Marxism is 'the same question, always, as final question'.

The second danger is that Marx – his radical thought – would now be tamed, 'depoliticize[d] profoundly...by putting on a tolerant face, to neutralize a potential force, first of all by enervating a corpus, by silencing in it the revolt.'[28] This defanged Marx then becomes just a philosopher like any other, and academics will 'treat him calmly, objectively, without bias: according to the academic rules, in the University, in the library, in colloquia!'[29]

Derrida ventriloquises:

'Marx, you see, was despite everything a philosopher like any other; what is more [and one can say this now that so many Marxists have fallen silent], he was a great-philosopher who deserves to figure on the list of those works we assign for study and from which he has been banned for too long. He doesn't belong to the communists, to the Marxists, to the parties, he ought to figure within our great canon of Western political philosophy. Return to Marx, let's finally read him as a great philosopher.'

'We have', notes Derrida, 'heard this and we will hear it again.'[30]

Derrida wishes to resist each of these temptations. His text opens, again surprisingly, with a scene from *Hamlet* – Act I, Scene V – in which Hamlet, having encountered his father's ghost, declares that 'time is out of joint.' Marx's love of Shakespeare, Derrida notes, is well known, and it is the spirit of Hamlet that seems, in Derrida's reading, to haunt Marx, in particular the Marx of *The Communist Manifesto*, that least depoliticisable of his works.

To his shame, Derrida admits having not read the *Manifesto* in decades, and to have found 'a ghost waiting there' – the first noun, 'specter.' 'A specter is haunting Europe – the specter of Communism.' It is of specters – ghosts, revenants, spirits – which Derrida wishes to speak. Triumphalism reveals its fears in the very manic mode of its avowals: 'Hegemony still organizes the repression and thus the confirmation of a haunting. Haunting belongs to the structure of every hegemony.'[31]

The positivistic hegemony advocated by Fukuyama (and Kojève, and Hegel, and Marx for that matter) has an absolutely transparent ontology – this is, after all, what Absolute Knowledge is. Opposing this, Derrida proposes his near homonym – 'hauntology'. Any hegemony is haunted from within by those 'things' which it is not (here again we hear echoes of the 'trace'), by pasts that can never quite cease to be past even under erasure, and those futures that were prophesied but never occurred. And by the 'starved and exterminated' who are the victims of its triumph.

We have, as Derrida notes, been here before. In 1919, after the Great War, Paul Valéry wrote *Crisis of the Mind*, in which he imagined a 'Hamlet of Europe' who is 'watching millions of ghosts' and staggering 'between two abysses – for two dangers never cease threatening the world: order and disorder.' Valéry writes:

> Every skull he picks up is an illustrious skull. This one was Leonardo. He invented the flying man, but the flying man has not exactly served his inventor's purposes ... And that other skull was Leibnitz, who dreamed of universal peace. And this one was Kant ... and Kant begat Hegel, and Hegel begat Marx, and Marx begat ...[32]

Presence/absence, ontology/hauntology, being/non-being or, in Shakespeare's formulation, 'to be' or 'not to be' – these are oppositions which must be undone through a discourse that Derrida names spectrality. As with the deconstruction of any binary opposition, this is not a simple overturning, but a recognition of mutual dependence, a putting into question, an encounter of the aporia, of the impossible. Like the ghost of Hamlet's father, the ghost of Marx is there and not there in the discourses of Western liberal democracy.

'Time is out of joint' – this is the deferral and delay that is différance. As Derrida notes, deconstruction was born from a previous 'end of history'. He drew on

> the canon of the modern apocalypse (end of History, end of Man, end of Philosophy, Hegel, Marx, Nietzsche, Heidegger ... [and] all the socio-economic disasters of Soviet bureaucracy, the

Stalinism of the past and the neoStalinism in process ... Such was no doubt the element in which what is called deconstruction developed – and one can understand nothing of this period of deconstruction, notably in France, unless one takes this histori- cal entanglement into account.[33]

While Derrida notes that 'deconstruction has never been Marxist, no more than it has ever been non-Marxist, although it has remained faithful to a certain spirit of Marxism, to at least one of its spirits ...', deconstruction 'would have been impossible and unthinkable in a pre-Marxist space'.[34]

The hegemonic state that Western liberal democracy aspires to is simultaneously performing its own version of spectralis- ing, in its *dissemination* – via the media. Today, notes Derrida, politicians and events are always already filtered through the media. Traditional political parties are 'radically unadapted to the new-tele-techno-media-conditions of public space, of political life, of democracy, and of the new modes of representation (both parliamentary and non-parliamentary) that they call up' and may disappear, become ghosts whose existence is effaced by politicians who 'were thought to be actors of politics, they now often risk, as everyone knows, being no more than TV actors'.[35]

If there is a tendency in all Western democracies no longer to respect the professional politician or even the party member as such, it is no longer only because of some personal insufficiency, some fault, or some incompetence, or because of some scandal that can now be more widely known, amplified, and in fact often produced, if not premeditated by the power of the media. Rather, it is because politicians become more and more, or even solely, characters.[36]

Derrida privileges Marx as one of the only thinkers of the tradition who, in his engagement with the space between his- torical diagnosis and a political prognosis, is able to 'converse with the specter' and to 'analyze the ambiguities of the event as the happening of the impossible'.[37] Deconstruction takes up this Marxism and radicalises it in two ways: first, it attempts to bring political reality closer to the Marxist ideal; second, as Derrida writes, deconstruction is 'a question of putting into question again, in certain of its essential predicates, the very concept' of the Marxist ideal.[38] Marxism should not be just another ideology competing for hegemonic completion, rather, radicalised by deconstruction, it should continue to work away as a form of engagement and a continual challenge to hegemony. It should continue to return, like Hamlet's father, to accuse its murderers.

Derrida is careful not to situate Marx as an empty signifier of resistance – the importance of Marx as political thinker cannot in any sense slew off the importance of Marx as an economic thinker. If it is *Hamlet* which Derrida invokes in *Specters of Marx*, he does not ignore another play, the one Marx himself invokes most often, *Timon of Athens*, Shakespeare's investigation of money, debt, obligation, gift and friendship. It is a play, writes Marx, about the 'power of money' and several times throughout his work he quotes from the opening speech of Act IV, Scene III. Timon, having started the play the most generous of men, giving away his money to all in need, forgiving his own debts and paying off those of others while being lavish to all and sundry, finds himself abandoned by his friends when his own debts pile up. Retreating to live in the woods, he soliloquises on the power of money, which makes 'black white, foul fair, wrong right, base noble, old young, coward valiant … Make the hoar leprosy adored, place thieves, and give them title, knee and approbation, with senators on the bench.'

Money is another specter which moves among us, a 'bodiless body'.[39] 'Marx', notes Derrida, 'always described money, and more precisely the monetary sign, in the figure of appearance or simulacrum, more exactly of the ghost.'[40] As Marx puts it in his *Critique of Political Economy*, 'The body of money is but a shadow.' But it has transformative power of exactly the sort Timon identifies, all is changed utterly by its presence or absence, by its promise to come or not to come, while debt, which can never be seen, nor precisely exacted ('a pound of flesh') is the foundation of all interactions.

Derrida also addressed money, and thus debt, and thus obligation, in a work composed at a similar time, *Given Time: I. Counterfeit Money*. In it, Derrida explores the idea of debt through the idea of the gift. Is it actually possible to give a gift? In such a way that does not implicate either the giver or the receiver in a cycle of repayment and indebtedness?

The key text is Marcel Mauss's influential *The Gift*.[41] Published in 1925, it is an anthropological investigation of the idea of reciprocity and gift-giving in a number of so-called archaic societies. The giving of gifts in these societies is often a very public act, often entailing a degree of prestige, and always entailing a sense of obligation and the need to reciprocate. These cultural forms are not, of course, simply the domain of 'the archaic' – gift-giving in all communities shares the same economy in one form or another.

But is a gift – which should carry no obligation – truly a gift if it is automatically part of a system of exchange? *The Gift*, argues Derrida 'speaks of everything *but* the gift: It deals with economy, exchange, contract, it speaks of raising the stakes, sacrifice, gift and countergift – in short, everything that in the thing itself impels the gift and the annulment of the gift.'[42]

A true gift, like true hospitality, can only occur outside this system, and have no possibility of entering into it. An unconditional gift would have to be given without being noticed, thus escaping the possibility of obligation. 'If the gift appears ... as gift ... it annuls itself' – a possible/impossible aporia. In addition, the giver of the gift would have immediately to forget the giving, to escape the possibility of ingratitude. 'At the limit, the gift as gift ought not appear as gift: either to the donee or to the donor. It cannot be gift as gift except by not being present as gift.'[43]

This is, of course impossible. The gift is, in fact, the experience of the impossible – like God, like unconditional hospitality, like undeconstructible justice – which, should it come, comes to disrupt the economy. It is the messianic again, and the economy, fiduciary or other, stretches between origin and telos. Here Derrida brings in Heidegger's (and Aristotle's and Hegel's) conception of time (also invisible, also impossible) as circular. Wherever, argues

Derrida, the concept of 'time as circle is predominant, the gift is impossible', as 'a gift is only possible only at the instant an effraction [breaking open] in the circle will have taken place,' time going out of joint.[44]

It is *à venir*, 'to come', and this is different from the future: the future is what we know because it is predictable, because we can be certain that it will occur. *À venir* is the time that haunts as a possibility of imminence or irruption, and that is what alters. Thus it cannot be presence, not even future presence; it is a promise, a 'perhaps', that moves and does without coming to be. Whether Hamlet knows it or not, notes Derrida in *Specters*, he is 'speaking in the space opened up by this question – the appeal of the gift, singularity, the coming of the event, the excessive or exceeded relation to the other when he declares the time is out of joint.'[45]

Marx(ism), then, posits an intervention which should it succeed, would change utterly all the terms of the exchange. Spectrally, this promise continues to haunt Western liberal democracy even, perhaps especially, at its most triumphal.

Improbably, Derrida's exploration of ghosts, specters, spirits and mourning had a new life that it is unlikely he could have imagined. In the 2000s the idea of hauntology was taken up by a number of critics of late modernity, who saw in it a sort of reverse nostalgia – a nostalgia for futures that never came to be, cancelled, for example by postmodernity or neoliberalism, and which haunt us by their absence. Theorists such as Mark Fisher drew attention to the shift into post-Fordist economies in the late 1970s, which Fisher argues has 'gradually and systematically deprived artists of the resources necessary to produce the new'. In Germany, thinkers such as Erich Hörl, in his *Sacred Channels: The Archaic Illusion of Communication*, related the idea to the way that logic, in its nineteenth-century incarnation, presented a world untethered from experience and intuition, which he linked to the early twentieth century's obsession with primitive magic in the anthropology of Durkheim, Mauss and Lévi-Strauss.[46]

More improbably, hauntology became a British music genre. Ambient artists such as Boards of Canada, Burial and the

Caretaker produced work that, in their use of cassette tapes and analogue synthesisers, foregrounded the hiss and crackle of the decaying medium, producing eerie soundscapes which evoke a nostalgia for a lost future. Incorporating found sounds, such as soundtracks of the BBC Radiophonic Workshop, incidental music from children's television of the 1970s and samples from public information films, these artists produced music which yearned for a lost utopia of the sort dreamed of by Stuart Hall and Raymond Williams. As Marxism continues to haunt the narratives of hyper-capitalism, so this dreamed future continues to seep into the interstices of Britain's dreaming, a relic of an imagined future.

If Derrida was grappling with the ghosts, he still had to deal with some corpses.

On 9 May 1992, a letter appeared in *The Times*. 'Sir,' it began, as letters to *The Times* do:

> The University of Cambridge is to ballot on May 16 on whether M. Jacques Derrida should be allowed to go forward to receive an honorary degree ...
>
> Derrida describes himself as a philosopher, and his writings do indeed bear some of the marks of writings in that discipline. Their influence, however, has been to a striking degree almost entirely in fields outside philosophy – in departments of film studies, for example, or of French and English literature.
>
> In the eyes of philosophers, and certainly among those working in leading departments of philosophy throughout the world, M. Derrida's work does not meet accepted standards of clarity and rigour ...
>
> Derrida's career had its roots in the heady days of the 1960s and his writings continue to reveal their origins in that period. Many of them seem to consist in no small part of elaborate jokes and puns ('logical phallusies' and the like), and M. Derrida seems to us to have come close to making a career out of what we regard as translating into the academic sphere tricks and gimmicks similar to those of the Dadaists or of the concrete poets ...

Many French philosophers see in M. Derrida only cause for silent embarrassment, his antics having contributed significantly to the widespread impression that contemporary French philosophy is little more than an object of ridicule ...

Many have been willing to give M. Derrida the benefit of the doubt, insisting that language of such depth and difficulty of interpretation must hide deep and subtle thoughts indeed.

When the effort is made to penetrate it, however, it becomes clear, to us at least, that, where coherent assertions are being made at all, these are either false or trivial.

The letter was signed by eighteen academics from around the world, of whom W.V.O. Quine was probably the best known. Judging by the made-up 'logical phallusies' none of them had taken the time to read any of Derrida's work – it is not as though neologisms ripe for this sort of mockery are hard to find. As Terry Eagleton noted, all that the dons who voted against him knew was probably that he was 'radical, enigmatic, French, photogenic and wildly popular with students'.[47] And quite what the 'accepted standards' Derrida failed to meet were anybody's guess, but one suspects thinkers as diverse as Nietzsche, Heidegger, Foucault and Kierkegaard might have had a struggle on their hands too – as would Descartes, Locke, Berkeley, Hume and later Wittgenstein, all of whom tended to drift from the analytic. Socrates and Plato might have struggled as well, though the latter might have agreed about excluding Dadaists and concrete poets were they minded to apply to join the academy. The 'French philosophers' who found Derrida's work a 'silent embarrassment' are indeed silent: the only Frenchman to sign was a mathematician, René Thom. But such was Derrida's fame that the very British scandal became front-page news, the *Independent* leading with the droll headline 'Cognitive Nihilism Hits English City'.

Whatever the stupidities and inanities of the letter, it once again highlighted the hostility towards Derrida, as well as how misinformed it tended to be. Despite this epistolary intervention, Derrida was awarded his doctorate – the vote in favour was 336 to 204 – without the walls of the academy collapsing when the trumpet sounded.

It was not Derrida's first run-in with Oxbridge. On his first visit to England, in February 1968, he had to contend with 'an explosion of wrath' from the venerable A. J. Ayer, whose 1936 text *Language, Truth and Logic* launched the logical positivism of the Vienna Circle into the Anglophone world. The logical positivists' basic thesis that only verifiable statements are meaningful statements was obviously as far from Derrida's as possible.[48]

Derrida kept a dignified silence during the Cambridge affair, but in later interviews spoke explicitly of what he felt was at stake.

The violence of these denunciations derives from the fact that the work accused is part of a whole ongoing process ... that's no doubt because 'deconstructions' query or put into question a good many divisions and distinctions, for example the distinction between the pretended neutrality of philosophical discourse, on the one hand, and existential passions and drives on the other, between what is public and what is private, and so on.[49]

This time he had not been expelled.

&

My shawl. Mine was white first, completely white, only white, virgin and without those black or blue stripes that are printed, it seems to me, on almost all the talliths in the world. It was in any case the only white tallith in my family. It was given to me by my mother's father, Moses. Like a sign of having been chosen. But why? ... After I left the house in El-Biar where I had left it, my father borrowed it from me for a few years. It is true that he still had reason to wear it, and he took it across the Mediterranean at the time of the exodus. After his death, I took it back as though I were inheriting it a second time. I hardly ever wear it ... I simply place my fingers or lips on it, almost every evening, except when I'm traveling to the ends of the earth, because like an animal it waits for me, well hidden in its hiding place, at home, it never travels.[50]

More and more, Derrida's reflections on ethics took him back to the self, his own self, and the place of inheritance and responsibility. His writings became more autobiographical. Philosophy is created from the vantage point of the philosopher, thrown into a historical setting, but nonetheless unique, singular. Derrida was attempting to write the book of himself and 'A Silkworm of One's Own', his meditation on the meaning of his inherited prayer shawl, explores ideas of veiling, and therefore truth, secrets, Judaism, Christianity and Islam. It is also written in the shadow not only of the death of philosophy, but in the 'to come' death of Derrida himself. It is written 'before the verdict, my verdict, before, befalling me, it drags me down with it in its fall, before it's too late, stop writing. Full stop, period.'[51]

Aimé Derrida had died in 1970, eight years after leaving his beloved Algeria. On 2 December 1989, just under a month after the fall of the Berlin Wall, Derrida was in Madrid, standing before El Greco's *Burial of the Count of Orgaz*. The painting is based on a Spanish legend that when the count, a noble philanthropist who had left considerable sums to the Church, died, St Stephen and St Augustine descended from heaven to bury him with their own hands. Burial, Derrida notes, 'is a reverse birth, return to the womb'.[52] The painting carries in it, like ghosts, four epochs – 'the old date of the count's death and the miracle, the inscribed date of birth, the date at which the canvas is painted ... and the fleeting, indeterminate epoch at which the spectator is watching.'[53] Derrida wonders why St Augustine has returned – to Earth for the burial, for himself as spectator at that moment – and notes wryly that 'all the characters in the picture, the contemporaries in fact, are looking in different directions, never crossing a glance, like my readers'.[54]

One year earlier, Derrida had believed his eighty-eight-year-old mother was about to die after a fall. In fact, Georgette lived for another two years. During that time Derrida wrote his own version of a confession, which he named 'Circumfession'. If his ethical and political writings were his most public response to the bruising years of the 1980s, this was his most personal response, although, as is the nature of any confession, it was not private.

The text takes St Augustine's own *Confessions* as its model (we remember Derrida was born in rue Saint-Augustin) and Derrida quotes him extensively, in particular the sections which deal with the death of Augustine's own mother, Monica. The word 'confession' also, of course, invokes Rousseau, and thus *Of Grammatology*. Derrida also quotes himself, drawing from a series of notebooks he had written between 1977 and 1984 about circumcision. Finally it is also a journal of his encounters with his mother as she dies – her fall, her inability to recognise him, her slide into a state which is not her, and the mourning that comes as much before death as after it. Derrida also charts the progress of an illness of his own, a virus which briefly prevented him closing his left eye, leaving it 'fixed open, like a glass-eyed Cyclops'.[55]

'Why do we confess to God, when he knows everything about us?' is the title of chapter 1 of book 9 of Augustine's *Confessions*, and it is this question of the secret, of confession, of testimony that frames the book. At a time when the attacks on Derrida were at their most personal, he turned to intimate public disclosure. But, as if to enact this authorised invasion of privacy, to implement its furtive and secretive public unveiling, the text itself appears as a 'sub' text, running like a footnote across the bottom of the essay 'Derridabase' by Geoffrey Bennington – the two works forming a whole (an auto/biography perhaps?) called *Jacques Derrida*. Bennington's essay is a valuable introduction to Derrida's thought, and its author a co-signatory on a contract between the two works. Where 'Circumfession' reveals itself in metaphor, allusion and quotation (double metaphoricity), in 'Derridabase', Bennington has promised Derrida he will 'do without any quotation and to limit himself to an argued exposition which would try to be as clear as possible.'[56]

For Derrida, circumcision is densely symbolic, overdetermined to a degree that almost cannot be borne. It is the original inscription on the body, a writing on it, a tattooing, by the other. It is the marker of Judaism, and therefore the perils of belonging and not belonging, a covenant, a consecration, the sexual organ turned into a sacrament. It is a rite of passage, a metaphor for nudity, a mark of shame. It enhances and decreases sexual pleasure (God

joins the circumcised in their most intimate act of intercourse),
and instils sexual discipline by reminding the Jew that God is
watching (God joins the circumcised in their most intimate act
of masturbation). It is the primal wound of patriarchy and mas-
culinity (Derrida like Freud refused to have his sons circumcised,
in part for this reason), and is a hypocritical unveiling set against
the veiling of women and their privates.

It is also the ever-present threat of maternal violence and/or
neglect. Derrida invokes the story of Zipporah in Exodus 5:24–
26, who circumcises her own son with her teeth to save Moses
from God's wrath 'before telling him, "You are a husband of
blood to me," she had to eat the still bloody foreskin, I imagine
first by sucking it, my first beloved cannibal, initiator at the
sublime gate of fellatio'; and Catherine of Siena who claimed
to wear Christ's own (invisible) foreskin as a wedding ring.[57] As
Derrida's mother dies, he is drawn back to this primal moment,
this mark of difference, this founding violence.

He is also drawn back to El-Biar, and the book contains some
of his richest descriptions of his childhood, again recalling his
tallith as his father makes the Yom Kippur sacrifice:

> The day of the Great Pardon, presence of white, my immaculate
> taleth, the only virgin taleth in my family. Like the feathers of
> the cocks and hens that Haim Aimé wants to be white for the
> sacrifice before Kippur, the Rabbi cuts their throats in the garden
> after feeling under their wings, holding the knife between his
> teeth, then passed them over our heads while saying our names,
> unforgettable bloodied white animals that I wanted to save.[58]

Blood runs through these narratives. Derrida structures a section
of the book around the exegetical schema known as PaRDeS:
Peshat, the literal meaning of a text; Remez, the allusive and yet
rational and logical meaning of a text, in the form of a puzzle,
a problem, an allegory; Derash, the homiletic, comparative
meaning, given by context, presented as sermon; and Sod, the
secret meaning, known only to initiates, often about the nature
of God – the last of which Maimonides in his *Guide* declares his

intention not to reveal, while pointing out that, in for instance the story of Eve being born from Adam, 'How great is the ignorance of those who do not see that all this necessarily includes some [other] idea [besides the literal meaning of the words]?'

In the case of blood, there is Peshat, his own blood, during circumcision; Remez, the blood of his cousin Simone whose 'sex' is injured in a scooter accident; Derash, his mother's menstrual blood, the sign for which is towels left lying around; and Sod, the blood of his mother, draining from her in death. There is also the blood of his cousin Jean-Pierre, whose death at the age of six was accidentally announced to Jackie at school as the death of his older brother; and the death of an actual older brother, Paul, eleven months before Jackie was born, which must 'have made me for her, for them, a precious but so vulnerable intruder, one mortal too many'.[59]

Derrida also meditates on his secret name, Élie, given to him at his circumcision but not recorded on his birth certificate, the 'hidden name without its ever being written on the official records, the same name as that of the paternal uncle Eugène Eliahou Derrida' – the unmarried uncle who would have carried him, Derrida speculates, to the mohel [circumciser]. Élie, then, is the founding secret, unknown even to himself for many years, a supplication and petition to Elijah, meaning 'My God is Yahweh', who in the Jewish tradition is invoked at circumcision and in Christian tradition, one who foretells the coming of the Messiah.

Secrets, as we have seen, those things of the crypt, had always haunted Derrida's work. If the trick to keeping a secret is not telling anyone, then confession is an abuse of the secret, unless it is produced to keep another secret. A secret must not be put into words, and yet I must tell it to myself, or it is not a secret – here again we encounter the auto-affection of the voice.

> The enigma ... is the sharing of the secret, and not only shared to my partner in the society but the secret shared within itself, its 'own' partition, which divides the essence of a secret that cannot even appear to one alone except in starting to be lost, to divulge itself, hence to dissimulate itself, as secret, in showing itself:

dissimulating its dissimulation. There is no secret as such; I deny it. And this is what I confide in secret to whomever allies himself to me. This is the secret of the alliance.[60]

But it is to his mother that the story keeps circling back. Georgette, this woman who 'along with billions of others forever knows nothing of what I write, never having wanted in all her life to read a single sentence of it.'[61] When he asks her, on 5 February 1989 whether she is in pain, she replies, 'Yes.' When he asks her where, she says, 'I have a pain in my mother' – as though, notes Derrida, 'she was speaking for me, both in my direction and in my place.'[62] Although he realises she may have been speaking about her own mother, the redoubtable Fortunée Temime, married in that back courtyard of a town hall to hide from the Algerian pogroms, whom Georgette more and more resembles. Later the same night she tears off all her clothes and when her son asks her why, she says, 'Because I'm attractive.' Such an 'improbable' sentence, he thinks, and then:

> I stop for a moment over this word 'improbable', over a pang of remorse, in any case over my admission that I owe the reader, in truth that I owe my mother herself for the reader will have understood that I am writing *for* my mother, perhaps even for a dead woman and so many ancient and recent analogies will come to my reader's mind even if no, they don't hold, those analogies, none of them, for if I were here writing for my mother, it would be for a living mother who does not recognize her son, and I am periphrasing here for whomever no longer recognizes me, unless it be so that one should no longer recognize me, another way of saying, another version, so that people think they finally recognize me, but what credulity, for here's the basis for the improbable, the improbable is here below the name.[63]

The book ends, improbably, with a series of photographs – Derrida at primary school, Derrida dreaming (like Camus) of being a professional footballer, Derrida at the Lycée Louis-le-Grand, Derrida at Cerisy, Derrida facing the press at Gare de l'Est, Derrida in *Ghost Dance*, Derrida with Borges. Then a bibliography interspersed with drawings, the 1973 cartoon of Derrida in *Le Monde*, the 1983 cartoon of Derrida which accompanied Searle's attack on him, the postcard of Socrates and Plato. And on the back cover a Judeo-Franco-Maghrebian two-year-old in a toy car, staring straight at the camera. 'Whatever precautions you take so the photograph will look like this or that,' notes Derrida, 'there comes a moment when the photograph surprises you. It is the other's gaze that wins out and decides.'[64]

11

An Event Has Occurred

The end approaches, but the apocalypse is long lived.
— 'Of an Apocalyptic Tone'

Such a caring for death, an awakening that keeps vigil over death, a conscience that looks death in the face, is another name for freedom.
— *The Gift of Death*

I was in Shanghai, at the end of a long trip to China. It was night-time there, and the owner of the cafe I was in with a couple of friends came to tell us that an airplane had 'crashed' into the Twin Towers. I hurried back to my hotel, and from the very first televised images, those of CNN, I note, it was easy to foresee that this was going to become, in the eyes of the world, what you called a 'major event'.[1]

An event had occurred, a singularity, an intervention of violence. For those who have now assimilated September 11 into a list of facts, or whose relationship to it is as an event from history, it is hard to describe the sense of doom that enveloped the world that day. Time was out of joint; there was a before and an after with an awful singular moment separating them. It was not long before competing narratives would attempt to enter the meaning of this moment, as they still do, but initially it lived in its uniqueness.

Derrida was on a tour of China, a place which had both fascinated and repelled him, its modernity, its strangeness. He was lecturing on the theme of 'Forgiveness and the Unforgivable and the Indefeasible', continuing to work away at the themes that had guided his work through the nineties. He also, where possible, spoke on the death penalty, the subject of his current seminars, although, in China there was little space for speculation such as:

> All discourses that legitimate the death penalty are first of all discourses of state rationality having a universal claim and structure; they are theorems of state right, of the machine of state ... the concept of the death penalty supposes that the state, the judges, society, the *bourreaux* and executioners, that is, third parties, have mastery over the time of life of the condemned one and thus know how to calculate and produce, in so-called objective time, the deadline to within a second ... Society, the state, its legal system, its justice, its judges and executioners, all these third parties are presumed to know, calculate, operate the time of death.[2]

The initial reaction of the Chinese state to September 11 was 'to circumscribe the importance of the event, as if it were a more or less local incident'.[3] On 12 September, Derrida spoke at Fudan University of a new phase in world history. He was himself due to be in New York shortly after, but had to go via Frankfurt, where he was to receive the Adorno Award – presented every three years, to recognise outstanding achievement in philosophy, theatre, music or film. Past winners included Jürgen Habermas, Pierre Boulez and Jean-Luc Godard; later it would be awarded to Judith Butler and Margarethe von Trotta. The award was always announced on 11 September, Adorno's birthday.

In accepting the award, Derrida read the first and last paragraphs of his essay 'Fichus', which concerned the dream of Adorno's friend and colleague Walter Benjamin. Benjamin had written to Gretel Adorno of a sentence in French that came to him in a dream – *Il s'agissait de changer en fichu une poésie*, 'It was about changing a poem into a scarf' – and from this Derrida weaves a rich tapestry of allusions about dreaming and waking, sleeplessness and melancholy. It also contained Derrida's first reaction to September 11. He called for a new way of thinking about Europe – 'a deconstructive critique that is sober, wide awake, vigilant, and attentive to everything that solders the political to the metaphysical, to capitalist speculating, to the perversions of religious or nationalist feeling, or to the fantasy of sovereignty'[4] – and set forth his position on what had occurred, a position he was to maintain.

> My absolute compassion for all the victims of September 11 will not prevent me from saying: I do not believe in the political innocence of anyone in this crime. And if my compassion for all the innocent victims is limitless, it is because it does not stop with those who died on September 11 in the United States. That is my interpretation of what should be meant by what we have been calling since yesterday, in the White House's words, 'infinite justice': not to exonerate ourselves from our own wrongdoings and the mistakes of our own politics, even at the point of paying the most terrible price, out of all proportion.[5]

One can imagine the effect of George W. Bush invoking 'infinite justice' on Derrida – Bush had already played a starring role in his seminars on the death penalty ('this Bush ... who dared to declare that the forty-five minutes of the execution of one of the 120 condemned ones he had not pardoned had been the worst in his life'), and now the president was making the ultimate apocalyptic promise, and with the military hardware to carry it out.[6]

That the event came to be named for its date was, of course, not insignificant for Derrida. A date is unique, it announces a singularity, it is something irreducible. But Derrida wanted to push this singularity further. This was not just a macro-event. The death of every one of the 2,996 individuals who died in the Twin Towers and at the Pentagon was itself a singularity, and the task – the infinite task – was to accord each death its own specificity, to face its unthinkability and not indulge in the 'affabulation' of real death. Derrida resisted totalising gestures here, as elsewhere. As he was to write about the death penalty, to impose a grand narrative is to distort. Naming is violence.

But in one of his later dialogues with Jürgen Habermas (collected as *Philosophy in a Time of Terror*) he was sensitive to other implications of designating this event by its date. First, the event is reduced to an 'intuition without a concept', just an empty incantation, where the date is substituted for the trauma, and the deaths of the victims and the trauma of the event are effaced.

Second, the date pins it to history – it is always already in the past, it can't happen again. This is, of course, a technique of psychoanalysis – by naming an event I archive it. Finally, the government and media, in their discourse, embrace the 'spectacularization' of the event such that the event is fully 'reified', to use an old Marxist term, as something coming from the outside, for which the body attacked has no responsibility and which is in no way 'encouraged'. Derrida uses corporeal and medical metaphors to speak of this, as 'the suicidal temptation, the autoimmunity' of a modern democracy: '9/11 is the symptom of an autoimmune crisis occurring within the system that should have predicted it. Autoimmune conditions consist in the spontaneous suicide of the very defensive mechanism supposed to protect the organism from external aggression.'[7] America had, after all, supplied weapons and training to the very hijackers who perpetrated the attack.

The event itself distilled for Derrida a great many of the themes of his ethico-political shift: justice, democracy to come, forgiveness. He had used the absence of the latter as a working definition of evil, 'capable of repeating itself, unforgivingly, without transformation, without amelioration, without repentance and promise.'[8] Thus the good is that which is able to forgive. Derrida chooses to speak of forgiveness as an 'Abrahamic concept' in order to bring together 'Judaism, the Christianities, Islam'. There are, he argues in 'The Force of Law', two types of forgiveness, parallel again with hospitality: the conditional and the unconditional. The former is a calculation about punishment and usually requires a promise from the forgiven not to do something again.

Unconditional forgiveness has no conditions, but it is also an impossible, mad idea:

> If, as I say, as I think, forgiveness is mad, that it must remain a madness of the impossible, this is certainly not to exclude or disqualify it. It is even, perhaps, the only thing that arrives, that surprises, like revolution, the ordinary sense of history, politics and law. Because that means that it remains heterogenous to the order of politics or of the juridical as they are ordinarily understood. One could never, in the ordinary sense of the words, found a politics or law on forgiveness.[9]

Derrida was in no way blind to the fact that these ideas were inseparable from the question of the Holocaust. This was of course the definitive singularity for a Jew of the twentieth century, although, controversially, he sometimes resisted what seemed to him to be an imperative to elevate it above other such tragedies: 'I know that it is unique, of course. But as to knowing whether one can make this uniqueness into an example and an exemplary point of reference, for me this remains very problematic with regard to other genocides.'[10] Again, this nuance was often not appreciated, nor was it allowed *as* nuance.

Similarly, his stance on Israel generated opprobrium, as is often the case with Derrida, from both sides. His position was, in a sense, classic (Jewish) left liberal, an ongoing attempt to divide anti-Semitism from disagreements with the Israeli government, an ongoing 'critical vigilance' to ensure this was done. Derrida remained sensitive to what he called 'left Judeophobia'. His own attitude towards the government of Israel was not censorious only for negative reasons. It also was 'an expression of respect for a certain image of Israel and as an expression of hope for its future.'[11]

Of the three Abrahamic religions, Islam was the one Derrida had engaged with least in his writings. In part this is, of course, in line with the Western (philosophical) tradition, which has, often unconsciously, but often brutally, aligned itself with the Judeo-Christian worldview, with its mania for assimilation of the other.

As Derrida pointed out, it is impossible to use the word 'Europe' without connoting 'Athens-Jerusalem-Rome-Byzantium'.[12] One still gets a jolt when Derrida is described laconically as an 'Arab philosopher', let alone as 'the African philosopher, Jacques Derrida', although both are correct. But there is a mimesis here, a repetition with the zones of exclusion which young Jackie had experienced growing up in El-Biar. Derrida was sensitive to this too, and, even before the event which generated such hyperbole as 'the clash of civilisations', had attempted to engage in dialogue, which was becoming his chosen way of communicating. But still we have no writing on, for instance, the event of the Prophet, whose writing down the dictated Word of God is rich with Derridean associations.

Derrida's most sustained engagement with Islam is a dialogue he conducted with Mustapha Chérif, then professor of philosophy and Islamic studies at the University of Algiers, in the spring of 2003 in Paris. In the shadow of September 11, the conversation is more political than religious. Derrida begins by insisting, 'I would like to speak today as an Algerian',[13] reiterating the influence his 'marginal' childhood had had on him:

> All the work I have pursued, with regard to European, Western, so-called Greco-European philosophical thought, the questions I have been led to ask from some distance, a certain exteriority, would certainly not have been possible if, in my personal history, I had not been a sort of child in the margins of Europe ... who had passed his time traveling between one culture and the other feeding questions he asked himself out of that instability.[14]

He is the search for the heterogenous, in his own identity, and in the political and geographical. Destabilise Judeo-Christian, by adding another hyphen, Judeo-Christian-Islamic.

Turning to September 11, Derrida argues that we can and must 'distinguish between the supposedly brute fact, the "impression", and the interpretation' of the attacks. What, he asks, would September 11 have been like if we did not have television? While not going as far as Jean Baudrillard's almost complete identification of the spectacle with the thing itself (as Bruno Latour wittily put it, for Baudrillard 'the Twin Towers destroyed themselves under their own weight, so to speak, undermined by the utter nihilism inherent in capitalism itself'), Derrida again wants to identify ways in which this singularity has been co-opted by the ideological state apparatus.[15] He retains his fidelity to a notion of reconciliation, of which South Africa's Truth and Reconciliation Commission is as close as we can get to an exemplar. Reconciliation is forgiveness is hospitality. As he had noted in his 2003 dialogues with Habermas:

> Pure and unconditional hospitality does not contain in an invitation ('I invite you, I welcome you into my home, on the condition that you adopt to the laws and norms of my territory [etc.]'). Pure and unconditional hospitality, hospitality itself, opens ... to someone who is neither expected nor invited, to whomever arrives as an absolutely foreign visitor ... I would call this a hospitality of visitation rather than invitation.[16]

Thus we must make room for the foreign, for the other. If all of this sounds overly idealistic, if Derrida's appeals to his Algerian boyhood sound overly nostalgic, there is a very good reason. Derrida had come to the dialogue straight from hospital where he had been told about his own unwelcome guest. Another event had occurred. He had pancreatic cancer.

Thoughts of death are, of course, an occupational hazard for philosophers; one cannot think philosophy without thinking of it. For Derrida, death was a constant preoccupation, haunting his work from its beginning: 'I think about nothing but death,' he once said. 'I think about it all the time, ten seconds don't go by without the imminence of the thing being there.'[17] Death is

> always the name of a secret, since it signs the irreplaceable singularity. It puts forth the public name, the common name of a secret, the common name of the proper name without name ... language about death is nothing but the long history of a secret

society, neither public nor private, semi-private, semi-public, on the border between the two.[18]

No one can experience someone else's death. It is the annihilation of the self, the messianic moment, the event. But death is a secret so secret that no one can experience their own either, until one can no longer experience. The sole keeper of it cannot access it, cannot hear it speak. It is the final end of that speaking self inside that we mistake for presence.

Derrida was seventy-three when he was diagnosed. Death had become more of an obsession for him in the few years before, especially since the death of Georgette. He found his seventieth birthday particularly confronting. It had also led to worries about his archive. All his life Derrida had kept everything he wrote, from shopping lists to *Of Grammatology*. What was to become of them? And his memories?

The notion of an archive was not simply a practical concern. In 1995 he had delivered the paper 'Archive Fever', in which he drew this association between archives and memory. Drawing on Freud and Foucault, he identifies the right to archive as an assertion of political power. Documents are made 'official' by 'publicly recognized authorities'. These private documents that are then given over to the public are, if held to be of sufficient import and interest, no longer our secret.

But archivisation does not simply record, it produces. By selecting what is important, it rejects what is not. This biography, for instance, adds another narrative version of the life of Jacques Derrida to other narratives of the life of Jacques Derrida. None of them regard, say, the car he drove in 1975 as important, nor can they access how things smelled for him at 10 a.m. on 5 June 1997. In choosing what of Derrida's to archive I assert a power over him. If this is the only book person *x* reads about Derrida, *this* is Derrida for them. As he put it in 'Cinema and Its Ghosts', 'The archive is a violent initiative taken by some authority, some power; it takes power over the future: it confiscates the past, the present, and the future. Everyone knows there is no such thing as innocent archives.'[19]

Drawing an analogy between this and the Freudian conscious/ unconscious (public/private) dichotomy, Derrida in 'Archive Fever: A Freudian Impression' anticipates some of the questions which will later be raised about the internet (this essay is his first to mention email). He asks:

Is the psychic apparatus better prepared or is it affected differently by all the technical mechanisms for archivisation and reproduction, for prostheses of so-called love memory, for simulacrums of things which already are, and will increasingly be, more refined, complicated, powerful than the 'mystic pad' (microcomputing, electonization, computerization, etc.)?[20]

Freudian psychoanalysis, argues Derrida, proposes a new theory of the archive, and it 'takes into account' the death drive. One who does not die does not need to archive, a society with no death does not need to keep records, although once the keeping of records *commences* (*arche* from which we get archive) it generates itself in a series of juridico-administrative moves (laws are refined by laws, texts by footnotes and secondary texts). Freud does not define a 'concept' of the archive, he gives the impression of it, a schema, of 'an infinite and indefinite process'.

But is Derrida talking about Freud? There are several times in the essay where his identification – transference – with this other controversial Jewish thinker feels almost total. In assessing Freud's archives, one cannot help but hear the echo of Derrida's own concerns.

What comes under theory or under private correspondence, for example? What comes under system? Under biography or autobiography? Under personal or intellectual anamnesis? In works said to be theoretical, what is worthy of this name and what is not? Should one rely on what Freud says about this to classify his works? ... In each of these cases, the limits, the borders, and the distinctions have been shaken by an earthquake from which no classificational concept and no implementation of the archive can be sheltered. Order is no longer assured.[21]

Order is no longer assured. In 1997 Derrida had started working with the Institut Mémoires de l'édition contemporaine (IMEC) to begin archiving his life's work, and in January 2002 he signed a contract allowing them to take charge of the material. They had done the same for Barthes, Foucault, Althusser and Genet. The Genet specialist Albert Dichy recalls Derrida saying, shortly after his seventieth birthday, 'You have to realize it's my life you are taking away.' There was, said Dichy, 'a sense of twilight about him.'[22]

As with Freud, it was not only order that was threatened.

> When it comes to thought, the question of survival has taken on absolutely unforeseeable forms. At my age, I am ready to entertain the most contradictory hypotheses in this regard: I have simultaneously – I ask you to believe me on this – the double feeling that, on the one hand, to put it playfully and with a certain immodesty, one has not yet begun to read me ... on the other hand, and thus simultaneously, I have the feeling that two weeks or a month after my death there will be nothing left.[23]

Derrida's nagging fear, that those who saw him as a charlatan were right, never left him. At any moment he might be thrown out of school, or photographed naked for a crime he didn't commit. Like Freud, his ideas were controversial, had spawned disciplines, generated fields of thought their originator could not have imagined, and had entered popular culture and everyday language to the point where their genesis had become invisible. He had millions of acolytes. But what if they were wrong? Sitting in his attic in Ris-Orangis, surrounded by his books and boxes of writings, typing at the 'little portable Macintosh on which I have begun to write', Derrida may have been thinking of himself when he typed, 'Freud can only justify the apparently useless expenditure of paper, ink, and typographic printing, in other words, the laborious investment in the archive, by putting forward the novelty of his discovery, the very one which provokes so much resistance, and first of all in himself.'[24]

࿒

Derrida continued to give public papers and to give his semi-nars. During 2001–3 the topic was 'The Beast and the Sovereign' where, carrying on his earlier work in *The Politics of Friendship*, he tried 'to think under the title of forgiveness, pardon, the death penalty, and sovereignty, what we were attached to was always … to try to think the living in life.'[25] This 'immense question of the living' could not be delimited to include only humans; the human/animal binary opposition was yet another to be deconstructed. The distinctions we use to separate the human species from the animal species are called into question, calling it 'necessarily indefinite' that we alone possess 'language, speech, reason, response, logos, the sense of death, technique, history, convention, culture, laughter, tears, work, mourning, burial, institutions, clothing, lying, pretence of pretence, covering of tracks, the gift, respect'.[26] This is, as with all Derridean decon-structions of binary oppositions, not a call for an overturning of the hierarchy, nor a call to obliterate one or the other of the categories (to obliterate one would necessarily be to obliterate the other anyway). Rather,

> as always, to stick to the schema of my recurrent and deconstruc-tive objections to this whole traditional discourse on 'the animal' (as though any such thing could exist in the general singular), one must not be content to mark the fact that what is attrib-uted as 'proper to man' also belongs to other living beings if you look more closely, but also, conversely, that what is attributed as proper to man does not belong to him in all purity and all rigor; and that one must therefore restructure the whole problematic.[27]

The seminar also took up themes Derrida had explored in his final trip to Cerisy in 1997, where he presented a ten-hour lecture, later published as *The Animal That Therefore I Am*. It was not the first time he had raised the question of the animal – the ani-mality of the letter appears back in *Writing and Difference*, while a later text '*Geslecht* 2: Heidegger's Hand' (1987) interrogates Heidegger's distinction between human and animal based on 'the hand' – roughly, that animals cannot 'make'. In his Cerisy lecture,

Derrida carries this interrogation across the whole of Western philosophy, teasing out the implications of the human/animal binary opposition. That which the human wishes to relegate from the self is given to the animal. But what happens when the animal gazes back?

If 'the animal' was a concern of Derrida's before his diagnosis, after it he was living in the awful corporeality of disease. Oral chemotherapy cost him the feeling in his fingers and toes and he was unable to write new texts. Instead he gave interviews and appeared on stage in dialogues. His seventy-fourth birthday was spent in Meina in Italy, where he holidayed with Marguerite and took part in a conference on 'How Not to Tremble' – neatly, movingly, bringing together his current physical state, what might have been his spiritual state and the moment, perhaps, that we heard the voice of Derrida for the first time, breaking through the text 'Violence and Metaphysics': 'It is at this level that the thought of Emmanuel Lévinas can make us tremble.'

In Meina, describing trembling as 'non-knowing', he added: 'The experience of trembling is always the experience of an absolute passivity, absolutely exposed, absolutely vulnerable, passive in the face of an irreversible past as well as in the face of an unpredictable future.'[28] This 'irreversible past' could be charted by the number of friends who had become ghosts. In *The Politics of Friendship*, Derrida invoked the 'law of friendship' – that every friendship is structured from its beginning, a priori, by the possibility that one of the two friends will die first and that the surviving friend will be left to mourn.

> To have a friend, to look at him, to follow him with your eyes, to admire him in friendship, is to know in a more intense way, already injured, always insistent, and more and more unforgettable, that one of the two of you will inevitably see the other die. One of us, each says to himself, the day will come when one of the two of us will see himself no longer seeing the other ... That is the ... infinitely small tear, which the mourning of friends passes through and endures even before death.[29]

This is of course reciprocal. 'I live in the present speaking of myself in the mouths of my friends,' he writes, 'I already hear them speaking on the edge of my tomb ... Already, yet when I will no longer be. As though pretending to say to me, in my very own voice: rise again.' Many of those whom he would have had gather would not be there. His 2001 *The Work of Mourning* – published in France under the considerably more evocative title *Chaque fois unique, la fin du monde* (Each time unique, the end of the world) – brought together fourteen meditations on the deaths of his friends for the past half-century, drawing a moving portrait of a particular moment in French and international thought, with celebrations and eulogies for Barthes, Foucault, Althusser, Lacan, Lévinas, Deleuze and Kofman, who had taken her own life on Nietzsche's 150th birthday. Hélène Cixous had referred to certain of them as the 'Incorruptibles' – they had, Derrida wrote, gone about their work 'without any concession even to philosophy, an ethos that does not let itself be scared off by what public opinion, the media or the phantasm of an intimidating readership might pressure one to simplify or repress.'[30] And now he had outlived them. 'Surviving – that is the other name for mourning,' he wrote. 'No one alive can get the better of this tautology.'[31]

On 16 August 2004, astonishingly, he went to Brazil, giving a three-hour address on 'Pardon, Reconciliation, Truth, What Genre?' On 19 August what would be his final interview appeared in *Le Monde*. In it he confessed to continuing to have a 'conversation – with Bourdieu, Lacan, Deleuze, Foucault, for example, who continue to interest me, more than those that the media focuses on these days.' In the interview he speaks of Europe and democracy, that there is a 'digression' in favour of gay marriage, and his difficulty in saying 'we'. And he talks for a final time about the ghost of death that runs through his work.

> All the ideas that have helped me in my work, notably those regarding the trace or the spectral, were related to the idea of 'survival' as a basic dimension. It does not derive from either to live or to die. No more than what I call 'originary mourning'. It is something that does not wait for so-called 'actual' death.[32]

A few days after the interview he found eating impossible, and was hospitalised, requiring morphine to deal with the pain. He told Marguerite he could hear Arab music, and smelled strange cooking odours. A six-hour operation to clear an intestinal blockage was successful, but that night Marguerite received a call to say he was in a coma. When she arrived, her Jackie was dead.

At home she found his funeral instructions. Not too many people, and, he joked, not too soon in case there was the possibility of resurrection. Perhaps it was in this letter that he asked for the name on his headstone to be Jackie – 'the name, to be distinguished from the bearer, is always and a priori a dead man's name, a name of death', he had written in 1982's *Ear of the Other*.[33]

The last thing he said in the interview in *Le Monde*, his last public pronouncement, was a sort of farewell.

> I am never more haunted by the necessity of dying than in moments of happiness and joy. To feel joy and to weep over the death that awaits are for me the same thing. When I recall my life, I tend to think that I have had the good fortune to love even the unhappy moments of my life, and to bless them. Almost all of them, with just one exception. When I recall the happy moments, I bless them too, of course, at the same time as they propel me toward the thought of death, toward death, because all that has passed, come to an end.[34]

The 'one exception' was his secret, which he took with him to the grave.

Jacques Derrida continues to divide opinion. Genius or charlatan? Philosopher or fraud? In his lifetime he was accused of corrupting youth, destroying academia, and of a relativism that is to be found nowhere in his writing. Now, he is accused of leading to post-truth, and the social and political implications of it.

Well, perhaps. In *The Politics of Friendship*, Derrida muses on the word 'perhaps', this 'dangerous perhaps'. Perhaps friendship, if there is such a thing, must honour what is impossible. Perhaps the impossible is the only possible chance of something new. A perhaps will perhaps always forbid its closing where it is in the very act of forming. The perhaps must open and precede, once and for all, the questioning it suspends in advance. The friends of the perhaps are the friends of truth. Of a mad truth ... perhaps.

If it is true that a theory proves its vitality by the number of controversies it provokes, then, perhaps, Derrida remains vital after the end, after the final undeconstructible:

> But to deconstruct death? Final period. And with the same blow, to come to blows with death and put it out of action. No less than that. Death to death. If death is not one, if there is nothing clearly identifiable and locatable beneath this word, if there is even more than one, if one can suffer a thousand deaths, for example through illness, love, or the illness of love, then death, death in the singular no longer exists. Why be anxious still? Stop taking seriously anxiety in the face of death – in the singular. Stop thinking of yourself as one condemned to death or the victim of a sentence of capital punishment. Your life is not a death row. That is perhaps what my angel might say to me. My angel, who is also my temptation. My angel is right, as always; it is necessary of course to deconstruct death and perhaps this is even the depth of the desire of what is called deconstruction. But the same guardian angel of deconstruction, or another guardian angel – for the problem of deconstruction is that it has more than one angel and that it is (this is its vigilance and its necessity) this knowledge of the multiplicity of angels – the same other angel of deconstruction just as implacably calls me back to order and says to me: *you will not get off so easily*.[35]

Acknowledgements

Thank you to my endless inspirations, Pearl and Olive Salmon-Watson; ditto Kerry Watson; to my saviours, Ivan Kolker, Charlie Davie, Bryan McCausland, Jason Pietzner and Garry Mansfield; ditto Guy Rundle; to my parents for supporting my baffling life; to Daniel Trilling, who commissioned me originally; to my agent, Markus Hoffman; to Leo Hollis for plucking me from obscurity and cutting out my nonsense; to Charlie and Fiona for reading this when it wasn't this. I would also like to acknowledge, in particular, Benoit Peeters, Edward Baring and Leonard Lawlor, whose work on Derrida was vital and illuminating. And to Fiona Sampson, who set me back on my feet and believed I had this in me, despite what I thought were powerful arguments against. Thank you all.

Notes

Introduction

1. 'Structuralism's Samson', *Johns Hopkins Magazine*, Fall 2012.
2. J. Derrida, 'Living On' in Derrida, *Parages*, trans. Tom Conley, James Hulbert and Avita Ronell, Stanford University Press, 2011, p. 104.
3. J. Derrida, *The Death Penalty: Volume 1*, trans. Peggy Kamuf, University of Chicago Press, 2014, p. 117.
4. J. Derrida, *Limited Inc*, trans. Samuel Weber, Northwestern University Press, 1977, p. 93.
5. J. Derrida, 'The Transcendental and Language' in Derrida, *Margins of Philosophy*, trans. Alan Bass, University of Chicago Press, 1982, p. 195.
6. J. Derrida, 'Roundtable on Translation' in Derrida, *The Ear of the Other: Otobiography, Transference, Translation: Texts and Discussions with Jacques Derrida*, trans. Avita Ronell and Peggy Kamuf, Schocken Books, 1985, p. 142.
7. G. Bennington, 'Derridabase' in Bennington and Derrida, *Jacques Derrida*, University of Chicago Press, 1993, p. 41.
8. Ibid., p. 264.
9. *The Times*, 9 May 1992
10. A. Pyle, *Key Philosophers in Conversation*, Routledge, 1999, p. 112.
11. M. d'Ancona, *Post Truth*, Ebury Press, 2017, p. 98.
12. André da Loba, 'Postmodernism Didn't Cause Trump, It Explains Him', *Washington Post*, 30 August 2018, 1.
13. J. Derrida, *Monolingualism of the Other; or, The Prosthesis of*

Origin, trans. Patrick Mensah, Stanford University Press, 1996, p. 5.

14. J. Derrida, 'White Mythologies' in Derrida, *Margins of Philosophy*, 1982, pp. 209–19.

15. Derrida, *Monolingualism of the Other; or, The Prosthesis of Origin*, 1996, p. 47.

16. Derrida, 'White Mythologies' in Derrida, *Margins of Philosophy*, 1982, p. 209.

17. J. Derrida, 'Violence and Metaphysics' in Derrida, *Writing and Difference*, trans. Alan Bass, Routledge & Kegan Paul, 1978, p. 79.

18. J. Derrida and M. Ferraris, *A Taste for the Secret*, Polity, 2001, p. 43.

19. J. Derrida, 'Violence and Metaphysics' in Derrida, *Writing and Difference*, 1978, p. 84.

20. Derrida, *The Ear of the Other*, 1985, p. 87.

21. J. Derrida, 'Taking Liberties' in G. J. J. Beista and D. Egéa-Kuehne, eds, *Derrida and Education*, Routledge, 2011, p. 178.

22. J. Derrida, 'The Time of a Thesis' in A. Montefiore (ed.), *Philosophy in France Today*, Cambridge University Press, 1983, p. 41.

23. Quoted in B. Peeters, *Derrida*, Polity, 2012, p. 159.

1 The Kid

1. C. Chaplin, *A Comedian Sees the World*, University of Missouri Press, 2014, p. 37.

2. M. Reeves and C. Goll, *The Intimate Charlie Chaplin*, McFarland and Company, Inc., 2001, p. 37.

3. J. Derrida, 'Circumfession' in Bennington and Derrida, *Jacques Derrida*, 1993, p. 119.

4. N. Oulebsir, *Les Usages du patrimoine: monuments, musées et politique coloniale en Algérie 1830–1930*, Maison des sciences de l'homme, 2004, p. 261.

5. M. McDougall, *A History of Algeria*, Cambridge University Press, 2017, p. 87.

6. F. Fanon, *The Wretched of the Earth*, trans. Constance Farrington, Grove Weidenfield, 1963, p. 40.

7. McDougall, *A History of Algeria*, 2017, p. 145.

8. M. Evans, *Algeria: France's Undeclared War*, Oxford University Press, 2012, p. 30.

9. J. Derrida, *Learning to Live Finally*, Palgrave Macmillan, 2007, p. 36.

10. Ibid., p. 35.

11. Ibid.

12. Derrida, *Monolingualism of the Other*, 1996, pp. 89–90.

13. Ibid., p. 52.

14. J. Derrida, *Points: Interviews 1974–1994*, Stanford University Press, 1995, p. 199.

15. Derrida, *Monolingualism of the Other*, 1996, p. 71.

16. Derrida, *Learning to Live Finally*, 2007, p. 35.

17. Derrida, *Monolingualism of the Other*, 1996, p. 55.

18. Ibid., p. 42.

19. Ibid., p. 37.

20. Ibid.

21. Derrida, 'Circumfession', 1993, pp. 169–70.

22. M. Chérif, *Islam and the West: A Conversation with Jacques Derrida*, University of Chicago Press, 2008, p. 31.

23. Derrida, *Monolingualism of the Other*, 1996, p. 60.

24. Peeters, *Derrida*, 2013, p. 13.

25. Ibid., p. 14.

26. Derrida, *Monolingualism of the Other*, 1996, p. 44.

27. Ibid., p. 42.

28. Ibid., p. 41.

29. Derrida, *Learning to Live Finally*, 2007, p. 37.

30. Ibid., p. 36.

31. Derrida, *Monolingualism of the Other*, 1996, p. 46.

32. R. Kearney, *Dialogues with Contemporary Continental Thinkers: The Phenomenological Heritage*, Manchester University Press, 1984, p. 123.

33. Derrida, *Monolingualism of the Other*, 1996, p. 50.

34. From an article in *Le Petit Oronais*, quoted in Peeters, *Derrida*, 2013, p. 16.

35. J. Derrida, *Sur Parole*, Editions de l'Aube, 1999, p. 12.

36. Derrida, *Monolingualism of the Other; or, the Prosthesis of Origin*, 1996, p. 16.

37. Derrida, 'Circumfession', 1993, p. 58.

38. Derrida, *Sur Parole*, 1999, p. 13.

39. Peeters, *Derrida*, 2013, p. 19.

40. F. Fanon, *Black Skin, White Masks*, Pluto, 2008, p. 69.

41. J.-P. Sartre, *Anti-Semite and Jew: An Exploration of the Etiology of Hate*, trans. George J. Becker, Schocken, 1948, p. 49.

42. J. Derrida, and H. Cixous, 'From the Word to Life', *New Literary History* 37(1), 2006, p. 4.

43. Ibid., p. 12.
44. Derrida and Ferraris, *A Taste for the Secret*, 2001, p. 59.
45. Bennington, 'Derridabase', 1993, p. 293.
46. J. Derrida, 'Cinema and Its Ghosts', *Cahiers du cinema* 37(1), p. 24.
47. Derrida, *Monolingualism of the Other*, 1996, p. 16.
48. Ibid., pp. 15–16.
49. Derrida, 'Cinema and Its Ghosts', 2015, p. 24.
50. Derrida, *Monolingualism of the Other*, 1996, p. 45.
51. J. Derrida, *Acts of Literature*, Routledge, 1992, p. 36.
52. Ibid., p. 38.
53. Ibid., p. 39.
54. Peeters, *Derrida*, 2013, p. 39.
55. 'Derrida on Sartre: Not a Strong Philosopher', YouTube.com, 20 July 2009.
56. E. Baring, *The Young Derrida and French Philosophy*, Cambridge University Press, 2011, p. 50.
57. Derrida, *Sur Parole*, 1999, p. 19.
58. Derrida, *Acts of Literature*, 1992, p. 34.
59. Peeters, *Derrida*, 2013, p. 32.
60. Ibid., p. 33.
61. Baring, *The Young Derrida and French Philosophy*, 2011, p. 65.
62. Peeters, Derrida, 2013, p. 35.
63. Ibid.
64. Baring, *The Young Derrida and French Philosophy*, 2011, p. 73.
65. Peeters, *Derrida*, 2013, p. 41.
66. Derrida, 'Phenomenologie et metaphysique du Secret,' sheet 1, in Baring, *The Young Derrida and French Philosophy*, 2011, p. 51.
67. Derrida, *Monolingualism of the Other*, 1996, p. 64.
68. Peeters, *Derrida*, 2013, p. 43.
69. Derrida, 'Cinema and Its Ghosts', 2015, p. 24.
70. Ibid.
71. Peeters, *Derrida*, 2013, p. 44.
72. Ibid., p. 43.
73. Ibid., p. 53.
74. Ibid.
75. Ibid., p. 54.
76. Ibid.

2 Husserl et al.

1. J. Derrida, *The Work of Mourning*, trans. Michael Naas, University of Chicago Press, 2001, p. 117.

2. E. Roudinesco, *Philosophy in Turbulent Times: Canguilhem, Sartre, Foucault, Althusser, Deleuze, Derrida*, trans. William McCuaig, Columbia University Press, 2010, p. 119.

3. L. Althusser, *The Future Lasts a Long Time*, trans. Richard Veasey, Vintage, 1994, p. 102.

4. Ibid., p. 339.

5. Baring, *The Young Derrida and French Philosophy*, 2011, p. 91.

6. Ibid., p. 108.

7. J. Derrida, 'The Politics of Friendship' in J. Derrida and E. Rottenberg, *Negotiations: Interventions and Interviews, 1971–2001*, Stanford University Press, 2002, p. 163.

8. Ibid., p. 152.

9. Ibid., p. 168.

10. Ibid., p. 191.

11. Baring, *The Young Derrida and French Philosophy*, 2011, p. 105.

12. A. Jaegerschmid, 'Conversation with Edmund Husserl, 1931–1938', trans. Marcus Brainard, *The New Yearbook for Phenomenology and Phenomenological Philosophy 1*, 2001, p. 339.

13. E. Husserl, *Philosophy of Arithmetic: Psychological and Logical Investigations with Supplementary Texts from 1887–1901*, trans. Dallas Willard, Kluwer Academic Publishers, 2003.

14. J. Derrida, *The Problem of Genesis in Husserl's Philosophy*, trans. Marian Hobson, University of Chicago Press, 2003, p. 16.

15. Quoted in D. Moran, *Edmund Husserl: Founder of Phenomenology*, Polity, 2007, p. 61.

16. Ibid., p. 22.

17. E. Husserl, *Ideas Pertaining to a Pure Phenomenology and to a Phenomenological Philosophy (Ideas 1)*, trans. Fred Kersten, Martinus Nijhoff, 1983, p. 84.

18. Ibid., p. 214.

19. Ibid., p. 55.

20. Ibid., p. 93.

21. Ibid., p. 49.

22. Derrida, *The Problem of Genesis in Husserl's Philosophy*, 2003, p. xv.

23. Baring, *The Young Derrida and French Philosophy*, 2011, p. 106.

24. T. Duc Thao, *Phenomenology and Dialectical Materialism*, trans. Daniel J. Herman and Donald V. Morano, D. Riedel Publishing Company, 1985, p. 39.

25. Ibid., p. 123.

26. Quoted in Derrida, *The Problem of Genesis in Husserl's Philosophy*, 2003, p. 54.

27. Husserl, *Ideas 1*, 1983, pp. 125, 83.

28. E. Husserl, *Analyses Concerning Passive and Active Synthesis: Lectures of Transcendental Logic*, trans. Anthony J. Steinbock, Kluwer Academic Publishers, 2001, p. 107.

29. E. Husserl, *The Phenomenology of Internal Time-Consciousness*, trans. James S. Churchill, Indiana University Press, 2019, p. 95.

30. Ibid., p. 23.

31. Derrida, *The Problem of Genesis in Husserl's Philosophy*, 2003, xvi.

32. Ibid., p. 90.

33. Ibid., p. 132.

34. Letter to Ludwig Landgrebe, quoted in D. Moran, *Husserl's Crisis of the European Sciences and Transcendental Phenomenology: An Introduction*, Cambridge University Press, 2012, p. 32.

35. As Heidegger's former student, Hans Jonas mocked his defenders in his searing inaugural lecture at a Drew University conference on Heidegger in 1964. Jonas had replaced Heidegger himself who had withdrawn for health reasons. Quoted in R. Wolin, *Heidegger's Children: Hannah Arendt, Karl Löwith, Hans Jonas and Herbert Marcuse*, Princeton University Press, 2015, p. 103.

36. Quoted in T. Kisiel and T. Sheehan (trans. and eds), *Becoming Heidegger*, Northwestern University Press, 2007, p. 413.

37. E. Husserl, *The Crisis of European Sciences and Transcendental Phenomenology*, trans. David Carr, Northwestern University Press, 1970, p. 389.

38. Derrida, *The Problem of Genesis in Husserl's Philosophy*, 2003, p. 178.

39. Peeters, *Derrida*, 2013, p. 69.

40. J. Derrida, 'Taking Liberties' in Beista and Egéa-Kuehne, *Derrida and Education*, 2011, p. 178.

41. Peeters, *Derrida*, 2013, p. 64.

42. Ibid.

43. Ibid., p. 72.

44. Ibid., p. 79.

3 Problems of Origin

1. Derrida, 'Circumfession', 1993, p. 329.

2. Peeters, *Derrida*, 2013, p. 81.

3. A. Horne, *A Savage War of Peace: Algeria 1954–1962*, New York Review Books, 2006, p. 183.

4. J. Caputo (ed.), *Deconstruction in a Nutshell: A Conversation with Jacques Derrida*, Fordham University Press, 1997, p. 25.

5. Derrida, 'Ulysses Gramophone: Hear Say Yes in Joyce', trans. François Raffoul, in A. Mitchell and S. Slate (eds), Derrida and Joyce: Texts and Contexts, SUNY Press, 2013, p. 150.

6. Ibid.

7. Derrida, *Sur Parole*, 1999, p. 21.

8. Peeters, *Derrida*, 2013, p. 95.

9. Ibid., p. 109.

10. E. Lévinas, 'The Name of a Dog, Or Natural Rights' in Lévinas, *Difficult Freedom: Essays on Judaism*, trans. Sean Hand, Johns Hopkins University Press, 1990, p. 153.

11. R. Davidson, 'Thinkers: Face to Face', *New Humanist*, 7 May 2008.

12. M. Heidegger, *Being and Time*, trans. Joan Stambaugh, SUNY Press, 1996, p. 27.

13. Ibid., p. 279.

14. E. Husserl, *The Crisis of European Sciences and Transcendental Phenomenology*, Northwestern University Press, 1970, pp. 108–9.

15. E. Lévinas, *Nine Talmudic Readings*, trans. Annette Aronowicz, Indiana University Press, 1990, p. 21.

16. Derrida, *The Work of Mourning*, 2001, p. 206.

17. E. Husserl, 'The Origin of Geometry' in J. Derrida, *Edmund Husserl's Origin of Geometry*, trans. John P. Leavey Jr., University of Nebraska Press, 1989, p. 159.

18. Ibid., p. 158.

19. Derrida, *Edmund Husserl's Origin of Geometry*, 1989, p. 17.

20. Husserl, 'The Origin of Geometry', 1989, p. 160.

21. Ibid.

22. Ibid., p. 161.

23. Ibid., p. 162.

24. Ibid., p. 164.

25. Ibid.

26. E. Husserl, *Logical Investigations*, trans. J. N. Findlay, Routledge, 2001, p. 60.

27. Derrida, *Edmund Husserl's Origin of Geometry*, 1989, p. 87.
28. Ibid., p. 88.
29. Ibid., p. 82.
30. Ibid., p. 100.
31. Ibid., p. 165.
32. Ibid., p. 102.
33. Derrida, 'Ulysses Gramophone', 2013, p. 149.
34. F. Nietzsche, 'On Truth and Lies in a Nonmoral Sense' in W. Kaufmann (ed.), *The Portable Nietzsche*, Viking, 1976, pp. 46–7.
35. J. Derrida, 'Des Tours de Babel' in J. Derrida, *Psyche: Inventions of the Other*, Stanford University Press, 2007, p. 197.
36. Husserl, *The Crisis of European Sciences*, 1970, p. 366.
37. Derrida, *Edmund Husserl's Origin of Geometry*, 1989, p. 153.
38. J. Derrida, 'Différance' in Derrida, *Speech and Phenomena and Other Essays on Husserl's Theory of Signs*, trans. David Allison, Northwestern University Press, 1973, p. 132.
39. J. Derrida, '"Genesis and Structure" and Phenomenology' in Derrida, *Writing and Difference*, trans. Alan Bass, Routledge, 2005, p. 157.
40. Peeters, *Derrida*, 2013, p. 119.
41. Ibid., p. 101.
42. J. Derrida, *Positions*, trans. Alan Bass, University of Chicago Press, 1982, p. 77.
43. Ibid., p. 41.
44. Ibid.
45. J. Derrida, '"Genesis and Structure" and Phenomenology', 2005, p. 207.

4 Jacques Derrida

1. J. Derrida, *Learning to Live Finally*, 2007, p. 31.
2. Derrida, *Sur Parole*, 1999, p. 19.
3. A. Camus, *Algerian Chronicles*, trans. Arthur Goldhammer, Harvard University Press, 2014, p. 18.
4. Fanon, *The Wretched of the Earth*, 1963, p. 61.
5. Peeters, *Derrida*, 2013, pp. 130–31.
6. J. Cavaillès, *On the Logic and Theory of Science*, trans. Knox Peden and Robin Macakay, Urbanomic, 2019, p. 65.
7. L. Lawlor, *Derrida and Husserl*, Indiana University Press, 2002, p. 146.

8. A. Badiou, *Philosophy for Militants*, trans. Bruno Bosteels, Verso, 2015, p. 12.
9. Derrida, 'Violence and Metaphysics', 2005, p. 141.
10. Ibid.
11. Ibid., p. 101.
12. Ibid., p. 111.
13. J. Derrida, *Of Grammatology*, trans. Gayatri Chakravorty Spivak, Johns Hopkins University Press, 1997, p. 99.
14. Derrida, 'Violence and Metaphysics', 2005, p. 97.
15. S. Wygoda, 'Levinas as reader of the Talmud', Ghansel.free.fr, 6 March 2001.
16. Lévinas, *Nine Talmudic Readings*, 1990, p. 4.
17. Derrida, 'Violence and Metaphysics', 2005, p. 101.
18. Ibid., p. 103.
19. Ibid., p. 126.
20. Ibid., p. 184.
21. Ibid.
22. Ibid., p. 192.
23. Peeters, *Derrida*, 2013, p. 147.
24. Derrida, *Positions*, 1982, p. 13.
25. E. Husserl, *Logical Investigations*, Routledge, 2001, p. 184.
26. Ibid., p. 187.
27. J. Derrida, *Voice and Phenomenon: Introduction to the Problem of the Sign in Husserl's Phenomenology*, trans. Leonard Lawler, Northwestern University Press, 2010, p. 6.
28. Ibid.
29. Ibid., p. 15.
30. F. Nietzsche, *Twilight of the Idols and The Anti-Christ*, trans. R. J. Hollingdale, Penguin, 1990, p. 6.
31. Derrida, *Speech and Phenomena*, 1973, p. 60.
32. Derrida, *Of Grammatology*, 1997, p. 13.
33. Hegel, *The Philosophy of Fine Art*, trans. F. P. Osmaston, 1920, Hacker Art Books, pp. 15–16.
34. Peeters, *Derrida*, 2013, p. 165.

5 An Event, Perhaps

1. K. Dwyer, 'Meet the Man Who Introduced Jacques Derrida to America', LitHub.com, 6 December 2018.

2. F. Saussure, *Course in General Linguistics*, trans. Wade Baskin, McGraw Hill, 1915, p. 7.

3. Ibid., p. 115.

4. C. Levi-Strauss, *The Raw and the Cooked*, trans. John and Doreen Weightman, Jonathan Cape, 1969, p. 92.

5. Derrida, 'Force and Signification' in Derrida, *Writing and Difference*, 1978, p. 1.

6. Ibid., p. 16.

7. Ibid., p. 26.

8. Ibid., p. 29.

9. Ibid.

10. Ibid., p. 22.

11. Ibid., p. 35.

12. M. Foucault, *The Order of Things*, Routledge, 2002, p. xxv.

13. J. Derrida, 'For the Love of Lacan' in Derrida, *Resistances of Psycho-analysis*, trans. Peggy Kamuf, Stanford University Press, 1998, p. 52.

14. J. Derrida, 'Structure, Sign and Play in the Discourse of the Human Sciences' in Derrida, *Writing and Difference*, 1978, p. 351.

15. Ibid., p. 352.

16. Ibid., p. 353.

17. Ibid.

18. Ibid.

19. Heidegger, *Being and Time*, 1996, p. 44.

20. Derrida, 'Structure, Sign and Play in the Discourse of the Human Sciences', 1978, p. 354.

21. Ibid.

22. Ibid., p. 362.

23. Ibid., p. 368.

24. Ibid.

25. Ibid., p. 369.

26. Ibid.

27. Ibid.

28. Ibid.

29. Ibid., p. 370.

30. Ibid.

31. Bret McCabe, 'Structuralism's Samson', *Johns Hopkins Magazine*, Fall 2012.

32. R. Macksey and E. Donato, *The Structuralist Controversy: The Languages of Criticism and the Sciences of Man*, Johns Hopkins University Press, 1972, p. 267.

33. Ibid., p. 265.
34. Ibid., p. 287.
35. J. Derrida, 'Some Statements and Truisms about Neologisms, Newisms, Postisms, Parasitisms, and Other Small Seismisms', trans. Anne Tomiche, in D. Carroll (ed.), *The States of 'Theory': History, Art, and Critical Discourse*, Columbia University Press, 1990, p. 80.
36. J. Derrida, 'Cogito and the History of Madness', in Derrida, *Writing and Difference*, 1978, p. 36.
37. Ibid., p. 60.
38. Ibid., p. 55.
39. Ibid., p. 39.
40. Ibid., p. 75.
41. Peeters, *Derrida*, 2013, p. 132.
42. M. Foucault, 'My Body, This Paper, This Fire' in Foucault, *Aesthetics, Method, and Epistemology*, The New Press, 1999, p. 417.
43. J. Derrida, 'To Do Justice to Freud' in Derrida, *The Work of Mourning*, 2001, p. 80.
44. Ibid.
45. Ibid., p. 90.

6 *Of Grammatology*

1. Derrida, *Of Grammatology*, 1997, p. 3.
2. Ibid., p. 310.
3. 'Derrida on the "Truly Exceptional Moment" when Writing "Of Grammatology"', YouTube.com, 5 January 2009.
4. Peeters, *Derrida*, 2013, p. 160.
5. Derrida, *Of Grammatology*, 1997, p. 6.
6. Ibid.
7. Plato, 'Phaedrus' in Plato, *The Collected Dialogues*, Princeton University Press, 1961, pp. 227a–279c.
8. Aristotle, *De Interpretatione*, 1:16a:3.
9. Derrida, *Of Grammatology*, 1997, p. 8.
10. Ibid., p. 11.
11. Ibid., p. 98.
12. Ibid., p. 35.
13. Ibid., p. lxviii.
14. Ibid., p. 30.

15. Ibid.
16. Ibid., p. 45.
17. Ibid.
18. Ibid.
19. Ibid., p. 46.
20. Ibid., p. 34.
21. Ibid., p. 53.
22. Ibid.
23. Ibid., p. 55.
24. Ibid., p. 56.
25. Ibid., p. 57.
26. Ibid., p. 61.
27. Peeters, *Derrida*, 2013, p. 28.
28. Derrida, 'Structure, Sign and Play in the Discourse of the Human Sciences', 1978, p. 369.
29. J.-J. Rousseau, *Emile, or On Education*, trans. Allan Bloom, Basic Books, 1979, p. 37.
30. Derrida, *Of Grammatology*, 1997, p. 101.
31. C. Lévi-Strauss, *Tristes Tropiques*, trans. John Russell, Hutchinson, 1961, p. 310.
32. Derrida, *Of Grammatology*, 1997, p. 113.
33. Ibid.
34. Ibid., p. 114.
35. Ibid., p. 59.
36. Ibid., p. 63.
37. Ibid.
38. Ibid., p. 108.
39. Ibid., p. 144.
40. Ibid., p. 17.
41. Ibid., p. 142.
42. Ibid., p. 163.
43. Ibid., p. 51.
44. Ibid., p. 154.
45. Ibid.
46. Ibid., p. 155.
47. Ibid., p. 159.
48. Ibid., p. 163.
49. Ibid., p. 166.
50. Ibid., p. 309.
51. Ibid., p. 292.

52. J. Derrida, 'Plato's Pharmacy' in Derrida, *Dissemination*, trans. Barbara Johnson, Athlone Press, 1981, p. 73.

53. Ibid., p. 95.

54. Ibid., p. 96.

55. Ibid., p. 171.

56. J. Derrida, 'Dissemination' in Derrida, *Dissemination*, 1981, p. 290.

57. Ibid., p. 304.

58. Peeters, *Derrida*, 2013, p. 207.

59. Ibid.

60. Ibid., p. 196.

61. Letter to Maria Antonietta Macciocchi in M. Macciocchi, *Letters from Inside the Italian Communist Party to Louis Althusser*, Verso, 1973.

62. Peeters, *Derrida*, 2013, p. 197.

63. Ibid.

64. A. Badiou, *Pocket Pantheon*, trans. David Macey, Verso, 2009, p. 137–8.

65. M. Heidegger, 'Letter on Humanism' trans. Frank A. Capuzzi, in Heidegger, *Pathmarks*, Cambridge University Press, 2014, p. 250.

66. Ibid.

67. Ibid., p. 247.

68. Derrida, *Of Grammatology*, 1997, pp. 23–4.

69. Ibid., p. 244.

70. Heidegger, *Being and Time*, 1996, p. 39.

7 Supposing That Truth Is a Woman – What Then?

1. S. De Beauvoir, *The Second Sex*, Vintage, 1973, p. 301.

2. H. Cixous, *Insister of Jacques Derrida*, trans. Peggy Kamuf, Stanford University Press, 2008, p. 31.

3. J. Derrida, *H.C. for Life, That is to Say ...*, trans. Laurent Milesi and Stefan Herbrechter, Stanford University Press, 2006, p. 21.

4. H. Cixous, 'The Laugh of the Medusa', trans. Keith Cohen and Paula Cohen, *Signs* 1(4), 1976, p. 880.

5. *Los Angeles Review of Books*, 9 October 2014.

6. J. Derrida, *Spurs: Nietzsche's Styles*, trans. Barbara Harlow, University of Chicago Press, 1981, p. 51.

7. A. Ronell, *Fighting Theory*, trans. Catherine Porter, University of Illinois Press, 2010, p. 161.

8. Badiou, *Philosophy for Militants*, 2015, pp. 15–16.
9. Derrida, *Spurs*, 1981, p. 37.
10. Ibid., p. 127.
11. Ibid.
12. Ibid., p. 129.
13. F. Nietzsche, *Beyond Good and Evil*, trans. Helen Zimmern, MSAC, 2008, p. 1.
14. J. Derrida, *Spurs*, 1981, p. 70.
15. L. Irigaray, *Marine Lover of Friedrich Nietzsche*, trans. Gillian C. Gill, Columbia University Press, 1993, p. 295.
16. Derrida, *Spurs*, 1981, p. 87.
17. Heidegger, *Nietzsche*, 1961, p. 70.
18. Derrida, *Spurs*, 1981, p. 135.
19. Peeters, *Derrida*, 2013, p. 296.
20. Ibid., p. 419.
21. Ibid., p. 284.
22. G. C. Spivak, preface to *Of Grammatology*, 1997, xvii.
23. J. Derrida, 'Proverb: "He That Would Pun…"', Foreword to John P. Leavey Jr, *Glassary*, Nebraska University Press, 1986, p. 17.
24. G. C. Spivak, 'Glas-Piece: A Compte Rendu', *Diacritics* 7(3), 1997, p. 23.
25. Peeters, *Derrida*, 2013, p. 158.
26. Ibid., p. 235.
27. Derrida, *Of Grammatology*, 1997, p. 26.
28. J. Sturrock, 'The Book Is Dead, Long Live the Book', *New York Times*, 13 September 1987.
29. Peeters, *Derrida*, 2013, p. 261.
30. J. Lacan, *Écrits*, trans. Bruce Fink, W. W. Norton & Company, 2006, p. 632.
31. J. Derrida, 'The Purveyor of Truth', *Yale French Studies* 52, 1975, p. 66.
32. J. Derrida, 'Fors' in N. Abraham and M. Torok, *The Wolf Man's Magic Word: A Cryptonomy*, trans. Nicholas Rand, University of Minnesota Press, 1986.
33. J. Derrida, 'The Time Is Out of Joint', trans. Peggy Kamuf, in A. Haverkamp and H. R. Dodge (eds), *Deconstruction is/in America: A New Sense of the Political*, New York University Press, 1995, p. 30.
34. Peeters, *Derrida*, 2013, p. 285.
35. J. Derrida, 'For the Love of Lacan' in Derrida, *Resistances of Psychoanalysis*, 1998, p. 69.

36. Derrida, *Spurs*, 1981, p. 35.

37. Peeters, *Derrida*, 2013, p. 357.

38. J. Derrida, *The Post Card: From Socrates to Freud and Beyond*, trans. Alan Bass, University of Chicago Press, 1987, p. 23.

39. Ibid., pp. 17–28.

40. Spivak, 'Glas-Piece: A Compte Rendu', 1977, p. 24.

41. Derrida, *The Post Card*, 1987, p. 87.

42. Ibid., p. 57.

43. Ibid., p. 38.

44. Ibid., p. 80.

45. Ibid., p. 98.

46. Ibid., p. 51.

47. J. Derrida, 'Khôra' in Derrida, *On the Name*, Stanford University Press, 1993, p. 109.

48. Althusser, *The Future Lasts a Long Time*, 1994, pp. 15–17.

49. Roudinesco, *Philosophy in Turbulent Times*, 2010, p. 101.

50. Peeters, *Derrida*, 2013, p. 321.

51. Ibid.

52. R. Seymour, 'The Murder of Hélène Rytman', versobooks.com, 24 July 2017.

53. G. Elliott, *Althusser: The Detour of Theory*, Brill Publishers, 2006, p. 328.

8 Here Comes Everybody

1. J.-F. Lyotard, *The Postmodern Condition*, trans. Geoff Bennington and Brian Massumi, Manchester University Press, 1984, p. 82.

2. Derrida, *The Ear of the Other*, 1985, p. 5.

3. Ibid., p. 49.

4. 'Derrida on Seinfeld', YouTube.com, 3 December 2014.

5. Peeters, *Derrida*, 2013, p. 227.

6. 'Critical Intimacy: An Interview with Gayatri Chakravorty Spivak', *Los Angeles Review of Books*, 29 July 2016.

7. Ibid.

8. S. Hall, 'Notes on Deconstructing "The Popular"' in R. Guins and O. Cruz (eds), *Popular Culture: A Reader*, SAGE, 2005, p. 70.

9. C. Clark, 'Jacques Derrida, a Cambridge Epiphany', opendemocracy. net, 25 October 2004.

10. Derrida, *The Ear of the Other*, 1985, pp. 119–20.

11. Derrida, 'Cinema and Its Ghosts', 2015, p. 27.

12. Villanova University, 'Roundtable Discussion with Jacques Derrida', hydra.humanities.uci.edu, 3 October 1994.

13. Peeters, *Derrida*, 2013, p. 306.

14. 'Jacques Derrida on Photography', YouTube.com, 5 July 2008.

15. J. L. Austin, *How to Do Things with Words*, Oxford Paperbacks, 1976.

16. J. R. Searle, *Speech Acts: An Essay in the Philosophy of Language*, Cambridge University Press, 1969, p. 55.

17. J. Derrida, *Limited Inc*, trans. Alan Bass and Samuel Weber, Northwestern University Press, 1988, p. 18.

18. Ibid., p. 7.

19. Ibid., p. 14.

20. Ibid., p. 12.

21. J. R. Searle, 'Reiterating the Differences: A Reply to Derrida', *Glyph* 2, 1977, p. 198.

22. Ibid., p. 201.

23. Ibid.

24. Ibid., p. 204.

25. Derrida, *Limited Inc*, 1998, p. 113.

26. Ibid, p. 8.

27. J. R. Searle, 'The World Turned Upside Down', *New York Review of Books*, 27 October 1983.

28. J. Derrida, *Limited Inc*, 1998, p. 114.

29. Ibid., 122.

30. Plato, *The Republic*, pp. 597–8.

31. Ibid.

32. Ibid.

33. Derrida, 'White Mythologies', 1982, p. 268.

34. Ibid., p. 266.

35. Ibid., p. 213.

36. C. Norris, *Derrida*, Harvard University Press, 1987, p. 18.

37. J. Derrida, *Acts of Literature*, 1991, p. 33.

38. Ibid., p. 47.

39. J. Derrida, 'Che cos'è la poesia' in P. Kamuf (ed.), *A Derrida Reader: Between the Blinds*, Harvester Wheatsheaf, 1991, p. 233.

40. P. Celan, *Selected Prose of Paul Celan*, Routledge, 2003, p. 34.

41. J. Derrida, 'Shibboleth for Paul Celan' in Derrida, *Acts of Literature*, 1991, p. 404.

42. Ibid., p. 378.

43. Ibid.

44. Ibid., p. 383.
45. Peeters, *Derrida*, 2013, p. 283.
46. C. Norris, *Paul de Man: Deconstruction and the Critique of Aesthetic Ideology*, Routledge, 1988, p. xvi.
47. B. Johnson, *A World of Difference*, Johns Hopkins University Press, 1988, p. 20.
48. Norris, *Paul de Man*, 1988, p. 59.
49. P. de Man, *Resistance to Theory*, Manchester University Press, 1987, p. 11.
50. P. de Man, *Blindness and Insight*, University of Minnesota Press, 1971, p. 231.
51. P. de Man, 'Shelley Disfigured' in P. de Man, *The Rhetoric of Romanticism*, Columbia University Press, 2000, p. 93–124.
52. F. Lentrecchia, *Criticism and Social Change*, University of Chicago Press, 1985, p. 44.
53. J. Hillis Miller, 'The Critic as Host', *Critical Inquiry* 3(3), 1977, p. 439.
54. H. Bloom, *The Anxiety of Influence: A Theory of Poetry*, Oxford University Press, 1997.
55. J. Hillis Miller, 'Stevens' Rock and Criticism as Cure', *Georgia Review* 30(1), 1976.
56. C. Campbell, 'The Tyranny of the Yale Critics', *New York Times*, 1986.
57. A. Bloom, *The Closing of the American Mind: How Higher Education Has Failed Democracy and Impoverished the Souls of Today's Students*, Simon and Schuster, 1988, p. 375.
58. Ibid., p. 379.
59. N. Chomsky, *Understanding Power*, New Press, 2002, p. 233.

9 Before the Law

1. Peeters, *Derrida*, 2013, p. 333.
2. Derrida, 'Circumfession', 1993, p. 300.
3. *El Polis*, 17 December 1987, quoted in B. Peeters, *Derrida*, 2013, p. 382.
4. J. Derrida, 'Heidegger, the Philosopher's Hell' in Derrida, *Points*, 1995, p. 182.
5. J. Habermas, *The Philosophical Discourse of Modernity: Twelve Lectures*, MIT Press, 1985, p. 156.

6. J. Derrida, 'Of Spirit: Heidegger and the Question', trans. Geoffrey Bennington and Rachel Bowlby, *Critical Inquiry*, 15(2), 1989, p. 464.

7. Ibid., p. 466.

8. Ibid., p. 467.

9. Ibid., p. 470.

10. G. C. Spivak, preface to *Of Grammatology*, 1997, p. xiv.

11. Derrida, 'Of Spirit', 1989, p. 471.

12. J. Derrida, *Memoires: For Paul de Man*, trans. Cecile Lindsay, Columbia University Press, 1989, p. 329.

13. Ibid., p. 219.

14. L. Menand, 'The de Man Case', *New Yorker*, 17 March 2014.

15. Quoted in M. Mazower, *Dark Continent: Europe's Twentieth Century*, Penguin, 1999, p. 144.

16. P. de Man, *Allegories of Reading: Figural Language in Rousseau, Nietzsche, Rilke, and Proust*, Yale University Press, 1979, p. 293.

17. J. Derrida, 'Like the Sound of the Sea Deep Within a Shell: Paul de Man's War', trans. Peggy Kamuf, *Critical Inquiry* 14(3), 1988, p. 594.

18. Ibid., pp. 646–7.

19. J. Derrida, *The Ear of the Other*, 1995, p. 28.

20. G. Hartman, 'Looking Back on Paul de Man' in L. Waters and W. Godzich, *Reading de Man Reading*, University of Minnesota Press, 1989. p. 18.

21. Derrida, *Points*, 1995, p. 139.

22. Peeters, *Derrida*, 2013, p. 401.

23. Derrida, *Memoires*, trans. 1989, p. 289.

24. J. Derrida, 'The Force of Law: The "Mystical Foundation of Authority"' in Derrida, *Acts of Religion*, Routledge, 2002, p. 231.

25. Ibid.

26. Ibid., p. 244.

27. Ibid., p. 233.

28. Ibid., p. 236.

29. Ibid., p. 243.

30. Ibid.

31. Ibid., p. 244.

32. Ibid., p. 247.

33. Ibid., p. 254.

34. Ibid., p. 252.

35. J. Derrida, 'Racism's Last Word', trans. Peggy Kamuf, *Critical Inquiry* 12(1), p. 291.

36. J. Derrida, *The Politics of Friendship*, trans. George Collins, Verso, 2005, p. vii.
37. C. Schmitt, *Political Theology*, trans. George Schwab, MIT Press, 1985, p. 5.
38. C. Schmitt, *The Concept of the Political*, University of Chicago Press, 2007, p. 26.
39. Derrida, *The Politics of Friendship*, 2005, p. 68.
40. Ibid., p. 84.
41. Ibid., p. 306.

10 Of ~~God~~

1. Derrida, 'Circumfession', 1993, p. 155.
2. J. Derrida, 'Edmond Jabès and the Question of The Book' in Derrida, *Writing and Difference*, 1978, p. 78.
3. H. Bloom, *Kabbalah and Criticism*, Continuum, 2005, p. 25.
4. J. Derrida, 'Adieu', trans. Anne Brault and Michael Nass, in Derrida, *Signature Derrida*, University of Chicago Press, 2013, p. 317.
5. John of Damascus, *An Exact Exposition of the Orthodox Faith*, CreateSpace, 2012, p. 19.
6. J. D. Caputo, *The Prayers and Tears of Jacques Derrida*, Indiana University Press, 1997.
7. E. Lévinas, 'Revelation in the Jewish Tradition' in Lévinas, *Beyond the Verse: Talmudic Readings and Lectures*, trans. Gary D. Mole, Indiana University Press, 1994, p. 142.
8. Interview, *New York Times*, 9 March 2014.
9. I. Kant, *Grounding for the Metaphysics of Morals*, trans. James W. Ellington, Hackett Classics, 1993, p. 30.
10. Ibid., p. 36.
11. Derrida, *Speech and Phenomena*, 1973, p. 35.
12. W. Benjamin, 'The Task of the Translator' in Benjamin, *Illuminations*, trans. Harry Zohn, Fontana, 1973, p. 21.
13. Ibid., p. 25.
14. Ibid.
15. J. Derrida, 'Des Tours de Babel' in Derrida, *Psyche: Inventions of the Other*, Stanford University Press, 2007, p. 220.
16. Ibid., p. 213.
17. Ibid., p. 220.
18. Ibid., p. 200.

19. Ibid., p. 208.

20. Ibid.

21. Derrida, *Memoires*, 1989, p. 18.

22. J. Derrida, *Specters of Marx: The State of the Debt, the Work of Mourning and the New International*, trans. Peggy Kamuf, Routledge, 2006, p. 109.

23. Ibid., p. 92.

24. Ibid., p. 87.

25. A. Kojève, *Introduction to the Reading of Hegel: Lectures on the Phenomenology of Spirit*, trans. James H. Nichols Jr, Cornell University Press, 1969, p. 159.

26. Derrida, *Specters of Marx*, 2006, p. 106.

27. Ibid., p. 16.

28. Ibid., p. 38.

29. Ibid.

30. Ibid.

31. Ibid., p. 46.

32. P. Valéry, 'The Crisis of Mind' in P. Valéry and James Lawler, *Paul Valéry: An Anthology*, ed. J. Mathews, Routledge & Kegan Paul, 1977, p. 99.

33. Derrida, *Specters of Marx*, 2006, p. 16.

34. Ibid., p. 115.

35. Ibid., p. 100.

36. Ibid., p. 99.

37. Ibid., p. 197.

38. Ibid., p. 108.

39. Ibid., p. 51.

40. Ibid., p. 73.

41. M. Mauss, *The Gift*, trans. W. D. Halls, Routledge, 2002.

42. J. Derrida, *Given Time 1. Counterfeit Money*, trans. Peggy Kamuf, University of Chicago Press, 1991, p. 24.

43. Ibid., p. 14.

44. Ibid., p. 9.

45. Derrida, *Specters of Marx*, 2006, p. 26.

46. E. Hörl, *Sacred Channels: The Archaic Illusion of Communication*, Amsterdam University Press, 2018.

47. T. Eagleton, 'Don't Deride Derrida', *Guardian*, 15 October 2004.

48. Peeters, *Derrida*, 2013, p. 189.

49. Derrida, *Points*, 1995, p. 409.

50. J. Derrida, 'A Silkworm of One's Own' in H. Cixous and J. Derrida,

Veils, Stanford University Press, 2001, p. 44.

51. Ibid., p. 21.
52. Derrida, 'Circumfession', 1993, p. 150.
53. Ibid., p. 151.
54. Ibid.
55. Ibid., p. 98.
56. Bennington, 'Derridabase', 1993, p. 1.
57. Derrida, 'Circumfession', 1993, p. 69.
58. Ibid., pp. 27–8.
59. Ibid., p. 52.
60. J. Derrida, 'How to Avoid Speaking: Denials' in H. G. Coward and T. Foshay (eds), *Derrida and Negative Theology*, New York Press, 1992, p. 95.
61. Derrida, 'Circumfession', 1993, p. 23.
62. Ibid.
63. Ibid., p. 25.
64. Derrida, *Points*, 1995, pp. 200–1.

11 An Event Has Occurred

1. G. Borradori, *Philosophy in a Time of Terror: Dialogues with Jürgen Habermas and Jacques Derrida*, University of Chicago Press, 2003, p. 109.
2. Derrida, *The Death Penalty*, 2014, p. 220.
3. Borradori, *Philosophy in a Time of Terror*, 2003, p. 109.
4. J. Derrida, 'Fichus' in J. Derrida, *Paper Machine*, trans. Rachel Bowlby, Stanford University Press, 2005, p. 179.
5. Ibid.
6. Derrida, *The Death Penalty*, 2014, p. 221.
7. Borradori, *Philosophy in a Time of Terror*, 2003, p. 153.
8. Ibid.
9. Ibid., p. 144.
10. Yad Vashem Holocaust Center, 'Interview with Jacques Derrida', yadvashem.org, 8 January 1998.
11. Derrida, *Acts of Religion*, 2001, p. 138.
12. Ibid., p. 45.
13. M. Chérif, *Islam and the West: A Conversation with Jacques Derrida*, University of Chicago Press, 2008, p. 29.
14. Ibid., p. 31.

15. B. Latour, 'Why Has Critique Run Out of Steam?', *Critical Inquiry* 30(2), 2004, p. 228.
16. Borradori, *Philosophy in a Time of Terror*, 2003, p. 162.
17. Derrida and Ferraris, *A Taste for the Secret*, 2001, p. 88.
18. J. Derrida, *Aporias*, trans. Thomas Dutoit, Stanford University Press, 1993, p. 74.
19. Derrida, 'Cinema and Its Ghosts', 2015, p. 39.
20. J. Derrida, 'Archive Fever: A Freudian Impression', *Diacritics* 25(2), 1995, p. 16.
21. Ibid., p. 11.
22. Peeters, *Derrida*, 2013, p. 501.
23. Derrida, *Learning to Live Finally*, 2007, p. 39.
24. Derrida, 'Archive Fever: A Freudian Impression', 1995, p. 11.
25. J. Derrida, *The Beast and the Sovereign. Volume 1*, trans. Geoffrey Bennington, University of Chicago Press, 2009, p. 219.
26. Ibid., p. 167.
27. Ibid., p. 56.
28. Derrida, 'How to Avoid Speaking: Denials', 1992, pp. 97–8.
29. Derrida, *The Work of Mourning*, 2001, p. 105.
30. Derrida, *Learning to Live Finally*, 2007, p. 27.
31. Derrida, *The Politics of Friendship*, 2005, pp. 13–14.
32. Derrida, *Learning to Live Finally*, 2007, p. 27.
33. Derrida, *The Ear of the Other*, 1985, p. 7.
34. Derrida, *Learning to Live Finally*, 2007, p. 52.
35. Derrida, *The Death Penalty*, 2014, p. 241.

Index